Japanese
Folk Literature

Japanese
Folk Literature

A Core Collection
and Reference Guide

Joanne P. Algarin

R. R. Bowker Company
New York and London, 1982

Published by R. R. Bowker Company
1180 Avenue of the Americas, New York, NY 10036
Copyright © 1982 by Xerox Corporation
All rights reserved
Printed and bound in the United States of America

Library of Congress Cataloging in Publication Data

Algarin, Joanne P.
  Japanese folk literature.

  Includes indexes.
  1. Folk literature, Japanese—History and
criticism—Bibliography. I. Title.
Z3308.L5A44 1982   [PL748]   016.3982'0952   82-9672
ISBN 0-8352-1516-4

Contents

Preface

Japanese Folk Literature is designed to provide an introduction to and general familiarity with the folklore and folktales of Japan. (*Folktale* is used in this work as an all-inclusive category, including genres such as myths, legends, and fairy tales.) The main body of this book will be of special aid to researchers, librarians, educators, storytellers, and other interested readers. Teachers also will find it most useful as an aid to selecting materials for the introduction of Japanese literature and culture to their classes.

Ideally, folk literature should be studied in the native language. However, most folklorists and interested readers in the United States do not possess the fluency in Japanese that is needed to read folktales and studies of folklore in that language. In addition, many readers are unfamiliar with English-language sources in this field. This work will be of special aid to those people.

Japanese Folk Literature is divided into the following sections:

Introduction: discusses the general areas of Japanese folklore with which researchers, scholars, educators, and other readers should be familiar.

Chapter 1, Works on Japanese Folklore: lists and abstracts studies that examine Japanese folklore, folktales, motifs that appear in the tales, and medieval tale collections.

Chapter 2, Japanese Folktale Anthologies: works whose basic purpose is to present Japanese folktales in English translation. Some of these anthologies have extensive notes explaining motifs that are not familiar to the average Westerner.

Chapter 3, Classic Folktales of Japan: lists and abstracts classic Japanese folktales.

Appendix A, Japanese-Language Sources: a brief introduction to Japanese-language sources, designed for use by researchers and others who have studied Japanese. Most of the entries listed are bibliographies from articles referenced in Chapter 1.

Appendix B, Glossary of Japanese Terms.

Also included are a subject index, an index of articles listed in Chapter 1, and an index of all the tales mentioned or annotated in this book.

All main titles in Chapters 1, 2, and 3 are listed by entry number, from entry 1 in Chapter 1 to entry 138 in Chapter 3. References to titles throughout the book are to entry number. The indexes, however, refer to page number.

Most of the research for this book was conducted at the Wason Library of Cornell University, Ithaca, New York. I wish to express my gratitude to Cornell for making its facilities available, and also to the University of California at Berkeley for granting access to its collection during the final stages of this work.

Thank you to Brett de Bary for her support and encouragement, Diane Perushek for her help and guidance, and Pat and Gerry McDonough for their limitless hospitality.

Finally, I wish to acknowledge the generous financial support provided by the Michael I. Current Foundation for the Study of Japanese Language and Literature.

Introduction

All those interested in the study and enjoyment of Japanese folklore should be familiar with at least three general areas: myths about the founding of Japan, general folklore studies, including types of tales, and anthologies.

The best sources for myths about the founding of Japan are two early chronicles, the *Kojiki* 古事記 and the *Nihongi* 日本紀. *Kojiki* was compiled in A.D. 712 and is the oldest extant Japanese book. Basil Hall Chamberlain first translated this work into English. It was published in the *Transactions of the Asiatic Society of Japan* in 1882 and reissued by Charles E. Tuttle in 1981. In 1968, a new translation, by Donald L. Philippi, was published by the University of Tokyo Press and Princeton University Press. Philippi's translation is an excellent work, which contains an informative introduction, many background notes, and an extensive glossary that includes the names of deities, people, and places.

Nihongi was compiled in A.D. 720. It was translated into English by W. G. Aston and first published in the *Transactions of the Asiatic Society of Japan* in 1896. A reprint edition was issued by Charles E. Tuttle in 1971. The *Nihongi* is also called *Nihon shoki* 日本書記.

In addition to these two histories, several of the classic literary works of medieval Japan are very important for the study of Japanese folklore. The Japanese did not develop their own writing system, but imported that of the Chinese during the late fourth and early fifth centuries. This simple, seemingly unrelated fact has had a tremendous impact on Japanese folklore, as well as Japanese literature.

Because the Japanese and Chinese languages are unrelated linguistically, some type of phonetic script had to be developed from the Chinese characters to express inflected endings of Japanese words and to record Japanese proper names. In fact, two syllabaries (sets of written characters) were developed, the *hiragana* script and the *katakana* script.

Japanese soon was written with a script that was a mixture of Chinese characters (kanji), hiragana, and to a lesser extent katakana.

During the medieval era in Japan, literacy increased dramatically, so that by 1600 well over half of the male population, and a good percentage of the female population, were at least semiliterate. (Semiliteracy existed in several stages: people who could read one or the other of the syllabaries, people who could read both syllabaries but virtually no kanji, and people who could read both syllabaries and some simple kanji.) As a result of this semiliterate state, many folktales, especially historical legends and Buddhist didactic tales, developed simultaneously in the oral and the written traditions. Books were written based on stories well-known to the general population; other books were composed precisely to provide tales that priests and entertainers could introduce into the oral tradition.

The work that most clearly developed from this side-by-side growth of oral and written tradition is the *Heike monogatari* 平家物語. This collection of tales is concerned with the fall from power and ultimate destruction of the Heike (or Taira) clan at the hands of the rival Genji (or Minamoto) clan in the Gempei War (1180–1185). The work contains not only stories of the battles, but also lyric tales about the friendships and love affairs of the men and women caught in this tumultuous time. The work is episodic and repetitive, demonstrating its multiauthorship and its use as oral entertainment. A complete translation, *The Tale of the Heieke*, by Hiroshi Kitagawa and Bruce T. Tsuchida, was published by the University of Tokyo Press in 1975.

Another important literary work is the *Gikeiki* 義経記, which tells the story of Yoshitsune, the Genji warrior who led the successful campaign against the Heike and who was subsequently driven to his tragic suicide by his suspicious older brother, Yoritomo, founder of the Kamakura shogunate. In contrast to *Heike monogatari*, *Gikeiki* possesses a cohesiveness of style that points to an individual author who collected the many legends about Yoshitsune from the oral tradition and compiled them in this work. Helen Craig McCullough's complete translation of this collection, *Yoshitsune: A Fifteenth Century Japanese Chronicle*, was published by the University of Tokyo Press and Stanford University Press in 1966.

Both the *Heike monogatari* and the *Gikeiki* were greatly influenced by popular Buddhist beliefs of the medieval era, and both works are permeated by Buddhist ideas and principles. During that time, numerous tale collections were compiled that contained straightforward Buddhist didactic tales. One work of both Buddhist didactic tales and secular tales and anecdotes is the *Konjaku monogatari shū* 今昔物語集. Here is a collection of more than 1,000 tales in 31 chapters (28 of which are still extant). The *Konjaku* was an extremely important and influential collection, and certainly the most massive. (Three works in English present translations of tales from this collection, listed as entries 66 [Brower], 82

[Jones], and 105 [Ury] in this book.) A collection often associated with the *Konjaku* is the *Uji shūi monogatari* 宇治拾遺物語 (for the complete translation of this work, see entry 84, Mills, in this book).

The earliest Buddhist tale collection in Japanese was the *Nihon ryōiki* 日本靈異記, compiled by the monk Kyōkai as a source of legends that could be used by priests to teach basic Buddhist principles and concepts. A complete translation of this work, *Miraculous Stories from the Japanese Buddhist Tradition: The Nihon Ryōiki of the Monk Kyōkai*, was done by Kyoko Motomochi Nakamura, published by Harvard University Press in 1973.

Many individual Japanese tales have been translated into English as picture books for young children. A work that lists many of these titles is *Japan Through Children's Literature: A Critical Bibliography* by Yasuko Makino. It was published by Duke University in 1978 as No. 5 in its series of Occasional Papers. The section entitled "Folklore and Legends" lists books that are translations and adaptations of Japanese tales; the section entitled "Fiction" lists books that were independently written, based on Japanese motifs and/or stories. Makino's main criterion for her critical evaluation is the accuracy with which a work portrays actual Japanese folk materials. This bibliography can be used as a guide by primary schoolteachers to select materials for introducing Japanese culture to their students.

Before beginning the study of the folklore of any given area, one should have some knowledge of general folklore studies. Japanologists who are not folklorists may be unaware of some of the classic works in this area. Some of them are discussed below.

On the Nature of Fairy Tales by Max Luthi (translated by Lee Chadeayne and Paul Gottwald; New York: Frederick Ungar Publishing, 1970; reprint edition Bloomington: Indiana University Press, 1976) is an excellent introduction to the literary study of the fairy tale. Luthi defines and describes fairy tales, animal tales, saints' legends, and local legends, and he discusses the form, function, content, style, and basic themes of fairy tales. Of the eleven chapters in the book, ten were originally lectures. In addition, this work contains a very good set of reference notes and an introduction by Francis Lee Utley that lists Luthi's publications from 1943 to 1969, all of which are in German.

The Folktale by Stith Thompson (Berkeley: University of California Press, 1977) is a far-reaching, detailed study that examines the folktale as a whole and its many motifs, discusses the numerous theories and methods used by folklorists, and investigates the role of the folktale in a particular culture, in this case, the native North American.

The most important work that applies the methods of structural analysis to the folktale is *Morphology of the Folktale* by Vladimir Propp (translated by Laurence Scott; Bloomington: Indiana University Research Center in Anthropology, Folklore and Linguistics, 1958; reprint edition Austin: University of Texas Press, 1968). This work outlines

Propp's method of analysis in which the actions performed by the characters ("functions of the dramatis personae") are the critical elements of a tale. Propp lists 31 major functions that can be found in fairy tales and describes how these functions compose the framework of a tale.

Many works apply psychological analysis to fairy tales. The best known is *The Uses of Enchantment* by Bruno Bettelheim (New York: Alfred A. Knopf, 1976). Bettelheim discusses the need for fairy tales in the lives of young children, the possible impacts of the tales on psychological development, and the Freudian psychological interpretations assigned to fairy tale motifs and to the story as a whole.

In contrast to Bettelheim's use of Freudian analysis, Marie-Louise von Franz has used Jungian psychoanalysis in her studies of the fairy tale. *An Introduction to the Interpretation of Fairy Tales* (Zurich: Spring Publications, 1973) is an excellent look at this type of analysis, giving a broad overview of the motifs considered important and of the meanings assigned to the motifs. Von Franz's second introductory work is *Shadow and Evil in Fairy Tales* (Zurich: Spring Publications, 1974). Part one explains the concepts of shadow, individual unconscious, and collective unconscious. (The analyses in this section are very complex, so it is advisable to read *Interpretation of Fairy Tales* before attempting the second book.) Part two examines various aspects of the conscious, evil, magic, magical competition, and supernatural possession in fairy tales.

Two other books on fairy tales by von Franz, *Problems of the Feminine in Fairy Tales* (1972) and *Individuation in Fairy Tales* (1976), were published by Spring Publications, Zurich.

Another approach to studying folk stories is to classify them into tale types. "The Types of the Folktale: A Classification and Bibliography" by Antti Aarne and Stith Thompson (*FF Communications* 75, 1961) is a cornerstone of Western folklore studies. The analyses in this work are of complete tales, with synopses and distributions of more than 2,000 tales and variants, and an index of synopses. Originally published in 1910, the first revised edition came out in 1928.

A classification of folktale motifs is presented by Stith Thompson in "Motif Index of Folk Literature: A Classification of Narrative Elements in Folktales, Ballads, Myths, Fables, Medieval Romances, Exempla, Fabliaux, Jestbooks, and Local Legends" (*FF Communications* 106–109, 116 and 117, 1932–1936; reprint edition [six volumes] Bloomington: Indiana University Press, 1955).

Because most of the work in Western folklore studies uses stories from the collection by the Brothers Grimm, a copy of their classic anthology is a vital research tool for any folklorist. *The Complete Grimm's Fairy Tales* (New York: Pantheon Books, 1972) is one of the finest texts available, and it is truly a joy to read and to use. This particular version was written by James Stern, based on the translation by Margaret Hunt.

Another fine anthology of fairy tales is *The Classic Fairy Tales* by

Iona and Peter Opie (New York: Oxford University Press, 1974). This work traces the histories of Western fairy tale literature and of 24 "classic tales." The versions of the tales in this anthology are the ones first published in English. This is a beautifully written and illustrated book.

The best source of folktales from individual countries is the Folktales of the World series published by the University of Chicago Press under the general editorship of Richard M. Dorson.

The earliest anthologies of Japanese tales in English translation were published in the late nineteenth and early twentieth centuries. Many of the compilers of these anthologies could not themselves read or speak Japanese, nor had they ever been to Japan. These authors simply relied on earlier works in English. For this reason there is a great deal of repetition of contents among these anthologies. The most influential works during this early period were Chamberlain's translation of *Kojiki* and Aston's translation of *Nihongi* (both discussed earlier). In some works, tales are reprinted verbatim from other sources. An example is entry 77 in this book, *Japanese Fairy Tales* by Lafcadio Hearn and others. One of the "other sources" was Grace James, author of *Green Willow* (see entry 80). James's stories, which appear in both *Green Willow* and *Japanese Fairy Tales*, are identical.

In some works, much of the material was taken from other previously printed English sources. An example is by F. Hadland Davis, entry 67 in this book, entitled *Myths and Legends of Japan*. Davis borrowed extensively from Aston's *Nihongi* and from *Ancient Tales and Folklore of Japan* by Richard Gordon-Smith (see entry 72). In fact, Davis adapts approximately one-fourth of the tales from the Gordon-Smith work for his own anthology.

The obvious problem with this reliance on secondhand sources is the fact that the author cannot judge the accuracy and authenticity of the materials being used. The most important case in this instance is the story of Raitaro, the son of the Thunder God. The tale of Raitaro first appeared in 1880, in William Griffis's *Japanese Fairy World* (see entry 74), and was adapted by many anthologizers after that. Not until Griffis published *The Fire-fly's Lovers* (see entry 73) did he include an introduction explaining that the story of Raitaro was an independent creation on his part with no actual version in Japanese folklore. (This did not stop people from adapting the story of Raitaro and other of Griffis's inventions for even later anthologies.)

In general, pre-World War II materials should be used with great caution by researchers and others not already familiar with Japanese folktales. This is not to say that none of the earlier anthologies is to be recommended. James's *Green Willow* (entry 80) and Ozaki's *Japanese Fairy Tales* (entry 89), for example, are very well-written anthologies. The easiest way to deal with the problem of nonauthentic folktales is to read these anthologies armed with a copy of Ikeda's index of Japanese tale types (see entry 25) and/or Seki's index (see entry 46).

The other clear-cut criterion for determining the authenticity of tales in a collection is to see whether the work lists a source (or sources) for the Japanese tales translated for the anthology. Many historical anecdotes and local legends are not included in these indexes, but the user can be assured of a tale's authenticity if it is translated from a Japanese original.

About the pronunciation of romanized Japanese words

Within each entry of this bibliography, the romanization system originally used by the author of each work has been maintained. The following key indicates the pronunciation of transliterations that do not reflect actual English sounds. Items not listed in this key are pronounced as in English, i.e., "k" as in kite, "g" as in go, "ya" as in yatch, "ch" as in chance, etc.

n, ñ, or n' before b, m, or p = m
"kwa" is an old orthographic form that is equivalent to the modern "ka"
    (Kwannon = Kannon)
"dzu" is an old orthographic form that is equivalent to the modern "zu"
    (Idzumo = Izumo)

hu = fu	"a" as in father
si = shi	"i" as in see
sy = sh	"u" as in too
ti = chi	"e" as in set
tu = tsu	"o" as in no
ty = ch	"ō" = "o" sound held for two syllables
zi = ji	"oo" = "o" sound held for two syllables
zy = j	

Works on Japanese Folklore

1. Adams, Robert J. "Social Identity of a Japanese Storyteller." Ph.D. dissertation, Indiana University, 1972.

This study of an individual storyteller of Niigata Prefecture examines not only the tales she tells but also the relationships among the story, the storyteller, and the cultural context. The contents include:

Chapter 1. The Life of Tsune Watanabe

Chapter 2. Folklore and Social Identity

Function, structure, social identity, rights and duties, status and role

Chapter 3. Storyteller as a Social Identity

Influence of social identity as listener on ultimate social identity as storyteller:

extent of passive exposure to stories

degree of identification with storytellers

amount of activity in precipitating storytelling events as listener

strength of desire to replace social identity as listener with that of storyteller

Formation of decision to assume social identity as storyteller:

acceptance of stories as valid embodiments of cultural values and beliefs

appropriation of stories as means of personal expression, which will include: reflection in the tales of the storyteller's attitudes toward herself (ability to remember, singing ability, education, work, illness, money); reflection in the tales of the storyteller's attitudes toward society (etiquette, cleanliness, drinking, repayment of obligations, family relationships); and reflection in the tales of the storyteller's attitudes toward forces beyond society (deity, fate)

activity in precipitating storytelling events as teller

Chapter 4. Technical Requirements for the Development of a Social Identity as Storyteller
    Ability to master techniques of storytelling:
        input 1, tale outline
        input 2, elements from other tales
        input 3, personal experience
        input 4, stylistic elements (repetitive exchanges of dialogue, pat-
        terning of time markers, opening and closing formulas, charac-
        terization of tale protagonists, development of dramatic tension)
    Ability to conceptualize and fulfill demands of listeners
    Opportunity to practice storytelling technique in reinforcing situa-
    tions

The study also contains conclusions, bibliography, and appendix—transcription of tapes.
    The tales included in this study are:

1. Bafuragonuya and Kurimutatari
2. The Serpent Bridegroom and the Frog's Skin
3. The Clam Wife and the Crane Wife
4. The Quarrel between the Monkey and the Crab
5. The Quarrel of the Monkey and the Frog over Mochi
6. Dan-ichi Whose Ears Are Bitten
7. The Bean, Charcoal and Straw
8. Momotarō (Peach Boy)
9. Snow-White
10. The Maiden in the Tower
11. The Man on a Quest for His Lost Wife
12. The Snake of Kumamoda Swamp (A)
13. The Snake of Kumamoda Swamp (B)
14. The Yamabushi and the Fox
15. The Treasure Ghost
16. The Heaven's Gift and the Earth's Gift
17. The Rich Man Who Bought a Dream
18. The Invisible Hood
19. The Search for a Lost Husband
20. The Two Girls, the Bear and the Dwarf
21. Three Horse Eyes
22. The Elder Sister Who Was Transformed into a White Bird
23. Hansel and Gretel
24. The Quarrel between the Monkey and the Frog over Mochi
25. The Quarrel between the Monkey and the Frog over Mochi
26. Uriko Hime (Melon Princess)

Sugisaki Version of The Quarrel between the Monkey and the Crab
Sekigawa Version of The Quarrel between the Monkey and the Crab
Yokoyama Version of The Quarrel between the Monkey and the
    Crab

Kurogi Version of The Quarrel between the Monkey and the Crab
Kurogi Version of The Monkey and the Crab Make Mochi Together
Standard National Reader Version of The Quarrel between the
Monkey and the Crab

2. Blacker, Carmen. "The Snake Woman in Japanese Myth and Legend." In
Animals in Folklore, pp. 113–125, edited by J. R. Porter and W. M. S.
Russell. Totowa, N.J.: Rowman and Littlefield, 1978.

Beginning with a discussion of divine marriage tales in which the
wife is really a snake woman, Blacker divides these tales into two
classes: those in which the man visits the snake woman in her home
under the water and those in which the snake woman leaves the water
to dwell in the world of humans. The first class is represented by the
stories *Urashima Tarō* 浦島太郎 and *Hanatare-kozō* 洟垂小僧. In *Urashima Tarō*, a young fisherman descends to the palace of the Dragon
King at the bottom of the sea and marries one of the ladies there.
Presumably she is a dragon-being. After Urashima has spent three years
in the palace, he decides to return home to his aged parents. His wife
gives him a box to take back to the human world, but she warns him that
he must not open it. When Urashima arrives on land, he discovers that
three centuries have passed. He opens the box, which contains the
passage of time from which he has been protected, and immediately he
ages 300 years and crumples to dust. In *Hanatare-kozō*, an old woodcutter is rewarded by the daughter of the Dragon King for throwing offerings of wood into the water; wood is very valuable because it is so rare
under the sea. The Dragon Princess gives the man an ugly little boy
who can grant his every wish. The only requirement is that the old man
feed the boy shrimp every day. The woodcutter eventually tires of car-
ing for the boy and drives him away, whereupon all of the man's new
riches disappear. (In this version of the story, the man neither marries a
snake woman nor visits her underwater domain.)

The second class of tales is represented by a story that begins with a
man saving the life of a snake. Later a beautiful woman comes to his
house and becomes his wife. When she is about to give birth to their
child, she tells the man that he must not look at her while she is in
labor. He breaks this taboo and sees that she is really a snake, so she is
forced to leave him. Blacker discusses the variants of this particular tale.
In the *Hagoromo* 羽衣 tale, a man discovers a feathered robe that belongs to a celestial maiden. She cannot return to heaven until she has
obtained her magic garment back from him.

Blacker also examines the bowl-lending legends, in which certain
caves and bodies of water would produce bowls for people who requested them. The only stipulation was that all the bowls had to be
returned in their original condition as soon as the borrower was done
with them. Once the taboo was broken, the lending of bowls ceased.

In the tales concerning snake husbands, a young woman is visited nightly by an unknown suitor and she finally becomes pregnant. She places a threaded needle into the hem of the suitor's kimono and follows the thread in the morning, only to discover that her lover is really a snake. In one group of tales, the woman gives birth to a powerful child who becomes a renowned warrior; in the second group, the woman hears the snakes talking in a cave, saying that she will give birth to unnatural offspring. The snakes mention the way in which the pregnancy can be aborted, and the woman carries out these instructions.

The next group Blacker discusses are the human pillar tales, in which a woman is buried alive as a sacrifice to a serpent water-deity. These stories are usually associated with the repairing of dams and dikes.

Last, Blacker discusses the relationship between snake-deities and female shamans.

3. Blacker, Carmen. "Supernatural Abductions in Japanese Folklore." *Asian Folklore Studies* 26, no. 2 (1967): 111–147.

Part one, The Theme, describes the Japanese belief that boys and young men who disappeared from a village were actually the victims of kidnapping by gods or other supernatural beings. When the boys were discovered back in the villages, they were often found in inaccessible places, such as the space between the ceiling and roof of a house or the eaves of a tall building. The boys were usually unconscious for a time, but upon recovering their senses, they would tell of being taken away by an old man who led them on a fantastic journey into the upper and lower worlds and across great geographic distances.

Women could also be the victims of supernatural kidnapping, most often by mountain men who made the women their wives. Boys and women who did not return to the villages would sometimes be seen once again under strange circumstances and then disappear forever.

Tengu were also known to kidnap people, but they were often forced to return their victims by a being who would appear as an old man dressed as a Buddhist priest.

Blacker examines case histories of such kidnappings and compares them with experiences of shamanistic initiation from the Asian mainland.

Part two, Hirata Atsutane and the "Strange Tidings from the Realm of Immortals," tells of the case history recorded by Hirata of Torakichi, a young man who claimed to have been the disciple of a strange old man who took him on supernatural journeys over a period of several years. The old man was thought to be a tengu. Torakichi told of the many places to which he had traveled, the experiences that he had, and the things that were told to him by his supernatural master. Hirata and his colleagues discussed with Torakichi many tales of unusual happenings, including stories of other supernatural kidnappings. Torakichi described the 100-day ordeal he was forced to undergo as an initiation to becoming the tengu's pupil. He also described the habits and great knowledge of the tengu.

4. Brower, Robert H. "The *Koñzyaku monogatarisyū*: An Historical and Critical Introduction, with Annotated Translations of Seventy-eight Tales." Ph.D. dissertation, University of Michigan, 1952.

Brower's dissertation is an important study of this monumental Japanese tale collection. Volume I (pp. i–362), which is abstracted below, discusses the *Koñzyaku monogatarisyū*, its literary predecessors, and the historical context of the late Heian era. Volume II (pp. 363–740) gives the tale translations, and Volume III (pp. 741–1062) provides the notes to the translations. (Volumes II and III are listed in Chapter 2 of this bibliography, entry 66.)

Volume I includes:

Chapter 1. Some Early Buddhist Tale Collections in India, China, and Japan

Chapter 2. Non-Buddhist Narrative Writing in Japan from the Beginnings to the Late Heian Period

Chapter 3. The Social and Literary Scene in the Late Heian Period (c. 1025–1160)

Chapter 4. The Contents of the *Koñzyaku monogatarisyū*, Their Topical Arrangement, and the Basis for the Selection of the Tales Translated

Chapter 5. The Sources of the *Koñzyaku monogatarisyū*, the Structure and Style of the Tales, and the Probable Purpose for Which the Collection Was Compiled

Chapter 6. The Problems of the Authorship and Date of the *Koñzyaku monogatarisyū*

Chapter 7. The Position of the *Koñzyaku monogatarisyū* in the Stream of Japanese Literature

The bibliography in Volume I lists many Japanese works on the *Koñzyaku* and on Japanese tale literature, as well as Japanese and English works on Buddhism.

5. Casal, U. A. "Far Eastern Monkeylore." *Monumenta Nipponica* 12, no. 1–2 (April/July 1956): 13–49.

The monkey was considered both an evil spirit and a deity, but it was most important as a fertility deity and as a talisman animal to drive away misfortune. This article cites monkey legends from India, China, and Japan.

The monkey was associated in Japan with the deity Sannō Gongen. Monkeys were thought to ward off evils such as illness and to bring prosperity to a family. The monkey was also important because of its role as one of the 12 animals of the Asian zodiac. The monkey often appeared as a motif in Japanese art and was often used for satirical and theatrical purposes during the Tokugawa era.

In the article, Casal examines the tales "How the Jellyfish Lost Its Shell," "The Battle of the Monkey and the Crab," and "Momotarō."

6. Casal, U. A. "The Goblin Fox and Badger and Other Witch Animals of Japan." *Folklore Studies* 18 (1959): 1–93.

Most of this article deals with beliefs concerning the fox, badger, cat, dog, and wolf. The sections on the rat, snake, spider, odd witch animals, and spooks are fairly short, about one to three pages each.

Fox: The Japanese had many superstitions concerning the fox, such as not using the word *kitsune* at night for fear that the animal would come as if called by the person who spoke the word. The fox was a very important animal in the religious system of the Ainu; fox skulls were often placed on poles outside the Ainu house to protect it from evil spirits.

The Japanese believed that the fox could be helpful to humans at certain times, as illustrated by a tale of a fox that carries a forgotten document from a government office to a courier bound for Edo (the ancient name for Tokyo). The government official who noticed that the document had been left behind offered a sacrifice to the fox and requested its help.

But most of the beliefs about the fox indicate that the animal was usually thought to be a danger to humans. A fox could bewitch a man and kidnap him from his village. When this happened, the villagers would gather after nightfall and beat on drums and shout for the fox to return the victim.

A fox could assume the shape of a human by placing a skull on its head, holding cow or horse bones in its mouth, covering itself with grass and leaves, and worshiping the North Star. Foxes who were disguised as humans could be recognized by various signs: Their bodies tended to be luminous, their faces were unnaturally long, they were unable to pronounce certain sounds, their true fox shape would appear as a faint shadow to one side of their human form or would be reflected in bodies of water and in mirrors, and their fox nature would always be recognized by dogs. Also, the fox would sometimes have difficulty hiding its long bushy tail under its kimono, so that the astute observer might see the tip of its tail sticking out from beneath the hem of the garment. If a person pinches him- or herself when in the presence of a fox in human guise, the person will not feel any pain. A fox could always be tricked into shedding its disguise by being offered one of its favorite foods, such as fried rat. The older a fox became, the more dangerous and powerful it grew. Foxes could cast spells to make phantom houses appear in desolate places and thus waylay weary travelers. Foxes could also lure travelers from the road by producing fires that looked like torches with their tails and breath.

Some tales tell of foxes assuming the shapes of trains or automobiles and of foxes tricking people in other ways. A popular motif is that of a fox assuming the shape of a beautiful young woman and marrying a mortal man.

Foxes were held or owned by certain families as magical "familiars." The foxes brought the family wealth and could be used to inflict damage on the family's enemies. The members of fox-holding families were shunned by non-fox-holders and were forced to marry among themselves. A non-fox-owner who married a member of a fox-holding family became a fox-holder and was similarly outcast. Certain means could be used to protect oneself from fox sorcery: eating the flesh or tongue of a fox, carrying a certain type of seed in one's sash, and using the services of a priest or exorcist.

Killing a fox was considered very dangerous, for the animal's angry spirit or its surviving relatives and friends would surely avenge the murder. Sometimes the performance of rites for the repose of the dead fox's soul could protect the killer from retribution.

Foxes were believed to arrange marriages in the same way that humans did, and many tales tell of elaborate weddings held by foxes. But by far the most dangerous power that the fox had was its ability to possess people. Those who were possessed by a fox spirit would begin to act like foxes and to show other signs of mental derangement. Fox possession could ultimately result in the death of the victim. Foxes could be exorcised by priests, who threatened and bribed the animal spirit to leave its victim. Casal gives numerous case histories of fox possessions and exorcisms, and he contrasts these cases of fox possession with those of deities and spirits possessing mediums.

The negative role of the fox as a bewitching animal is contrasted by the positive role assigned to this animal by its association with the deity Inari.

Badger: The badger appears in Japanese folklore most often as the practical joker, usually simply seeking to terrify people with its pranks. Like foxes, badgers were able to assume human shape. Their deception could be detected by the luminosity of their bodies or by the fact that their kimonos would stay dry even in a heavy rainstorm. The badger's favorite human guise was that of a Buddhist priest. Badgers delighted in swindling people of their goods, paying for purchases with gold coins that would later turn into dead leaves. But the badger was also known to reward those who helped it or who offered it food. And the badger was quite renowned for its love of saké.

Badgers were able to transform themselves into inanimate objects, as illustrated by the tale in which a badger takes the shape of a teakettle and uses this strange form to accumulate a fortune for the poor tinkerer who had taken the creature under his protection.

Another favorite trick of the badger was to inflate its belly and play it like a drum, often singing a type of accompaniment. The badger was also thought to have a very large scrotum, which the creature could enlarge even beyond its normal size to the point of using it as the flooring for an eight-mat room.

Cat: Most of the beliefs concerning the cat are very negative. Cats were thought to be ungrateful, evil, and dangerous creatures. A common superstition warned against leaving a cat in a house where a corpse was laid out, as the cat could transform the corpse into a vampire by jumping over it. The cat itself was often cast in the role of a vampire creature; a cannibalistic witch could assume the shape of a cat, move in as a pet with some family, and begin preying on the family's members.

Cats possessed different magical powers, depending on the color of their fur. Old cats, cats with more than one tail, and cats with unusually long tails were particularly dangerous.

The cat has a more positive role in the tale of the origin of the "beckoning cat" statue. A young courtesan's pet cat once followed her around, crying incessantly, until the woman's patron angrily killed the animal. Whereupon the cat's severed head flew up to the ceiling and killed a huge snake that was hiding there. To soothe the young woman's grief at the loss of her dutiful pet, one of her admirers had a statue made in the likeness of the slain cat. So many people heard this story and came to see the famous statue that the courtesan became quite successful.

Some superstitions about the tiger were known in Japan, but this animal is not native to the Japanese islands and plays a minor role in Japanese folklore.

Dog: The article gives several legends that explain the origin of the animosity between the dog and the cat. Dogs protected the houses in which they lived and were especially good at sniffing out and exposing ghosts and bewitching animals. Dogs were offered up as sacrifices, and the actions and howlings of dogs were interpreted as omens.

Dogs could be supernatural beings or the embodiments of deities. Dogs could be owned or held by families as magical familiars similar to the holding of foxes, and dogs could possess people in the same way that foxes did.

Wolf: The wolf plays a minor role in Japanese folklore. A wolf could be a deity or a messenger of a deity, or it could be a spectral creature that attacked humans. Casal includes in this section a short discussion of European beliefs about werewolves.

Rat: Rats, like foxes, were thought to be fond of imitating human marriage customs. The nineteenth day of the first moon was the rat's preferred wedding day. There was also a belief in very large supernatural rats that were evil and would prey upon humans.

Snake: Snakes were worshiped throughout Japan. They would often take on human shape and parent human offspring.

Spider: Large supernatural spiders would attack and devour humans. Small "vampire" spiders would suck the blood of their victims.

Odd witch animals: Casal mentions the monkey, kappa, frog and toad, turtle, and wild boar. Each animal is discussed for only two or three sentences, except for the wild boar, which takes up one and one-half pages.

Spooks: The spirits of dead animals could appear as ghosts.

7. Casal, U. A. "The Kappa." *Transactions of the Asiatic Society of Japan,* series 3, 8 (December 1961): 157–199.

This excellent article is a general review of tales concerning kappa. Casal provides detailed physical descriptions of kappa, names by which kappa are known throughout Japan, and speculations as to the origin of these creatures, including tales of kappa migrations from mainland Asia and a story saying that kappa were originally dolls made by a carpenter to help him in his work. Casal discusses tales of kappa transforming themselves into humans and catching and drowning victims, tales of kappa dragging young boys into the water and eating parts of their bodies, and tales in which kappa are actually helpful to humans.

The antagonisms between kappa and monkeys and between kappa and clams are examined. One tale tells of the kappa and Lord Kiyomasa. When a kappa drowns one of the lord's favorite pages, the daimyo sets an army of monkeys against the kappa, determined to kill all the kappa in his domain. A Buddhist priest finally intervenes, obtaining from the kappa a promise never again to harm anyone. Other tales concern kappa being captured and forced to make such promises. Casal also describes the kappa's fondness for wrestling and gives instructions on how one can protect oneself and win the wrestling match if confronted by the creature.

Kappa are also associated with horses, the kappa most often trying to drag the horses into the water and drown them. Also, certain festivals and religious practices are associated with kappa.

The last pages of the article examine the use of the kappa motif in merchandising in Japan.

8. Casal, U. A. "Magic Vengeance in Old Japan." *Asiatische Studien* 10 (1956): 114–129.

This article is in two parts. The first part, Anchin and Kiyohime, discusses two tales involving the Dōjōji temple. In the first tale, while diving in the sea, a fisherman is terrified by an unnatural light underwater. Upon reaching the surface, he finds a tiny gold statue in his hair knot. A deity appears to him in a dream and says that she is Kannon, the Buddhist goddess of mercy. The old man and his wife worship the gold image of Kannon, asking only that their daughter, who is very ugly, be made beautiful. This gift is granted, and in due course the girl comes to the attention of the emperor, who makes her his concubine. The emperor orders that the Dōjōji temple be constructed to house the statue of Kannon.

In the second story, two centuries later, a priest named Anchin goes on a pilgrimage to visit the Kumano Gongen. While he is lodging at a certain place, the daughter of the house tries to seduce him, claiming that he must have been her lover in a former incarnation. He says that he cannot break his ritual purity before reaching the shrine, but he promises to come for her on his return journey. Anchin, however, remembers his priestly vows and does not stop on his way home. When the girl Kiyohime learns of this, she becomes furious and vows to pursue him. She is so angry that when she meets Anchin, she begins to breathe fire at him. The terrified Anchin flees to Dōjōji, and Kiyohime is transformed into a huge fire-breathing snake or dragon. When Anchin finally reaches Dōjōji, he is hidden by the priests under the huge bronze bell of the temple. The dragon Kiyohime easily finds the bell, winds herself around it, turns it red hot, and burns Anchin to ashes. Soon after, two serpents, who are really the spirits of Anchin and Kiyohime, appear in a dream to the old priest of the temple and entreat him to pray for their salvation. The priest does so, and later two celestial beings appear to him and say that they are the serpents whom he has saved by his devotions.

In this section, Casal also describes the rituals *hyaku do mairi* 百度詣り (walking 100 steps) and *sen do mairi* 千度詣り (walking 1,000 steps), which are performed at Dōjōji by terminally ill patients in the hope that Kannon will miraculously cure them.

The second part of the article, *Ushi no toki mairi* 丑の時詣り, describes the Japanese ritual of sympathetic magic that was practiced by women to avenge wrongs by an unfaithful lover. The woman would visit a Shinto shrine, most often one of Fudō Myōō or Kompira, at the hour of the ox (1:00 A.M. to 3:00 A.M.). Casal details the elaborate preparations that the woman had to make before leaving for the temple, such as arranging her bedding in a certain way on the night when she is going to the temple, wearing a certain type of kimono in a certain way, and wearing or carrying various ritual objects. When the woman reached the shrine, she would nail a bamboo puppet that represented her lover and/or her rival to the sacred tree in the shrine's compound. She then went into the sanctuary and told the deity that the nails would be removed when her lover and rival were dead. This ritual was performed nightly for 3 to 49 consecutive nights. When the woman drove the last nail into the puppet, her victims would die.

9. Chigusa, Steven. "Hachikazuki: A Muromachi Short Story." *Monumenta Nipponica* 32, no. 3 (autumn 1977): 303–331.

The first part of this article examines the genre of *otogi zōshi* お伽草子, summarizes the plot of "Hachikazuki" 鉢かづき, compares it with the stories "Hanayo no hime" 花世の姫 and "Ubakawa" 姥皮, and analyzes the folklore motifs such as the bowl and garments that appear in these three stepdaughter tales. The latter part of the article is a translation of the standard version of "Hachikazuki."

10. Daniels, F. J. "Snake and Dragon Lore of Japan." *Folklore* 71 (September 1960): 145–164.

This is a general survey of folk beliefs concerning snakes and deities that appeared in snake and/or dragon shape. Daniels names the types of snakes found in Japan, describes the uses of snakes in Japanese folk medicine, and discusses the methods that were used to keep snakes away from people (and thus avoid snakebites). Footwear dyed with indigo, covering oneself with cypress branches when sleeping in a forest, and reciting certain spells were all thought to be efficacious. Some of the spells threatened to report any molesting snake to the local mountain deity, some threatened straightforward physical violence from the person reciting the spell if any snake approaches, and others simply sought to mollify the snake so that it was less likely to attack. Certain shrines sold amulets and special rice cakes that were supposed to protect people from snakes.

In different parts of Japan, certain actions regarding snakes were considered taboo: pointing at a snake, indicating the length of a snake with one's hands, killing or wounding a snake, and burying a snake near any vegetation. In some cases the ill effects caused by breaking the taboo could be avoided by performing certain prescribed rituals.

Daniels also describes beliefs concerning mallet snakes and *uwabami* 蟒, monstrously large serpents. He discusses deities that had snake or dragon form, or that were associated in some way with snakes. Many snake deities, such as Ōmononushi, were associated with mountains, but most were linked with bodies of water. Local snake deities were worshiped primarily as controllers of weather and water. The most important of the dragon deities were Ryūjin and Hachidai-ryūō. Many rituals were dedicated to snake deities; some made use of straw snake figures.

The article ends with stories of one-eyed fishes that originated from one-eyed snakes and of very small snakes that grew into tremendously large serpents.

11. Daniels, F. J. "Snakes as Wives and Lovers in Japanese Myth, Legend, and Folk Tale." *Japan Society of London Bulletin* 75 4, no. 20 (February 1975): 12–20.

This is a survey of the many classes of tales concerning marriages between humans and snakes. Most of the text is devoted to versions of various tales. The first part deals with snake wives and the second part with snake lovers.

The *Kojiki* and the *Nihongi* both record the story of the daughter of the Sea God marrying a mortal man. When she is about to give birth to their child, she enters a parturition hut on the seashore, telling her husband not to look at her while she is in there. He ignores her order and sees that she has resumed her true shape, which is some form of sea serpent. The wife returns to the sea, leaving her child behind. Her younger sister comes to care for the child. (In some versions the wife takes the child with her to her underwater home and returns him to land later.) In another tale from the *Kojiki*, an imperial prince takes a wife who proves to be a serpent. In a modern tale a woman from the Dragon Palace marries a poor but honest onion seller. When the lord of the province tries to steal her for himself, she kills him.

In another class of tales, the snake wives are not women from the Dragon Palace under the sea, but are from bodies of water throughout Japan, particularly in the mountains. In one group the snake wife leaves one of her eyes behind for use in nursing her child when she is forced to leave because her true identity has been discovered. When the lord of the province steals the eye, the wife sacrifices her second eye. In one version she tells her husband to flee the town, for she will cause a great earthquake to punish the lord; in another the snake wife does not seek any revenge, but goes to live in a lake near the Miidera temple after she is blinded. She asks that her husband arrange for the bell of Miidera to be rung every day for her.

Also discussed is a tale of the Dōjōji temple in which the spirit of a lustful woman turns into a snake and pursues the young priest who has spurned her. When he reaches the temple, the priest hides under the temple bell. The snake winds herself around the bell and causes it to become red hot, thus burning the priest to death. In a related tale the spirit of the woman turns into a snake and goes to live in a body of water. When the priest is passing by, she drags him into the water, and he also turns into a snake. Many tales about snake lovers involve a man secretly visiting a woman at night. In a tale from the *Kojiki*, the girl's parents tell her to stick a threaded needle into her lover's kimono so that they can follow it in the morning and discover his identity. When they do so, they find that the thread leads to the shrine of the deity Ōmononushi.

In a tale from the *Nihongi*, a woman tells her lover that she wishes to see him in the light of day. He tells her to look into her comb box in the morning, but warns her not to be frightened by what she sees. When she looks, she sees a small snake and cries out in surprise. The lover leaves and does not return, and the woman eventually kills herself.

Other stories tell of snakes founding important families or fathering guardian deities through their liaisons with mortal women.

One tale tells the origin of the sweet-flag-bath of the fifth month festival. A woman becomes pregnant by a snake. She hears that she will give birth to snake offspring, but that the pregnancy can be aborted if she takes such a bath. Thus, the sweet-flag-bath was thought to help against evil influences.

Daniels discusses the possibility that serpent bridegroom tales were an outgrowth of marriage practices in early Japan and of possession of female mediums by deities.

Another group of tales tells of women who, at least somewhat willingly, go to live with snakes as their wives. Finally, in some tales a woman is promised to a snake in exchange for the snake's performing some task. The girl thwarts the snake either by tricking and killing it herself or by being saved by some crabs whose lives she had previously saved.

12. de Visser, M. W. "The Dog and Cat in Japanese Superstition." *Transactions of the Asiatic Society of Japan* 37, part 1 (1909): 1–84.

This is a general survey of tales concerning dogs and cats in Japan and, to a lesser extent, China.

Chapter 1, The Dog and Cat in China, presents tales of dogs transforming themselves into humans, describes *ku* sorcery 蠱, and tells of the use of dogs as protectors against this form of magic and other evils. It also gives tales of cats transforming themselves into old women, describes several cases of cat specter sorcery, and discusses the beliefs that vengeful souls are transformed into cats after death and that a corpse will be reanimated if a cat jumps over it.

Chapter 2, The Dog and Cat in Japanese Legend, contains tales from a wide variety of sources, including the *Nihongi*, the *Kojiki*, the *Konjaku monogatari*, diaries, and literary collections. The tales tell of white dogs, of faithful dogs who stay with their masters even after their masters' deaths, and of dogs who are omens or who bring ritual uncleanliness, especially in the palace. There are many tales of *nekomata* 猫股, cat demons that can possess people and make them ill, even to the point of death, and that can assume the shapes of people whom they have killed and then attack and eat other people.

Chapter 3, The Dog's Protective Power, is subdivided into six sections. In section A, The Character 犬 (*inu*, dog) Written on the Foreheads of Babies, the practice is described that was believed to protect children from demons, especially from the demon bird *kisacho* 鬼車鳥.

This mythological creature of Chinese origin was believed to have ten heads, one of which had been devoured by a dog. This section also describes similar Chinese practices used against the *kisacho*.

Section B, The Inu-hariko 犬張子, describes the use of a dog-shaped box as a talisman in the lying-in room where a woman was giving birth. The box contained the child's first clothes, charms, white powder, a brush, and paper. The box was also used when the child was first brought to the temple and introduced around the neighborhood.

Section C, The Dog as a Bestower of Easy Birth, discusses the belief that the dog could ease the labors of childbirth because the dog itself was thought to have a relatively easy birth.

Section D, Dog-Charms, describes the talismans against fox possession that could be obtained from the temple at Mount Mitsumine where sacred dogs were kept; section E, The Hayato 隼人, describes the special group of guards at the Imperial Palace who would bark like dogs to drive away evil demons; and section F, The Koma-inu 拍犬, describes the use of lionlike dog statues for protection in the Imperial Palace and in temples.

Chapter 4, Sorcery by Means of the Dog-God, discusses the use of the dog essentially as a magic familiar by a sorcerer to bring illness and even death upon his victims. De Visser examines the belief that certain families hold or own supernatural dogs and pass this power on hereditarily, and he describes the ceremony by which a person can obtain such a dog familiar. He also discusses the *inugami-bito* 犬神人, men who were associated with several temples in Kyoto and who performed various ritual functions.

Chapter 5, Conclusions, summarizes and restates the material presented in the body of the paper.

In this work, de Visser cites more than 30 Chinese sources and more than 80 Japanese sources. He gives kanji for titles and authors, dates of publication and/or dates of authors, and volume, chapter, and/or page for each reference.

13. de Visser, M. W. *The Dragon in China and Japan*. Amsterdam: Johannes Muller, 1913.

This excellent book is a comprehensive study of folk beliefs and local legends concerning dragons. Book I deals with the dragon in China, and Book II discusses the dragon in Japan.

Introduction. The Nāga in Buddhism, with Regard to His Identification with the Chinese Dragon
   The Nāga according to European scholars
   The Nāga according to some translated texts
   The Nāga as a giver of rain
   Sūtras recited in rain ceremonies

Book I. The Dragon in China
Chapter 1. The Dragon in the Chinese Classics
  Yih king
  Shu king
  Li ki
  Cheu li
  I li
Chapter 2. Divination and Geomancy
  Lucky omens
  Bad omens (fighting dragons, dead dragons, dragons appearing
    at wrong times, dragons appearing in wrong places)
  Dragon-horses
  Geomancy
Chapter 3. General Information
  Enormous light-giving mountain-gods
  Nature of the dragons
  What dragons like and dislike
  Shape of the dragons
  Male and female dragons
  Different kinds of dragons
  Kiao lung
  Rearing and taming dragons
  Dragons ridden by *sien,* or drawing the cars of gods and holy
    men
  Dragon-boats
  "Dragon-tail-rod" and other words connected with the dragon
  Dragon-gate
  Dragon's den
  Dragon herds
  Dragon's pearls
  Dragon's eggs
  Dragon's bones, skins, teeth, horns, brains, livers, placentas,
    and fetuses used as medicines
  Dragon's blood, fat, and saliva
Chapter 4. Ornaments
  Symbols of imperial dignity and fertilizing rain, represented on
    garments, honorary gates, coffins, etc.
  Nine different kinds of dragons, used as ornaments
  Ornaments used by Wuist priests and mediums
  The dragon and the ball
Chapter 5. Causing Rain, Thunder, and Storm
  The gods of thunder, clouds, and rain
  Violent rains accompanied by heavy winds and thunderstorms
  Rain magic and prayers
  Buddhist rain ceremonies
Chapter 6. Emperors Connected with Dragons

Hwang Ti rode on a dragon
Yao and Kao Tsu, sons of dragons
Shun visited by a yellow dragon
Yü drove in a carriage drawn by dragons, assisted by a *ying-lung*
Ming Hwang's vessel moved forward by a dragon
Two yellow dragons threatened to upset Yü's vessel
Shi Hwang died for killing a dragon
Chapter 7. Transformations
Dragon's transformations unlimited
Appearing as old men or beautiful women
Appearing as fishes
Appearing as snakes, dogs, or rats
Cow transformed into a dragon
Appearing as objects
Chapter 8. The Indian Nāga in China
Reborn as dragon
Ponds inhabited by dragon-kings
Temples of dragon-kings
Palaces of dragon-kings
Book II. The Dragon in Japan
Chapter 1. The Original Dragon-Gods of Rivers, Seas, and Mountains
Okami
Yamatsumi and *Mitsuha*
Watatsumi
Mizuchi, the river-gods
Oho-watatsumi, the sea-god
Wani
The jewels of flood and ebb
Take-iwa Tatsu no Mikoto, the dragon-god of a sacred pond in
   Higo Province
An emperor's dragon-tail
Chapter 2. The Chinese Dragon and the Dragon-Horse as Omens in
Japan
Flying dragons as horse of a ghost or of a *sien*
Dragon-horses
Carriage of a ghost drawn through the air by eight dragons
Dragon appeared as good omen
Chapter 3. Causing Rain
Shinto gods
Horses offered to Shinto gods
Buddhism wins the field
The Sacred Spring Park
The "dragon-hole" on Mount Murōbu
Reborn as a rain-giving dragon

14. de Visser, M. W. "The Fox and the Badger in Japanese Folklore."
Transactions of the Asiatic Society of Japan 36, part 3 (1908): 1–159.

Chapter 1, The Fox in China, presents tales of werefoxes who could
turn themselves into humans, of foxes who caused various evils such as
madness, fire, and death, of foxes who appeared as Buddhas, and of
foxes who bewitched people. Foxes could be forced to resume their true
shapes by being wounded, by being confronted by dogs, or by incantations or other ritual means. Foxes could transform themselves into humans by using human bones, charms, or spells. This chapter also tells of
foxes who were interpreted as good omens and of foxes who became
Celestial Foxes and ascended into heaven.

Chapter 2, The Fox and the Badger in Japanese Laws, Divination,
and Legends, is in three sections. The first section, Laws, tells of edicts
that forbade the disinterring of corpses and the burning of corpses,
graves, and coffins to smoke out foxes and badgers.

The second section, Divination, tells of the appearances of foxes
being interpreted as omens. Nine-tailed foxes, white foxes, and black
foxes were considered good omens. A fox's crying out or discharging
bodily wastes had different meanings, depending upon the zodiacal day

on which the event was witnessed, but in almost all cases these events portended death or other disaster. Foxes would sometimes enter the Imperial Palace, in which case it was almost always interpreted as a bad omen.

The third section, Legends, is in ten parts. Part A deals with the eighth, ninth, and tenth centuries, and parts B through J deal with one century each in chronological order. In almost all parts, there are tales of bewitching foxes who tricked people, of foxes who possessed people, and of foxes who appeared as beautiful women and seduced men. A person who was possessed by a fox spirit would suffer illness, madness, or even death. The person could often be cured by being threatened by a knife, by being beaten, or by having the fox spirit "channeled" into a medium and bribing it with offers of food. A bewitching fox that appeared as a human, as a Buddha, or as some other object could be forced to resume its true shape by being shot with an arrow or threatened by a sword, by being attacked by dogs, or by the reciting of Buddhist prayers. Some stories tell of certain families who held or owned foxes as magical familiars and who thrived financially because of this. The members of such a family could only marry someone from another fox-holding family. Several tales tell of people who obtained material wealth or magical power by worshiping foxes.

Foxes were associated with the deity Inari and were believed to be her messengers. In some cases of fox possession, notice would be sent to the Inari shrine asking the deity to stop her subject's evil deeds against humans.

Foxes would reward people who spared their lives and could even become a person's guardian deity. Foxes were noted for their keen sense for revenge when they felt that they had been wronged. It was also believed that foxes could produce fires from their tails.

De Visser gives far fewer tales of the badger. In general, the badger was thought to bewitch people and to possess them in much the same way as did foxes, but the badger was considered not quite as skillful as the fox. Badgers could make music by puffing up their bellies and beating on them like drums. Badgers disguised as men liked to write and draw, and many tales claim that certain artworks were really produced by badgers.

Chapter 3, Ideas about Foxes and Badgers Prevalent in the Seventeenth and Eighteenth Centuries, is a summary of common folk beliefs of the time. Foxes and badgers were considered to be omens and were thought to be capable of possessing people and of assuming human form. Foxes could act as magical familiars, could produce fire from their tails, from bones, or from horses' hooves, and were the messengers of Inari. The fox's soul was thought to be in the shape of a pearl or jewel. The fox's liver and the badger's skin were used as medicines.

Chapter 4, Fox Sorcery, Izuna, and Dagini Ten, discusses in greater detail the belief that people employed foxes as magical familiars, the practice of worshiping foxes in cults other than that of Inari, and the possible connection between foxes and tengu. De Visser also compares fox sorcery and dog sorcery. He describes how certain families owned foxes and passed this power on hereditarily and why these families, although they were usually quite wealthy, could not marry into families other than other fox-holding families.

Chapter 5, Inari, the Fox-Shaped Spirit of the Rice, describes the worship of fox deities, the rise of the cult of Inari, and Inari's association with foxes. The chapter ends with a brief summary of the material presented in the rest of the paper.

Synopses for each of the tales presented in this article are not given here, because many of the tales are very similar, particularly those about foxes. The stories about badgers tend to be unique, but the tales of badger enchantment are similar to those of fox enchantment.

15. de Visser, M. W. "The Snake in Japanese Superstition." *Mitteilungen des Seminars für Orientalische Sprachen an der Koniglichen Friedrich-Wilhelms Universitat zu Berlin*, pp. 267–322. Berlin: Kommissionsverlag von Georg Reimer, 1911.

This is a general survey of folk beliefs concerning snakes in Japan and, to a much lesser extent, in China.

Chapter 1, The Snake in China, gives tales of snakes assuming human form and of humans turning into snakes, of snakes parenting human offspring, and of plant spirits that could appear as snakes. The souls of children who were murdered by their mothers were thought to be reincarnated as snakes to seek revenge. Snake demons could haunt and possess people and cause disease. Snakes were used in sorcery, especially in *ku* sorcery 蠱. The leaves and roots of a certain plant, the head bones of spotted or striped cats, musk, and centipedes were all used as antidotes against *ku* sorcery.

Chapter 2, Serpent-Shaped Gods, contains: Shinto gods, including serpent-shaped mountain-gods (examines the legends of Yamato no Orochi and Oho-mono-nushi no kami, among others), serpent-shaped gods of the water (examines the legends of Mitsu-ha-no Me, Princess Hinaga, and the god of Lake Suwa, among others), serpent-shaped tree spirits, and various serpent-shaped Shinto gods. Chapter 2 also discusses Buddhist snake-shaped gods, including Benzaiten, as well as sorcery by means of snake-gods.

Following are Chapter 3, Snakes as Omens; Chapter 4, Reborn as Snakes; and Chapter 5, Snakes as Embodied Passions (lust, hatred, jealousy, and desire of snakes). Chapter 6, Transformations, contains snakes assuming human shapes, bewitching metamorphoses of the spirits of serpents, women changing into snakes, and objects changing into snakes.

Chapter 7, Charms against Snakes, discusses how metals (particularly iron), Buddhist prayers, music, and amulets were all used as protection against snakes. Chapter 8 contains the conclusions.

16. de Visser, M. W. "The Tengu." *Transactions of the Asiatic Society of Japan* 36, part 2 (1908): 25–99.

This is a historical survey of legends about tengu.

Chapter 1, The Celestial Dog in China, proposes a Chinese antecedent of the tengu in the *t'ien keu* 天拘, the Celestial Dogs, which lived in the heavens or on mountain tops. The *t'ien keu* could appear as omens that war or other catastrophe was imminent, as guardian spirits of a citadel, or as predators of human infants. Chinese tales tell of young boys being abducted by mountain demons.

Chapter 2, The Celestial Dog in Japan, is a chronological examination of tengu legends in Japanese sources. The first section, Eighth Century, suggests that the idea of the Celestial Dog came to Japan from China with a Buddhist priest, and by the time of the *Nihongi*, the Celestial Dog was being associated with the Celestial Fox, *Ama tsu kitsune*, which the Japanese wrote with the same characters 天拘. The second section, Tenth and Eleventh Centuries, begins with a tale in which the Minister of the Right was lured into the woods in Kitayama by the sound of skillful koto playing. He found a beautiful girl there, but the incident was later ascribed to a tengu. Nine stories are presented from the *Konjaku monogatari*.

1. A tengu was lured to Hieizan by the sea singing a Buddhist text. Although he originally wanted to make the singing stop, the tengu became a convert to Buddhism, resolved to become a priest, and was reincarnated as a man.
2. A tengu from China tried to defeat the Buddhist priests of Japan, but the power of one bishop was too much for him. The tengu was defeated and sent back to China.
3. A tengu appeared as a Buddha in a tree. After seven days his powers ended, the illusion ceased, and the tengu was killed.
4. A priest of Takayama was renowned for his spiritual powers, but it was discovered that his powers came from the worship of tengu, not of the Buddha.
5. A tengu who was disguised as a nun tried to steal some vestments from a temple, but he was discovered and stopped.
6. A tengu possessed a young woman in order to seduce a priest. Through prayers to Fudō Myōō, the priest defeated the tengu and cured the woman.
7. A young man, who sought to learn the power of magic, went with a sorcerer to an old priest in the mountains. He took a sword with him, contrary to the sorcerer's instructions. When the sword was discovered, the old priest disappeared (he was really a tengu), and the sorcerer's power was broken.

8. A tengu abducted a dragon in the form of a small snake. The dragon could not resume its true shape unless it had some water available. The tengu then abducted a priest from Hieizan and took him to where the dragon was being kept. The priest gave the dragon some water, and the dragon resumed its true shape. The dragon returned the priest to Hieizan and killed the tengu.

9. A devout but uneducated priest was tricked into believing that a tengu was actually the Amida Buddha. The priest thought that he was to be taken to the Western Paradise, but in fact the tengu tied him to the top of a tree. A week later, the priest was found, but he had become a raving lunatic, and he soon died.

Using these tales as examples, de Visser discusses the prominent role of the tengu as an opponent of Buddhism.

In the third section of chapter 2, Twelfth and Thirteenth Centuries, it was feared that tengu would interfere with the construction of a Buddhist temple. The Emperor Sanjo was thought to have been made blind by the angry spirit of the priest Kansen, and he was not cured even after he had abdicated the throne and retired to Hieizan. Several tales from various sources tell of tengu who possessed people and who proved to be the spirits of clerics who had been turned into tengu as punishment for the sins that they had committed in life. In particular, sins of vanity and heresy could cause people to become tengu after their death. One priest, who had vowed to serve his teacher in the afterlife, became a tengu because his teacher had become one, and he was bound by his oath. Another priest became a tengu because he had built a marvelous temple simply to satisfy his vanity. An empress was possessed by a tengu who proved to be the spirit of a bishop who had served Fudō Myōō; this bishop had been made a tengu as a punishment for heresy. De Visser also discusses the legend of Yoshitsune, who supposedly received his training in the martial arts from tengu. The deposed Emperor Sutoku became a dreadful demon after his death because of his hatred for his brother. A spirit who claimed to be the dead Emperor Go Shirakawa possessed several people and demanded that he be worshiped as a god; the demands were ignored, and the people recovered. An apparition of the god of Sumiyoshi explained that the souls of proud people or those of bad principles became tengu, especially the souls of proud Buddhist clerics. Many tales tell of tengu abducting priests and children and of tengu suffering the punishments of the Buddhist afterlife because of their sins. De Visser stresses the belief that tengu involved themselves in politics and religion so as to cause wars and bring disorder to the world.

The fourth section is not marked in the text, but the fifth section, Fifteenth Century, tells the story of two boys from Miidera who were on their way to Hieizan when they were abducted by tengu; the tengu thus caused a battle between the two monasteries.

Sections six, Seventeenth Century, and seven, Eighteenth Century, also contain tales of boys being kidnapped by tengu. Villagers would beat gongs and drums and call out to the tengu to return the boys. In contrast to previous stories, there are also tales of tengu actually promoting and protecting Buddhism. In some stories the tengu show people the evil in sins such as pride and the murdering of animals; in others they act as guardians for temples against disasters such as fire and theft.

The eighth section, Nineteenth Century, describes *kuhin mochi* 拘賓餅, rice cakes that were offered by the woodcutters of Mino Province to the tengu as a protection against these demons. Section nine, Statements of Japanese Scholars of the Seventeenth, Eighteenth, and Nineteenth Centuries, discusses various theories about the tengu that were presented by Japanese writers of that time. This section includes physical descriptions of tengu, names of famous tengu, types and origins of tengu, and deeds ascribed to tengu.

Chapter 3, The Tengu and the Garuda, examines the theory that the tengu is actually derived from a Buddhist demon of Indian origin. Chapter 4, Conclusions, summarizes and restates the information given in the body of the text.

17. Dorson, Richard M., ed. *Studies in Japanese Folklore*. Bloomington: Indiana University Press, 1963.

Most of the articles in this book deal with folk culture and folk religion; one article deals with tales of "inborn luck" (including the origin of the Hearth God), and one article concerns a particular subtype of the serpent bridegroom tale.

There are two introductions, "Bridges between Japanese and American Folklorists," by Richard M. Dorson, and "Opportunities for Folklore Research in Japan," by Kunio Yanagita.

"Seasonal Rituals Connected with Rice Culture," by Toshijiro Hirayama, details several agricultural rituals, in particular those associated with the transplanting of the rice seedlings.

"Mysterious Visitors from the Harvest to the New Year," by Ichirō Hori, describes several festivals in which supernatural beings are believed to visit the earth. Hori also describes the rites associated with these mysterious visitors and discusses the various groups of people, many of them members of the outcasts, who visited homes during the New Year's celebration and performed magico-religious rituals.

"The Taboos of Fishermen," by Tokihiko Ōtō, discusses two kinds of taboo, ritual taboos and those associated with death and childbirth.

"The Ebisu-gami in Fishing Villages," by Katsunori Sakurada, tells of this patron deity of fishing and its association with various objects and marine animals.

"Drifted Deities in Noto Province," by Manabu Ogura, describes the beliefs that deities from the sea either come ashore on various objects or are brought ashore by fishermen.

"Japanese Metalworkers: A Possible Source for Their Legends," by Nobuhiro Matsumoto, discusses the practice of corpse worship by metalworkers and the legend on which it is based. It gives versions of several tales in which poor men obtain great wealth by discovering precious metals in the areas where they work (tales of "inborn luck"). This type of tale is related to stories of the origin of the Hearth God, which are also mentioned. Matsumoto explains the theory that these tales were originally from mainland Asia, brought to Japan by metalworkers who migrated from the mainland to the Japanese islands.

"The Double-Grave System," by Takayoshi Mogami, describes the burial custom in which two graves are constructed for the same person, one for the actual interment of the corpse and the other as a site for memorial services.

"The Concept of *Tamashii* in Japan," by Narimitsu Matsudaira, examines the Japanese idea of soul or spirit; and "A Study of *Yashiki-gami*, the Deity of House and Grounds," by Hiroji Naoe, describes the family tutelary deity and its worship.

"The Village Tutelary Deity and the Use of Holy Rods," by Toshiaki Harada, explains the practice of choosing from among the villagers a person who is responsible for the services to the village tutelary deity for one year and describes the use of the holy rods in the services to the deity.

"The Position of the Shinto Priesthood: Historical Changes and Development," by Tatsuo Hagiwara, discusses the regulations governing professional priests, the duties of the priest, and the effects of political changes on the priesthood. "Menstrual Taboos Imposed upon Women," by Kiyoko Segawa, describes the rules of seclusion and abstinence that traditionally had to be observed by women when menstruating. "*Ahiire-kon*, Putting-One's-Feet-in-Marriage," by Tokuzō Ōmachi, describes the matri-patrilocal marriage customs of Toshima.

"The Spool of Thread: A Subtype of the Japanese Serpent-Bridegroom Tale," by Keigo Seki, is an analysis of tales in which a woman is visited nightly by an unknown suitor who is really a snake, and in which the woman discovers his true identity by sticking a threaded needle into his clothes and following the thread in the morning. Also discussed are the distributions of the variants, the versions of the tale that appear in Japanese written literature, and the story's social and religious background.

"Initiation Rites and Young Men's Organizations," by Taro Wakamori, describes the rites of passage that mark the attainment of adulthood by young men and, to a lesser extent, young women and the youth organizations that serve to integrate young men into the general society of the village, in particular the adult labor force, and to help them to obtain wives and arrange marriages.

This book also contains an excellent 24-page glossary of Japanese names and terms.

18. Dykstra, Yoshiko Kurata. "Jizō, the Most Merciful: Tales from *Jizō Bosatsu Reigenki*." *Monumenta Nipponica* 33, no. 2 (summer 1978): 179–200.

This article describes the cult of Jizō in China and its introduction to Japan and gives translations of seven stories from the *Jizō Bosatsu Reigenki* 地蔵菩薩霊験記. (The double numbers in the list below refer to book and story numbers.)

I, 1: How the Jizō of Shōbōji Appeared in a Dream to Jitsuei, the Head Priest
I, 5: How Mochikata Received a Miraculous Revelation
I, 7: How Ninkō Delivered the First Jizō Sermon
II, 9: How Moritaka of Kamo Came Back to Life
II, 10: How an Ascetic Priest Was Given a Miraculous Sign
II, 12: How Koretaka of Suhō Made the Statues of the Six Jizō
III, 5: About the "Malt Jizō" of Kanuki in Suruga

19. Dykstra, Yoshiko Kurata. "Miraculous Tales of the Lotus Sutra: The *Dainihonkoku Hokkegenki*." *Monumenta Nipponica* 32, no. 2 (summer 1977): 189–210.

This article describes the cult of the Lotus Sutra and gives translations of eight stories from the *Dainihonkoku Hokkegenki* 大日本国法華験記, a Heian collection of 129 Buddhist tales in three books. (The double numbers in the list below refer to book and story numbers.)

I, 13: How a Corpse Recited the Hokekyo on Mount Shishigase in Kii Province
I, 22: About Priest Shunchō
I, 32: About the Hokekyo Reciter of the Tada-in
III, 81: About Priest Jin'yū of Echigo Province
III, 110: About the Government Official of Higo Province
III, 113: About a Hawk Catcher of Mitsu Province
III, 125: About the Rat and Snake of Shinano Province
III, 128: About the Guardian of Travelers in Minabe District of Kii Province

20. Dykstra, Yoshiko Kurata. "Tales of the Compassionate Kannon: The *Hasedera Kannon Genki*." *Monumenta Nipponica* 31, no. 2 (summer 1976): 113–143.

This article describes the cult of the Kannon of Hasedera and gives translations of 11 stories from the *Hasedera Kannon Genki* 長谷寺観音験記, a collection of 52 tales in two books. The first volume contains tales of the teachings of Kannon; the second volume gives tales of the various manifestations of Kannon. Some stories tell of the origin of the Hasedera and its ceremonies, and some tell of the benefits obtained by the faithful worshipers of the Hasedera Kannon. (The double numbers in the list below refer to book and story numbers.)

> I,   4: How Sadanori Prayed to the Kannon and Was Blessed with a Son, Haseo, Who Re-established His Clan
>
> I,   5: How Emperor Montoku Cured the Illness of Emperor Seiwa and Established Three Priestly Positions in the Temple
>
> I, 15: How a Son's Ulcer Was Cured and a New Elevated Corridor was Built at Hasedera
>
> II, 15: How Both Takemitsu and His Wife, Inspired by Faith, Practiced Ascetic Ways and Finally Entered the Buddhahood
>
> II, 16: How Ono no Muko, of the Junior Fifth Rank, Encountered Mountain Bandits and Quickly Escaped
>
> II, 21: How a Priest Discovered the Reason for His Being Dark and Was Reborn in the Tosotsu Heaven
>
> II, 27: How the Great Holy One Caused the Theft of a Silk Robe in Order to Benefit a Man and Two Women
>
> II, 28: How the Wishes of Five Persons Were Immediately Realized after They Had Seen and Worshiped the Kannon
>
> II, 31: A Story about Praying for a Child and Receiving a Filial Daughter
>
> II, 32: How a Poor Woman Dedicated a Poem to the Kannon and Was Instantly Blessed with a Fortune
>
> II, 33: How a Priest Prayed for the Mitigation of His Sins, Changed Grave Sins into Lesser Ones, and Attained Enlightenment

Jizō, Kannon, and the Lotus Sutra are often mentioned in Japanese folktales. Folklorists who are not familiar with these Buddhist cults will find these three articles (18, 19, 20) by Dykstra to be very helpful introductions.

21. Eder, Matthias. "Reality in Japanese Folktales." *Asian Folklore Studies* 28, no. 1 (1969): 17–26.

Eder examines the extent to which Japanese tales are an expression of religious beliefs. The tales presented here tell of the origins of animals, of demons, of magical powers, of nonhuman marriage partners, and of the special powers of Buddhist priests.

22. Harada, Violet H. "The Badger in Japanese Folklore." *Asian Folklore Studies* 35, no. 1 (1976): 1–6.

This short article describes the illusionary shapes that the badger can assume and examines the three major roles of the badger in Japanese folktales: vengeful transformer, grateful friend, and roguish prankster. Harada includes brief synopses of 17 tales to illustrate the roles.

23. Ikeda, Hiroko. " 'Kachi-Kachi Mountain'—A Japanese Animal Tale Cycle." *Humaniora: Essays in Literature, Folklore, Bibliography,* pp. 229–238, edited by Wayland D. Hand and Gustave O. Arlt. Locust Valley, N.Y.: J. J. Augustin, 1960.

This is an excellent analysis of the tale "Kachi kachi yama" かちかち山, "The Crackling Mountain." Ikeda gives a synopsis of the standard version of the story as it appears in *Nippon Bungaku Daijiten* 日本文学大辞典. She notes that there are still many local variants, 89 of which appear in Seki's *Nippon mukashibanashi shūsei* 日本昔話集成 (see Appendix A in this book).

Ikeda divides the tale into ten component parts:

1. An evil badger mocks an old man who is working. The man traps the badger and brings it home to make into soup.
2. The badger tricks the old man's wife into releasing it, kills her, makes her into the soup, and serves it to the old man. (In this section, Ikeda tells an Arapaho Indian tale that is very similar to "Crackling Mountain.")
3. The rabbit seeks to revenge the old woman's death, getting the badger either to carry some firewood on its back or to work inside a grass hut, then sets the wood or grass on fire. When the badger asks what the noise of the fire is, the rabbit says that the mountain is called "crackling" because it makes a sound like that.
4. The rabbit gives the badger a plaster of some painful substance to put on its burns.
5. This is a group of minor variants. The rabbit tricks the badger into being bound with vines, or the rabbit offers to carry the badger if the badger closes its eyes. The rabbit then delivers the badger to the old man.
6. The rabbit and the badger go boating. The rabbit uses a wooden boat and gives the badger a mud boat. When the mud boat dissolves, the badger drowns. (This is the end of the standard version.)
7. The rabbit takes the badger to a farmhouse, makes it into soup, and eats it all.
8. The wife of the farmhouse is going to kill the rabbit. She sends

her child to fetch a knife, but each time he brings the wrong object. The wife finally goes for the knife herself, leaving the child to guard the rabbit.
9. The rabbit tricks the child into releasing it and escapes.
10. The wife throws the knife at the rabbit and cuts off its tail.

Ikeda gives 33 different combinations formed by these parts and the distribution of the combinants.

24. Ikeda, Hiroko. "Relationship between Japanese and Korean Folktales." *Internationaler Kongress der Volkserzahlungsforscher in Kiel und Kopenhagen*, pp. 118–123. Berlin: Walter de Gruyter, 1961.

At the time of this article, about 8,000 Japanese folktales had been recorded for use by scholars, while less than 200 Korean tales had been cataloged. For this reason, the article is really a preliminary study, and Ikeda does not make any broad generalizations about the relationship between the two groups of tales. What she does do is list the types of tales that were then known to overlap between the two countries. Ikeda first eliminated those Japanese tales known to be derived from Chinese literary sources. She gives three groups of Japanese tales that show similarities with those from Korea: tales in Japan that have very old traits, tales found only in the outlying islands of southern Kyushu, and tales known to be popular in Japan, Korea, and China.

25. Ikeda, Hiroko. "A Type and Motif Index of Japanese Folk Literature." *FF Communications* 89, no. 209 (1971): 1–377.

This is an invaluable reference work on Japanese folklore. Ikeda has assigned an Aarne-Thompson number to each of the 439 types listed in this index. Each entry gives the type number, an English title for the tale, Romanized Japanese titles, geographic distribution, number of known versions and their sources, and a plot synopsis that notes possible variations of motifs. The single most important source for these tales is Seki's *Nippon mukashibanashi shūsei* 日本昔話集成 (see Appendix A).

There are four main appendixes. The first is an Index of Motifs. Each motif is assigned a number from Stith Thompson's *Motif Index of Folk Literature* (see Introduction), and the motifs are arranged alphanumerically according to this number. Each entry has the Thompson motif number, a descriptive phrase summarizing the motif, and the type numbers of the tales in which the motif appears. The motifs are divided into 23 major categories:

Mythological Motifs
Animals
Tabu

Magic
The Dead
Marvels
Ogres
Tests
The Wise and the Foolish
Deceptions
Reversals of Fortune
Ordaining the Future
Chance and Fate
Society
Rewards and Punishments
Captivity and Fugitives
Unnatural Cruelty
Sex
The Nature of Life
Religion
Traits of Character
Humor
Miscellaneous Groups of Motifs

The second appendix is a General Index and Glossary. It lists catchwords and names in English, sometimes followed by a brief explanatory note, and the numbers of the tale types in which the item appears.

The third appendix is a Japanese Index. It lists Japanese catchwords and titles in romaji and the numbers of the tale types in which the item appears.

The fourth appendix is a bibliography containing many Japanese and English sources, with some Chinese sources. Japanese titles and authors are given only in romaji. This section also explains the title abbreviations used throughout the work.

In addition to the appendixes, there are two cross-reference tables that correlate Ikeda's numbering system with the one done by Keigo Seki (entry 46), and a map of Japan for use in studying the geographic distribution of the tales.

26. Ishida, Eiichiro. "The Kappa Legends: A Comparative Ethnological Study on the Japanese Water-Spirit Kappa and Its Habit of Trying to Lure Horses into the Water." *Folklore Studies* 9 (1950): 1–152.

Most of this article deals with legends of supernatural or marvelous horses and oxen from around the world. It also examines the associations between horses and dragons, between horses and water-deities, and between oxen and water-deities. The latter part of the article deals with kappa and with the relationships among kappa, monkeys, and horses.

Following is an abridged table of contents.

Chapter 1. Horses and Water-Gods
    The Japanese islands
        kappa luring horses into the water
        pastures by the waterside
        fine horses sired by dragons
        fine horses appear out of the water
    China and its borders
        dragon-horses
        dragons turn into horses and horses into dragons
        dragons and Celestial Horses
        pasturing mares by the waterside so that they may bear fine
          steeds
        divine horses in the water
        water-gods on horseback
        horses and floods
        river-gods seek to draw horses into the water
        sacrifice of horses to water-gods
    The Caucasus, etc.
    The Finnic peoples
    The Germanic peoples
    Scotland
    Ireland
    France
    Spain
    Russia
    Bohemia
    Lausitz
    Hungary
    Southern Slavs
    The Greeks and the Mediterranean
Chapter 2. Oxen and Water-Gods
        The ox and the horse
        The female principle, the moon, the ox, and agriculture
        Fertility and ox worship
        The moon and water
        Water and the ox
        Oxen and horses sacrificed to water-gods
    The Turks
    The Finno-Ugric peoples
    The Germanic peoples
    The Celts
    The Semites
    Persians
    India
    China and border regions

thunder and the dragon
wicked dragons destroyed by thunder
the *chiao*-dragon in the form of oxen
an iron ox quells a river flood
oxen and wind and rain
heaven is represented by the horse, and the earth by the ox
The Japanese islands
agriculture and the ox
divine oxen in the water
the ox and the ceremony of praying for rain
The Nakoshi festival, etc.
riddle of the kappa trying to lure horses into the water
Chapter 3. Monkeys and Water-Gods
Boy water-gods
Bowl on the head
Monkeys
Monkeys by the waterside
Monkeys are considered as enemies of the kappa
Monkeys, horses, and kappa
Monkeys kept in stables
Conclusion
Fine steeds obtained by the waterside
Water-gods in the form of horses
Oxen and water
Ox worship
The moon, the earth, the female principle, oxen, the power of
fertility and water
The southward advance of the horse
Oxen replaced by horses
Western Europe and Eastern Asia
Oxen and agriculture
Dragon-horses cum Celestial Horses versus river-oxen cum
earth-oxen
Continuity of the human culture
God of thunder and rain
Megalithic culture
Taboo of iron
The need of vision from the standpoint of world history

27. Ishida, Eiichiro. "Unfinished but Enduring: Yanagita Kunio's Folklore
Studies." *Japan Quarterly* 10, no. 1 (January/March 1963): 35–42.

This article is a tribute to Yanagita. It gives a brief biographical
sketch and outlines Yanagita's basic attitudes toward folklore studies.

28. Ishiwara, Yasuyo. "Celestial Wife in Japanese Folk Tales." *Journal of East Asiatic Studies* 5, no. 1 (January 1956): 35–41.

Ishiwara classifies tales of *tennin nyōbō* 天人女房 into two groups, legendary and entertaining, and gives an example of each.

In the legendary tale a Celestial Maiden from Mount Rokkoushi is trapped on earth when a mortal man steals her magic robe, which she had left on a rock while bathing. She follows him to his home and requests that he return her robe, but he refuses, saying that he will present it to the lord of the province. The woman then builds a hut on the man's land, lives there, and cultivates lotus plants. She spins the fibers and weaves a beautiful brocade, which the man also presents to the lord. The woman then goes to live in the palace. When the clothing in the palace is hung out to air, the maiden recovers her robe and returns to Mount Rokkoushi.

In the entertaining tale, the maiden is again trapped by the theft of her robe. In this story, however, the man makes her his wife, and several children are born. The maiden discovers, from a lullaby that her oldest child sings to her baby, that her robe is hidden under a pile of rice. The woman returns to the sky, but she leaves instructions for her husband to follow. When the man reaches the sky, he is given superhuman tasks to perform by his father-in-law. The man accomplishes them with the help of his wife. He is then given one final task. The man ignores his wife's advice, and they are separated.

Ishiwara divides this tale into seven parts: (1) man finds maiden, (2) man steals robe, (3) birth of children, (4) recovery of robe, (5) return to heaven, (6) pursuit by husband, and (7) tasks assigned by father-in-law. The different variants for each part are given and parts that can be omitted are noted.

The footnotes for the article give some versions of this tale from other parts of Asia.

29. Johnson, T. W. "Far Eastern Fox Lore." *Asian Folklore Studies* 33, no. 1 (1974): 35–68.

This article outlines Chinese, Japanese, and, to a lesser extent, Korean beliefs concerning the fox. Johnson discusses the names, words, and kanji used to refer to foxes, the early literary references to the fox, beliefs in the medicinal uses of parts of the fox's body, and the interpretation of the appearances of foxes as omens.

The types of fox tales found in the three countries are examined. Tales from China is divided into four categories according to a classification proposed by Wolfram Eberhard in 1948:

1. Erotic experiences with foxes
2. Experiences with evil fox ghosts

3. General experiences with foxes
4. Experiences with good foxes

There are tales from Japan to represent each of these four categories, but the tales from Korea are almost always of foxes who assume human shape and kill people.

Johnson describes the methods by which a fox is able to assume human shape and the ways in which such enchantments can be detected. He also discusses the phenomenon of fox possession, giving some case histories and examining the methods used to exorcise the fox spirit. He describes the belief that certain families held or owned foxes as magical familiars. The article ends with a brief look at fox worship and the cult of Inari.

Throughout this article, Johnson refers to Casal's "The Goblin Fox and Badger and Other Witch Animals of Japan" (entry 6), de Visser's "The Fox and the Badger in Japanese Folklore" (entry 14), and Nozaki's *Kitsune: Japan's Fox of Mystery, Romance and Humor* (entry 45).

30. Kelsey, W. Michael. "*Konjaku Monogatari Shū:* Toward an Understanding of Its Literary Qualities." *Monumenta Nipponica* 30, no. 2 (summer 1975): 121–150.

This is an examination of the literary value of the stories found in the *Konjaku,* especially the didactic ones, and of the collection as a whole. Kelsey discusses the organization of the tales within the collection and the importance of their order. He also gives his translations of four consecutive tales, numbers one through four of Book 19.

19.1: The Conversion of Yoshimine no Munesada
19.2: The Conversion of the Governor of Mikawa
19.3: The Conversion of Yoshishige no Yasutane
19.4: The Conversion of Minamoto no Mitsunaka

The literary value of each tale is discussed, and the relationship and development of theme between the consecutive stories are analyzed.

31. Kobayashi, H. "The 'Ashikari Tale,' a Tenth-Century Japanese Story of a Reed Cutter and Its Possible Source." *Journal of the Oriental Society of Australia* 11 (1976): 19–36.

This article examines the story type in which a husband and wife separate and later meet again, with the wife having become very wealthy and the husband poverty-stricken. The oldest extant version of "Ashikari setsuwa" 葦刈リ説話 is from the *Yamato monogatari* 大和物語, but different versions of the tale are found in later anthologies.

Other very similar tales to the Ashikari are "Kamagami no koto" 竈神のこと (On the Kitchen God), "Sumiyaki chōja" 炭焼長者 (The Millionaire Charcoal Burner), and "Ubigami mondō" 産神問答 (Dialogue with the Guardian Deity of the Newly Born). The article gives versions of these tales and compares them.

Kobayashi also discusses tales of the origin of the worship of the Kitchen God and the sending off of the God of Poverty, describes the worship of the Kitchen God in China, and relates the retention of the "Kamagami" theme in Okinawan tales (but not in Japanese tales) to the fact that the Okinawans worship the Kitchen God in a manner similar to that of the Chinese, while the Japanese do not.

32. Krappe, Alexander H. "Far Eastern Fox Lore." *California Folklore Quarterly* 3, no. 2 (April 1944): 124–147.

This is a study of fox tales that were available in English translation at the time.

The article begins with tales from China:

1. A man marries a woman. She always goes to bed with her clothes on, but one night he sees that she has a fox tail. Thus he learns that she is really a fox.
2. Two farmers who had threatened to smoke out some foxes are possessed by them, but the fox spirits release their victims when threatened with a knife.
3. A farmer steals a magic elixir from a fox. After 30 years the fox manages to recover it.
4. A fox disguised as an old man takes another man to a banquet. When the enchantment is broken, the man discovers that he is a great distance from his home.
5. Despite the gifts of silver given to him by a fox maiden, a man remains poor and ill-lucked. This is finally ascribed to his inevitable fate.
6. A fox benefits the fortunes of a family that worships the fox god.
7. The fox god, disguised as an old man, prevents a group of thieves from stealing some sacred vessels from an imperial temple.
8. A man chases off a bewitching fox with a whip and is later able to cure a possessed woman by the same means.
9. Two fox spirits that have enchanted a young man are bound into vessels by a traveling stranger. The younger fox is finally released by the young man and becomes a Celestial Fox. When the young man is about to die, the fox reappears and promises that she will see him safely to the other world.
10. A tutor asks for his employer's daughter for his wife. When he is refused, he haunts the family until he is defeated.
11. A renowned scholar is exposed as a fox when he is found teaching a class of young foxes.

Two Ainu tales are included:

1. A man overhears two foxes plotting to get some money, interferes with the plan, and takes the money himself. When the angry foxes seek revenge, the frightened man propitiates them by promising to worship them. This explains the origin of fox worship.
2. The mole, disguised as an old man, traps two foxes, who are also disguised as men, trying to sell false goods. The foxes repent and promise to stop such evil antics.

One Buryat tale from Eastern Siberia follows:

God gives a wolf some livestock that belong to a wealthy sorcerer, but the man continually prevents the wolf from obtaining his goods. Finally the wolf transforms itself into a beautiful girl, tricks the sorcerer into taking her into his carriage, and devours the sorcerer instead of his animals.

Next the article describes tales from Japan:

1. A wolf takes the shape of a beautiful girl, waylays travelers, and devours them.
2. A man who has questioned the validity of fox stories sees a fox turn itself into a young woman. He beats her to force her to assume her true shape, but she remains a young woman and is killed. As the man is about to be convicted of murder, a Buddhist priest offers him holy orders as an alternative to the death sentence. As soon as the man's head is shaved, he discovers that the entire incident was just a trick by the foxes to punish him for his skepticism.
3. A fox who had been frightened by a farmer avenges itself by telling the farmer that a great treasure is buried in his yard, when in fact nothing is there.
4. A cryptomeria tree turns into an old fox when it is shot with arrows.
5. A young man and his father save the life of a fox from two other men, but in the quarrel the father is killed. The fox comes to the young man disguised as a beautiful girl, marries him, and bears him a son. She then reveals her true identity and leaves her husband and child.
6. A man's wife is attacked by a puppy and turns into a fox. The man tells her that even though she is a fox, he wishes her to remain with him.
7. A Buddhist priest is bewitched by a fox into going to a mansion and feasting and drinking, but the fox is ultimately revealed in its true form.
8. A maid is tricked into going to a distant house by some foxes who are disguised as her employers. When the maid meets her true

employers at the main house some days later, they realize that she has been bewitched by foxes.

The article also tells the tale of the fox Tamamo no mae, who is disguised as a beautiful court lady and becomes the consort of the emperor in order to destroy him. When she is discovered and killed, her spirit enters a rock, which becomes deadly poisonous until it is exorcised by a Buddhist monk. Other tales are given of foxes seducing and killing men and of foxes becoming wives of men. In a Labrador Eskimo tale, a man finds a fox girl in his hut. He makes her his wife, but she disappears one day when he complains of a strange odor.

Krappe discusses many Chinese and Japanese superstitions about foxes. It was believed that meeting a fox or having a fox enter a house was bad luck, that foxes produced fire from their tails, and that various parts of the fox's body were useful in curing different illnesses. Foxes were worshiped in China largely to protect the household from their evil deeds. Certain families were thought to hold foxes as magical familiars and to pass this power on hereditarily through the female line. Spirits of the dead were thought to assume the shape of foxes or to possess foxes that were in cemeteries and then return to haunt the living.

Krappe describes the cult of Inari in Japan and compares the foxes of Inari with the animals associated with home and crops in Western countries. He analyzes the role of the fox as an animal that transforms itself into human shape. He tries to trace the origins of the fox cult and to link Eastern fox tales with European tales of weasels and European, Indian, and Asian tales of snakes transforming themselves into women.

33. Lanham, Betty B., and Shimura, Masao. "Folktales Commonly Told American and Japanese Children: Ethical Themes of Omission and Commission." *Journal of American Folklore* 80, no. 315 (January/March 1967): 33–48.

This interesting article presents analyses of ten representative American tales and ten representative Japanese tales. (The tales were selected based on responses to questionnaires distributed to parents, in which they were asked to list stories they told to their children.) The tales were analyzed in terms of age and sex of hero and villain, occurrence and type of supernatural characters, and ethical themes presented.

The ten American tales are:

The Three Bears
Three Little Pigs
Little Red Riding Hood
Cinderella
Snow White
Jack and the Beanstalk

Sleeping Beauty
Hansel and Gretel
Rumpelstiltskin
Rapunzel

The ten Japanese tales are:

Momotarō
Hanasaka jijii (The Old Man Who Made Withered Trees Blossom)
Urashima Tarō
Shitakiri suzume (The Tongue-Cut Sparrow)
Kachi kachi yama (The Crackling Mountain)
Issun-boshi
Kaguya-hime (The Tale of the Shining Princess)
Saru-kani kassen (The Battle of the Monkey and the Crab)
Kobutori jijii (The Old Man Who Lost His Wen)
Bunbuku chagama (The Lucky Tea-Kettle)

34. Makita, Shigeru. "World Authority on Folklore: Yanagita Kunio." *Japan Quarterly* 20, no. 3 (July/September 1973): 283–293.

This article describes the popularity achieved by Yanagita's work in the years following his death in 1962 and the acknowledgment afforded Yanagita as a major intellectual figure of his time. Makita gives a sketch of Yanagita's life, outlines his many projects involving folklore, literature, and education, and speculates on the possible reasons for Yanagita's renewed popularity.

35. Manabe, Masahiro, and Vidaeus, Kerstin. "The Old Fox and the Fairy Child: A Study in Japanese Folklore and Miyazawa Kenji." *Journal of Intercultural Studies* 2 (1975): 5–28.

This article examines the motifs of the old fox and the fairy child in Japanese folklore and the use of these motifs by Miyazawa Kenji 宮沢賢治 in his works *Tokkobe Torako* 甚米虎子 and *Zashiki bokko no hanashi* 座敷ぼっこの話 (Tales of the zashiki-bokko). The words *bokko* and *warashi* are both from the northeastern dialect and mean "child"; they are used interchangeably in the article.

The first section is a brief introduction that lists the types of tales in which foxes are found. The second section, a translation of the story *Tokkobe Torako*, has two episodes. In the first, a greedy moneylender named Roppei meets a young samurai who says that he is leaving for a distant province and wants Roppei to take charge of his fortune. In the event of the samurai's death, Roppei may keep the money for himself. The samurai gives him ten chests filled with gold, which Roppei carries away with great difficulty. When he finally arrives home, Roppei discovers that the chests of gold are really baskets filled with pebbles. The samurai was really the old fox.

The second episode takes place at a party at the home of the village assemblyman Heiemon. One guest, feeling that he has been slighted, leaves the party early. When he reaches the village talisman statue, which is made of paper strips on bamboo, he moves it into the middle of the road. When the rest of the guests (who are quite drunk) return home, they see the figure in the road and think that it is the old fox. They run back to Heiemon's house, dropping their presents in the road. The old fox, Tokkobe Torako, then steals the presents (or so the people think).

The third section, in five parts, analyzes the theme of the old fox in Japanese folklore. Part one gives three tales in which people are bewitched by foxes into believing that worthless objects (funeral urns, leaves, or horse manure) are gold, and one tale in which a fox tries to cheat a man of his money. Part two lists the names of famous foxes throughout Japan. Part three gives tales of some famous foxes who appeared as human beings. Part four discusses tales of Tora foxes who possessed people. Part five traces the possible origins of the names Torako and Tokkobe.

The fourth section is a translation of *Zashiki bokko no hanashi*. These four stories tell of the antics of the fairy child who haunts the tatami room. In the first story, two children hear a broom sweeping in the tatami room. When they go to investigate, no one is there, but the sweeping sound continues. In the second story, 10 children are playing together. Suddenly there are 11. No face is unknown, yet no two faces are the same. In the third story, a family party is delayed because one of the children is ill. The other children are annoyed and decide not to play with him. When they see him approaching, they all run and hide, but then they look back into the tatami room and see that he is already there. In the fourth story, a man finds a beautiful, richly attired boy on the riverbank. The child says that he is leaving his first home because it has become boring there and he is going to live in a new house. Soon after the fortunes of the first house decline and those of the second house improve.

The fifth section, in two parts, analyzes the theme of the fairy child. Part one gives 15 short local tales of *zashiki warashi* and compares these to the *Zashiki bokko no hanashi*. Part two summarizes the attributes of the fairy child, lists other names by which he is known, and traces the relationship between the *warashi* and the child of the Sea God's palace, *ryūgū dōji* 竜宮童子.

The appendix contains a brief sketch of Miyazawa's professional life.

36. Mayer, Fanny Hagin. "Collecting Folktales in Niigata, Japan." *Midwest Folklore* 9, no. 2 (summer 1959): 103–109.

This is a brief report on Mayer's field trip to Niigata in July 1958 with Ken'ichi Mizusawa and Banzo Yuki. Mayer names the places she visited and the people from whom she heard tales, as well as the sources from which her informants had heard the tales. A sample story, "Kani Kani, Koso, Koso" 蟹蟹こそこそ (A Crab Tale), appears at the end of the article.

37. Mayer, Fanny Hagin. "Fauna and Flora in Japanese Folktales." *Asian Folklore Studies* 40, no. 1 (1981): 23–32.

This is a statistical survey of the animals and plants mentioned in 3,000 folktales from Niigata Prefecture. Fauna are subdivided into five categories: four-legged animals, birds, fishes, miscellaneous animals, and insects. The article contains a bibliography of 35 collections of Niigata folktales; titles and authors are given only in romaji.

38. Mayer, Fanny Hagin. *Introducing the Japanese Folk Tales: Studies, Essays, and an Annotated Bibliography*. Taipei: Chinese Association for Folklore, 1973.

This book contains 16 articles; 13 of them were published previously, and 2 are conference reports.

"The Discovery of the Japanese Folk Tale" is from *KBS Bulletin* (81 [December 1966/January 1967]: 5–15). It is a survey of late nineteenth- and very early twentieth-century translations of Japanese tales into English, French, and German.

"Available Japanese Folk Tales," from *Monumenta Nipponica* (24, no. 3 [1969]: 235–247), is an annotated bibliography that details materials available in Japanese (see Appendix A). The original article translates titles and authors into the kanji script; this reprint does not.

"In Search of Folk Tales," from *Japan Quarterly* (6, no. 2 [April/June 1959]: 175–182), discusses Ken'ichi Mizusawa's efforts in collecting folktales and details a particular field trip on which he and Mayer collected tales. Mayer also gives three short tales: one about a disagreement between a flea and a louse, one about a wife who is really a frog, and one about an endless tale that finally cures an old woman's addiction to hearing stories (at least for the moment).

"Ken'ichi Mizusawa, a Modern Collector of Japanese Folk Tales" is from *Asian Folklore Studies* (26, no. 2 [1967]: 149–159). It details the many contributions that Mizusawa has made to Japanese folklore studies.

"The Japanese Folk Tale," from *Kansai Asiatic Society Occasional Papers* (3 [1955]: 14–17), begins with a brief history of Japanese folklore studies, then gives an analysis of the types of the folktale in Japan. Mayer divides the tales into four major groups: complete folktales, subdivided into ten major divisions; derived tales, subdivided into five major divisions; story substitutes, such as endless tales; and set expressions used in telling tales. The remainder of the article examines the ten divisions of the complete folktale.

"Characters Appearing in the Japanese Folk Tale" is from *Transactions of the International Conference of Orientalists in Japan* (4 [1959]: 23–36). It deals with the human characters that appear in the tales and gives the many roles and positions assigned to them.

"Character Portrayal in the Japanese Folk Tale" is from *Anthropos* (55 [1960]: 655–670). It examines the types of character traits that are often illustrated in Japanese folktales as represented by ten types of characterizations for old women in the tales.

"Family Stories Appearing in the Background of the Folk Tale," from *Nihon minzokugaku* 日本民俗学 (59 [1969]: 26–28), divides family stories into five groups depending on the appearance in the tales of human beings, supernatural beings, and/or animals and discusses each type.

"Takada *goze* 瞽女: A Living Tradition," from *KBS Bulletin* (99 [December 1969/January 1970]: 9–12), tells about the blind women singers of traditional ballads, in particular three women who are still living in Takada, Niigata Prefecture.

"Tales for the Little New Year" is from *Japan Quarterly* (13, no. 1 [January/March 1966]: 76–79). It presents four tales traditionally told on the night of the first full moon of the New Year.

"Mushroom Ghosts," from *Japan Quarterly* (13, no. 4 [October/December 1966]: 292–295), gives three tales; two are about spirits that actually were mushrooms and one is about a mushroom that grew because of the anger of a dead snake. (Marvelous stories!)

"Even a Mudsnail" is from *Japan Quarterly* (17, no. 2 [April/June 1970]: 191–194) and contains four tales about mudsnails, one about a crab, and one about a frog.

"The Devoted Fox Wife" is from *Japan Quarterly* (18, no. 4 [October/December 1971]: 463–466). It deals mostly with tales in which a fox turns itself into a woman and marries a man, but it also touches on tales in which the fox turns itself into a man.

"About Trees and Plants" discusses the relationship between humans and trees as it is depicted in Japanese folktales. "The Setting of the Japanese Folk Tale" is a report given to Asian Studies on the Pacific Coast in 1971. It discusses the human habitations—dwellings, shrines, and temples—that appear in the tales and examines the effect of the physical setting on the story. "The Japanese Folk Tale as Oral Literature: Views of Society" is a report given to the Western Conference of the Association for Asian Studies in 1972. It describes the roles assigned to samurai, feudal lords, Buddhist priests, and chōja in the tales.

The final entry in this collection is an annotated bibliography that gives many Japanese sources for anthologies of tales and works on Japanese tales and German and English translations of Japanese tales. The assembling of these varied and widely dispersed articles into a single volume has resulted in a valuable and easily utilized reference work on the Japanese folktale. The translations of tales that Mayer presents in these articles (36, 37, 38) are a reader's delight.

39. Mayer, Fanny Hagin. "Ken'ichi Mizusawa, a Modern Collector of Japanese Folk Tales." *Asian Folklore Studies* 26, no. 2 (1967): 149–159.

This article outlines Mizusawa's work on the folklore of Niigata Prefecture. Mayer discusses in some detail each of the 11 volumes that Mizusawa had produced by 1967 and gives titles (with kanji), publishers, and dates for each. This is a valuable annotated bibliography for anyone interested in Mizusawa and in the folklore of Niigata. (This article is included in the anthology *Introducing the Japanese Folk Tales*, entry 38.)

40. Mayer, Fanny Hagin. "Religious Elements in Japanese Folk Tales." *Studies in Japanese Culture*, pp. 1–16, edited by Joseph Roggendorf. Tokyo: Sophia University Press, 1963.

Mayer examines the Buddhist and Shinto motifs and the supernatural creatures that appear in the folktales collected by Sasaki Kizen. The Buddhist deity Kannon helps people out of difficult situations, bestows children, takes the sufferings of her worshipers upon herself, and grants rewards for self-sacrifice. In one story a young couple learn that their blind, aged mother will regain her eyesight if she is fed the liver of a child. The couple sacrifice their only son, but when the old woman's sight is restored, the child is found to be unharmed. Blood is seen running from the temple of Kannon, and the statue has assumed the terrible wound from the child.

The Buddhist deity Jizō is another important character in many tales. One story tells of an old man who gave his sedge hat to a stone statue of Jizō to protect the idol from a snowstorm. The man was rewarded with a great fortune for this act of piety. Another tale concerns an old woman who entered the underworld while following a bean that rolled down a rat hole. Jizō helped her to secure a fortune from some demons who were there gambling. Jizō himself likes to gamble, and he once lost so much that he had to settle his debt by parting with a magic ladle.

A young man once set himself up in a temple as a talking Jizō statue. When the local landlord came to seek advice, "Jizō" told him to take the young man's friend as his son-in-law; in this way both men became wealthy.

An old man is once mistaken for a Jizō statue by some monkeys. Wishing to please the deity, the monkeys move him to a more pleasant location and present him with offerings of money.

Some tales do not involve particular deities, but they present Buddhist ideas. A man who was not at all pious in this life was given a bag of gold by a deity. The man had been an ox in his previous incarnation and had been used in the work to build the god's shrine.

A wooden Buddha statue once defeated a golden statue in a wrestling match. The servant who owned the wooden statue had worshiped it three times a day, while the rich man who owned the gold statue had not worshiped it and had used it only to satisfy his vanity.

A certain girl's karmic bond to her parents was so weak that when she died suddenly, her body was not found and properly buried. For this reason she was prevented from entering Paradise.

Mayer also gives synopses of tales that involve trips to the upper and lower worlds and examines the various ways in which mortals can reach these places. Among Shinto deities, Inari is important, especially with respect to her association with the fox.

The mountain goddess Yama-no-kami oversees childbirths in villages. Once two men who spent a night in her shrine hear the goddess talking about a boy child and a girl child who were just born in their village. The goddess prophesies good fortune for both if they are married to each other. The men soon discover that it is their own children of whom she is speaking and accordingly arrange the betrothal. Yama-no-kami is known to give bodily strength to her worshipers, as illustrated by the story of a successful wrestler who performed devotions on Mount Rokkoushi. Yama-no-kami is also the patron deity of hunters.

Local deities and divine objects appear often in Japanese tales. A magic listening hood allows an old man to understand the speech of trees. He learns that a rich man's illness was due to the resentment of a tree stump whose growth was stopped by the construction of an addition to the rich man's house.

Sentient animals are also important. A cat who lives in a temple knows that the acolytes are being killed by a big rat. The cat sends for her sister, and together they defeat the monster.

Other creatures that Mayer mentions are nushi, demons, tengu, kappa, and ghosts. Ghosts in Japanese tales are not only the spirits of deceased humans, but they can also be the spirits of animals, plants, or even discarded objects. One story tells of a ghost that is really a carnivorous mushroom. A more orthodox ghost story tells of a woman who died in childbirth. The woman returned every night to buy candy. When the shopkeeper followed her to her grave, he discovered that a child had been born after the woman had been buried; the man rescued the child and returned it to its father.

In this short article Mayer demonstrates the complexity of the religious motifs that appear in Japanese folktales.

41. Mills, D. E. "Medieval Japanese Tales Part I." *Folklore* 83 (winter 1972): 287–301; and "Medieval Japanese Tales Part II." *Folklore* 84 (spring 1973): 58–74.

Part one covers tales from the late Heian and early Kamakura eras from the *Konjaku monogatari* and the *Uji shūi monogatari*. This genre is referred to as "tale literature"; it is called *setsuwa bungaku* 説話文学 in Japanese. Mills discusses the Buddhist origin of this type of literature, outlines the many kinds of tales found in the *Konjaku*, and gives two stories from this collection:

1. A wooden statue of Jizō descends into Hell to save the soul of a sinful priest who had occasionally shown some respect to the statue.
2. A wild boar haunts a man by calling out his name when he is out hunting at night. The spirit is finally discovered and killed by the man's brother.

Mills next outlines the kinds of tales found in the *Uji shūi*, compares them with those found in the *Konjaku*, and presents two stories from the *Uji shūi*:

1. A deer with a five-colored body and white horns saves a man from drowning. As a reward, the deer asks only that the man never tell anyone of the deer's existence, since someone will surely come to kill it for its rare hide. When the queen has a dream about the deer, the man tells the king his story, and a large hunting party is outfitted to capture the deer. The deer comes before the king and tells how it saved the man's life and was promised that the man would never reveal the deer's existence. Thereupon the king orders the man's execution, releases the deer, and outlaws deer hunting in his domain.
2. A man who is attacked by a band of ruffians near the Kiyomizu temple escapes by jumping from the temple platform into the deep valley below, using a shutter as a kind of parachute. (In some versions, the man or a child, who had been dropped by its mother, is saved through the intervention of the Kiyomizu Kannon.)

Mills also discusses the *Uji dainagon monogatari* 宇治大納言物語, which is attributed to Minamoto Takakuni, and the possible connection between this work and the other two anthologies discussed in the article.

Part two covers tales from the late medieval period found in the entertainment booklets called *otogi zoshi*. Mills gives a classification system for these tales that was devised by Ichiko Teiji. The tales are divided into six major types:

1. Tales of Court Nobles (three subdivisions)
2. Tales of Priests (four subdivisions)
3. Legends of Warriors (three subdivisions)

4. Tales of the Common People (four subdivisions)
5. Foreign Tales
6. Tales about Nonhuman Creatures and Things (five subdivisions)

The article ends with Mills's excellent 14-page translation of the story "Yoshitsune's Voyage Among the Islands." (For a complete translation of *Uji shūi monogatari*, see Mills, *A Collection of Tales from Uji*, entry 84.)

42. Morse, Ronald A. "The Search for Japan's National Character and Distinctiveness: Yanagita Kunio (1875–1962) and the Folklore Movement." Ph.D. dissertation, Princeton University, 1975.

This work traces the development of Japanese folklore studies through the life, work, and ideas of Yanagita Kunio, the individual who shaped and directed that movement for most of the twentieth century. Contents include:

Chapter 1. The Formative Years
Chapter 2. Policy and Agrarian Society
Chapter 3. Yanagita Folklore: Structure and Influence
Chapter 4. The Source for Yanagita's "New National Learning"
Chapter 5. The Folklorist's Craft
Chapter 6. Folklorist as Hero

Also included are notes, appendix, bibliography, and dissertation abstract. The bibliography of this dissertation contains an outline of the contents of *Teihon Yanagita Kunio shu* 定本柳田国男集, a 36-volume compilation of Yanagita's writings, a guide to Yanagita's works available in English translation, a list of essays on Yanagita in English, and a list of Japanese sources for works on Yanagita in Japanese.

43. Mulhern, Chieko Irie. "Cinderella and the Jesuits: An *Otogizoshi* Cycle as Christian Literature." *Monumenta Nipponica* 34, no. 4 (winter 1979): 409–447.

Mulhern presents the theory that tales of the persecuted stepdaughter, which appeared in the literature of late medieval Japan, were actually the work of Christian converts and missionaries. The tales are separated into three types:

1. Hanayo no hime (Princess Blossom) 花世の姫
2. Hachikazuki (The Princess Who Wore a Bowl on Her Head) 鉢かづき
3. Ubakawa (The Bark Gown) 姥皮

Mulhern analyzes the characters and geographical locations that appear in each type and associates the characters with Japanese Christian converts of high social position who lived during the late sixteenth and early seventeenth centuries. Much of the article details the complex politics and events that involved Japanese Christians at that time. Mulhern also gives a short comparison of the Japanese Cinderella cycle with the Italian cycle, which the Catholic missionaries would have used for their inspiration.

44. Mulhern, Chieko Irie. "Otogi-zoshi: Short Stories of the Muromachi Period." *Monumenta Nipponica* 29, no. 2 (summer 1974): 181–198.

This article is a study within the historical context of the *otogi zoshi*, the entertainment booklets. Mulhern gives the classification system for the tales worked out by Ichiko Teiji and examines each of the six categories in detail.

Tales of Aristocrats
Religious Tales
Tales of Warriors
Tales of Commoners
Tales of Foreign Countries
Tales of Nonhumans

45. Nozaki, Kiyoshi. *Kitsune: Japan's Fox of Mystery, Romance and Humor.* Tokyo: Hokuseido Press, 1961.

This is a general and far-encompassing study of Japanese foxlore, in 23 chapters.

Chapter 1, A Background for Appreciation, gives a very brief sketch of the Japanese context in which the fox is found.

Chapter 2, Concerning the Inari Shrine, presents a physical description of the shrine and gives some tales that explain how the fox became associated with this deity.

Chapter 3, Concerning the *Konjaku monogatari*, discusses the roles of the fox in the tales found in this anthology.

Chapters 4, 5, and 6 present eight fox tales from the *Konjaku:*

"The Story of a Young Samurai Who Copied the Sutra of the Lotus for the Repose of a Fox's Soul." A fox maiden dies as a result of having spent the night with a young samurai. When he learns of her true identity and her fate, he offers Buddhist prayers on her behalf and causes her to be reborn in Paradise.

"The Story of a Fox Coming Disguised as a Wife." A man is faced by two women who look exactly like his wife. Realizing that one of them must be a fox, he draws his sword and threatens them with it. The imposter resumes its fox shape and escapes.

"The Story of a Fox Repaying Kindness for Returning Its Treasured Ball." A samurai steals a ball that belongs to a fox from a woman whom the fox has possessed. The fox demands its return, vowing to become the man's guardian. The man returns the ball. Later when the man feels that he is in danger, he calls the fox. The fox comes and leads the man home down a back path, thus protecting the man from a band of robbers who were waiting in ambush on the main road.

"The Story of a Fox Who Got Killed Assuming the Form of a Cedar Tree." Two men come upon an unfamiliar, gigantic cedar tree in the middle of the night. They decide to shoot the tree with an arrow and return in the daytime to examine it. As soon as the arrow strikes, the tree disappears. The terrified men run home, then return the next morning. They find an old fox, which has been shot dead by their arrow. The fox had assumed the shape of the tree.

"The Story of a Fox Fond of Riding on a Horse's Buttocks." A pretty girl would stop any traveler going to the capital at night and ask for a ride on his horse. After riding a short distance, it would jump down, assume its true fox shape, and run off. A young officer decides to capture the fox. He succeeds, but the fox manages to escape by casting an enchantment on him. He decides to capture the fox again, but this time he brings along several companions. They capture the fox and bring it back to the palace, where they burn it with pine torches until it resumes its true shape. They finally release it, but the incident cures the fox of its habit of bothering travelers.

"The Story of a Man Infatuated with a Fox Saved by the Goddess of Mercy." A rich man meets a beautiful girl on a lonely road at night. She brings him to her home, and he stays there with her. Meanwhile the man's family prays to Kannon for help in their search for him. The goddess, in the shape of a Buddhist priest, appears at the girl's house. All the members of the household run away, and the man discovers that he has actually been under the floor of his own warehouse. Several foxes are seen running away.

"The Story of an Imperial Household Officer Disillusioned by an Act of a Fox." A young officer meets a pretty girl in a pine grove at night. He walks her to her home, which proves to be a place where foxes were thought to live. Realizing that she must be a fox, the officer attacks her. The girl resumes her fox shape and escapes.

"The Story of General Toshihito Who Employed a Fox for His Guest, Exercising an Influence upon It." A man expresses a wish to eat a large quantity of a particular delicacy, and General Toshihito decides to fulfill his wish for him. The general takes the man to his palace in a distant province. On the way, the general captures a fox and sends it to his house with a message that he is returning with a guest and wishes to be met by some of his men. The fox delivers the message by possessing the general's wife. When the two men reach the general's mansion, a host of strange-looking servants prepare so much of the delicacy for the guest that the man loses his appetite at the sight and never eats that particular food again.

Chapters 7 and 8 concern the fox in other works by famous authors:

"The Story of the One-Eyed God." A young man from eastern Japan wishes to go to Kyoto to study poetry. Just before reaching the capital, he is forced to spend the night at an old shrine in the forest. While he is lying beneath a tree, he sees two female foxes dressed as court ladies, a tall godlike creature with a long nose, and a mountain priest come to the shrine and conjure up the resident deity, a grotesque, one-eyed being. They order the terrified young man to join their saké drinking party. The one-eyed god then lectures the young man, convincing him that he should return to his home and give up any vain ideas of studying in the capital.

"The Story of a Fox Sucking Up the Energy of a Feudal Lord." An innkeeper sees a fox turn itself into a young girl. She tells the man that her family has all been killed during an attack on her home, and the man offers to take her in as his daughter. She proves to be most satisfactory and dutiful, so the man never reveals that he knows that she is really a fox. One day a general who is staying at the inn falls in love with the girl. He pays the innkeeper a large sum of money for her and takes the girl to his home. She is respectful to his wife, talented, and industrious. Soon, however, the general falls into a grave decline. A priest comes to offer prayers for his recovery. The fox is forced to resume its true shape and is killed as a result of the prayers.

"The Story of a Samurai Entertained by Foxes." A young samurai finds a girl who has lost her way. He escorts her home, where he is entertained graciously. When dawn comes, however, he is rather unceremoniously pushed out of the mansion, and he discovers that he was actually in a cave in the mountains inhabited by foxes.

"The Story of a Rich Merchant Deceived by a Girl Impersonating Kitsune." A rich merchant sees a tame fox cub and wishes to buy it. The owner says that he obtained the cub when its mother was killed and that he promised the mother fox that he would care for the cub. The merchant says that he will establish the fox cub as the guardian deity of his house and construct a shrine for the worship of the fox-god; thereupon the owner gives the cub to the merchant, refusing any payment. When they return to the merchant's house, the cub refuses to eat and becomes weaker every day. A young woman comes for the cub, claiming that she is its aunt. The merchant gives her the cub and a large sum of money. Later the merchant learns that the woman is not a fox but a conspirator with the original owner, who uses the fox cub to swindle people.

Chapter 9 discusses the role of the fox in fairy tales:

"The Noh Player and the Fox." A player who is wearing a Noh mask to protect himself from the cold encounters a fox in the shape of a man. Seeing the player, the fox mistakenly thinks that he can assume the shape of a man just by wearing a mask, and he beseeches the actor to give the mask to him. When the fox appears before a feudal lord wearing only the mask as a disguise, he is instantly recognized as a fox and killed.

"The Fox and the Branches of a Big Tree." A fox who lives under a big tree is struck by one of its branches during a storm. The fox stalks off, determined to find a new place to live. However, he soon thinks better of it and returns to his old home under the tree.

"The Gift of a Fox." An old man secures some horse meat for a lame, skinny fox. The fox later takes the old man to its home and gives him a magic book that allows him to understand the speech of animals. The old man learns from some crows why the daughter of a rich man is sick and how she can be cured. By using his new power, the old man becomes wealthy.

"The Carpenter and the Foxes." A carpenter who is skeptical about foxes goes to a haunted moor on a bet with his fellow carpenters. He sees a girl whom he thinks is a fox and kills her, but she does not assume a fox shape. The man is attacked by the girl's parents. A Buddhist priest arrives and offers to make the man his disciple. As soon as the man's head is shaved, the people disappear, and the carpenter realizes that he has been bewitched by foxes.

There is also a short paragraph on stories about fox weddings.

Chapter 10 discusses the role of the fox in kabuki. Nozaki examines the plays *Kuzu-no-ha, or the Fox Wife in Shinoda Wood, Tamamo-no-mae, Sembon Zakura, or Romance of Yoshitsune,* and *Honcho Nijyu-shiko.*

Chapter 11 concerns the role of the fox in Noh. Nozaki examines the plays *Sanjyo Kokaji, or Munechika, the Swordsmith, Tsurigitsune, or Trapping a Fox, Tamamo-no-mae, Sado-gitsune, or the Fox of Sado Island,* and *Kitsune-zuka, or the Earth of Foxes.*

Chapter 12 discusses the role of the fox in poetry. Chapters 13 and 14 give tales of foxes bewitching people:

Some courtiers who are playing a game of *go* find a fox just outside their room. When the fox realizes that he has been discovered, he runs off.

"The Chief Abbot of the Higashi-Honganji Temple Bewitched Together with His Followers by Kitsune." A fox shrine is destroyed to build a new villa for the abbot. When the abbot and a large group of men are returning home after inspecting the construction, they are bewitched into going in the wrong direction. They walk all night, and the exhausted party does not realize the mistake until the morning, by which time they are very far from their original destination.

Two stories are said to be true incidents reported by reliable sources:

"Fox Bewitching a Man by Wagging Its Tail." A traveler stumbles upon a farmer who is acting strangely. Although he is alone, the farmer is going through the motions of sharing saké with a companion. The traveler sees a fox that is rotating its tail and casting glances at the farmer, thus bewitching him. The traveler drives the fox off, and the farmer recovers his senses.

"Fox Luring a Pedlar by Its Occult Power." A man looking out his window sees a medicine pedlar walking back and forth over the same stretch of path. The man then sees a fox, which is wagging its tail back and forth to bewitch the pedlar. When the man drives the fox off, the pedlar continues on his way down the path, apparently unaware that he had been bewitched.

"Fox Making a Fish Dealer Intoxicated." A fox follows behind a man and causes him to walk as if he were sleepwalking.

"Fox Kidnapping a Girl." A fox disguised as an old woman calls a young girl out of her house and leads her into a pine forest. The girl's family calls a medium, who becomes possessed by the fox's spirit and says that the girl had dislodged a rock while walking in the woods and had blocked the entrance to the fox's lair. Because the girl's parents are so concerned about her, the fox agrees to release her from its spell. The girl is found the next day by her father.

"Fox Sends an Old Woman Insane." An old woman curses a fox because it stole a fish bone that the woman had been saving for her cat. While her son and daughter-in-law are out visiting, the woman becomes overwhelmed by a dreadful feeling of loneliness and sets out on the road to meet her children. As she is walking along, she is struck by a bamboo pole and rendered senseless. Her children find her and realize that she has been bewitched by a fox.

"Fox Turning Itself into a Stag." A hunter shoots a large stag, but when he goes to collect his game, he discovers that it is really an old fox who had been trying to trick him.

Three tales tell of foxes bewitching animals:

"Fox Bewitching a Horse." A fox that is sitting on a stable wall kicks its hind legs, thus causing the horse in the stable to do the same.

"Fox Bewitching a Rooster." A fox beckons to a rooster and tries to lure it into a bamboo grove.

"Fox Bewitching Crows." A fox would "bind" crows in a certain tree and cause them to move parts of their bodies in accordance with the fox's actions.

"Fox Imitating a Maid's Voice." A maid often leaves scraps out for foxes. When she neglects to do so, one fox comes up to her door and makes a series of noises to sound out her name.

"Fox Calling for Help in a Human Tongue." A fox who is caught in a snare screams out loudly for help in a woman's voice.

Chapter 15 concerns the fox's intelligence and lewdness:

"Fox Outwitting a Famous Artist." An artist tries to capture a fox that has been raiding a chicken coop. The artist sets up a snare and baits a trap, but the fox cleverly gets the bait without becoming ensnared.

"Fox Locating a Hunter's House." A hunter kills a female fox several miles from his home. The male fox comes to retrieve the body of its mate, and it manages to locate the hunter's house among all the houses in the valley.

"Fox Robbing a Man of His Food by Using Its Brains." A fox repeatedly jumps at a man who is returning home from a wedding carrying a box of food gifts. The fox simply frightens the man so badly that he abandons his food and flees.

"Fox Retrieving Its Horse Bone by a Trick." A fox is startled by some young men and drops the horse bone that it was carrying in its mouth. The men take the bone back home, thinking that the fox will surely try to retrieve it. The fox slips into the house and gets the bone, then it props a piece of bamboo against the sliding door so that the men cannot open the door and pursue the fox. The fox thus escapes with its horse bone.

"How a Man Is Captivated by a Fox." A licentious man meets a beautiful woman one evening drinking saké at a restaurant. He takes her to the house of a friend, where they spend the night together. When the man awakes, he finds that the woman is gone. He realizes that she had actually been a fox. Soon after the man becomes seriously ill and dies.

"How a Sozu Is Ruined by a Fox." A Buddhist cleric receives romantic overtures from a beautiful woman. He goes to her mansion and lives with her. One day a Buddhist priest runs into the house. The house and its inhabitants vanish, and the cleric discovers that he is actually under the floor of the temple.

"How a Maid Is Seduced by a Fox." A maid is carrying on an affair with her employer in a shed outside the main house. A fox assumes the shape of the man and takes the maid to the shed. However, the actions of the fox cause the girl so much pain that she is forced to call out to her mistress for help. The wife and the employer are together, and they both run out to the shed to see what is wrong. They find the maid alone and in terrible pain.

Chapter 16, Dakini-ten Faith and the Record of Foxes with Uncanny Power, discusses the practice of worshiping Dakini-ten to obtain foxes as magical familiars:

"Kitsune Are Averse to Accepting Unwilling Charity." Foxes refuse rice offerings from a particular street because some of the people there had complained about making the offering.

"Kitsune Suffer from a Guilty Conscience." A fox cub dies from eating some poisoned rats that a farmer had discarded. The farmer's daughters are then killed by fox possession. The farmer chastizes the foxes, saying that the cub's death had been accidental. The old foxes are then filled with remorse and die.

"Family Fortunes Decline Because of Kitsune." The New Year's rice cakes of a particular prosperous family keep disappearing. The wife sees that they are being taken by phantom foxes that herald the family's decline.

Nozaki also gives tales of famous foxes whose names have been recorded: Koan, Jingoro, Gengoro, Genkuro, Hakuzo, and Kojoro.

Chapters 17 and 18 contain tales of foxes producing fires and of fox weddings. Chapters 19 and 20 discuss the use of the fox in cartoons and other works of art. Chapters 21 and 22 discuss fox possession and give some sample case histories. Chapter 23 lists things that have been named after kitsune.

46. Seki, Keigo. "Types of Japanese Folktales." *Asian Folklore Studies* 25 (1966): 1–220.

This excellent work lists synopses of 470 tale types. It has a very good bibliography, citing over 100 Japanese sources, and a short glossary of Japanese terms used in the tale titles and synopses. (Titles, authors, and Japanese words are given in romaji only.)

The tale types are numbered from 1 to 470; each has a type number, an English title for the tale, the tale synopsis with possible variations indicated, geographic distribution, and literary sources. The types are divided into 18 major categories (see also entry 25):

1. Origin of Animals, numbers 1–30
2. Animal Tales, 31–74
3. Man and Animal:
   Escape from ogre, 75–86
   Stupid animals, 87–118
   Grateful animals, 119–132
4. Supernatural Wives and Husbands
   Supernatural husbands, 133–140
   Supernatural wives, 141–150
5. Supernatural Birth, 151–165
6. Man and Water Spirit, 166–170
7. Magic Objects, 171–182
8. Tales of Fate, 183–188
9. Human Marriage, 189–200
10. Acquisition of Riches, 201–209
11. Conflicts:
    Parent and child, 210–223
    Brothers or sisters, 224–233
    Neighbors, 234–253
12. The Clever Man, 254–262
13. Jokes, 263–308
14. Contests, 309–326
15. Osho and Kozo (priest and his acolyte), 327–344

47. Smith, Robert. "On Certain Tales of the *Konjaku monogatari* as Reflections of Japanese Folk Religion." *Asian Folklore Studies* 25 (1966): 221–233.

Smith emphasizes the importance of knowing the cultural context for understanding folktales. This article deals in particular with the portrayal of folk beliefs and practices in Japanese folktales. He uses the stories of Jones's *Ages Ago: Thirty-seven Tales from the "Konjaku monogatari Collection"* (entry 82) and examines in detail story number 29, How in Mimasaka Province a God Was Trapped by a Hunter and Living Sacrifice Stopped. Smith also discusses Mayer's "Religious Elements in Japanese Folk Tales" (entry 40).

48. Sugiyama, Yoko. "Time and Folk Literature: A Comparative Study." *East-West Review* 1, no. 1 (spring 1964): 13–37; and "Time and Folk Literature: A Comparative Study II." *East-West Review* 1, no. 2 (autumn 1964): 145–166.

This two-part article examines the motif of supernatural time lapse in folktales and literary works from around the world. There are two kinds of supernatural time lapse: that in which the hero experiences a short time lapse when, in fact, a very long period of time has gone by (the more common type), and that in which the hero experiences a very long time lapse when, in fact, a very short period of time has gone by.

The hero who experiences a supernatural time lapse is usually doing one of four things:

Sleeping
Dancing or feasting with supernatural creatures
Talking with the dead
Journeying to the Other-World

Part one of the article examines the Epimenides legend of ancient Greece, tales from the early Christian era of Europe, Celtic tales of faeries, "Rip Van Winkle" by Washington Irving, *Doldrum* by John O'Keefe, and "The Wedding Jest" by James Branch Cabell. Part two examines tales from China, Formosa, and Okinawa and the story "Urashima Taro." Sugiyama discusses the story in detail and gives numerous versions from Japanese literary sources.

49. Takayanagi, Shun'ichi. "In Search of Yanagita Kunio." *Monumenta Nipponica* 31, no. 2 (summer 1976): 165–178.

This is a review article of Ronald A. Morse's translation *The Legends of Tōno* (entry 110) and of Yanagita's original Japanese work *Tōno monogatari* 遠野物語. Takayanagi examines Yanagita's overall view of folklore studies and fits *Tōno monogatari* into the context of Yanagita's other works.

50. Takayanagi, Shun'ichi. "Yanagita Kunio." *Monumenta Nipponica* 29, no. 3 (autumn 1974): 329–335.

This is a survey of writings published between 1972 and 1974 on Yanagita and his work.

51. Wakamori, Tarō. "Folklore." *Japan at the XIIth International Congress of Historical Sciences in Vienna*, pp. 119–133. Tokyo: Nihon Gakujutsu Shinkōkai, 1965.

The first section, History and Folklore, argues for the use of folklore materials as valid sources for some historical information. The second section, The Making of the Japanese People, discusses the possible cultural and racial origins of the Japanese.

Section three, Efforts for Clarifying Ancient History, traces the introduction of rice culture to Japan, the role of Shinto rites in agricultural life, the adoption of Buddhism, and the process of fusion of indigenous folk beliefs with Buddhism. The fourth section, Common People's Life under Feudalism, studies the changes in the family system and in craft organizations from ancient to medieval times.

This article includes a bibliography of more than 50 Japanese works on Japanese folklore. Most of the references are on folk religion. Entries include kanji for titles.

52. Wakamori, Tarō. "The Study of Folklore." *Le Japon au XIᵉ Congrès International des Sciences Historiques à Stockholm*, pp. 219–229. Tokyo: Nippon Gakujutsu Shinkōkai, 1960.

Section one, Origins, discusses the attempts to convince historians in Japan that folklore materials are valid historical sources.

Section two, Research during the War, describes the problems of isolating genuine folk religious practices from the mandated rites of state Shinto, expecially those rites involving village shrines and festivals.

Section three, Post-war Trends, presents the problems of methodology and interpretation facing folklorists in Japan, and section four, Future Tasks, outlines the plans at that time for further folklore research in Japan, particularly in the field of folk religions. Wakamori names several Japanese folklorists and gives their areas of interest.

The 45 notes at the end of the paper list many Japanese sources. Titles and authors are given only in romaji.

53. Yen, Alsace. "Thematic Patterns in Japanese Folktales." *Asian Folklore Studies* 33, no. 2 (1974): 1–36.

Yen describes the method of "story pattern" or "thematic pattern" analysis, applies it to seven Japanese tales, and compares their structural similarities. The tales used for this study are from Mayer's *Japanese Folk Tales* (entry 109) and Adams's *Folktales of Japan* (entry 97).

1. The Boy Who Had a Dream (Mayer no. 41)
2. The Listening Hood (Mayer no. 78)
3. The Mountain God and the Boy (Mayer no. 80)
4. The Monkey's Liver (Adams no. 11)
5. Shippei Taro (Adams no. 15)
6. The Swamp Nushi's Messenger (Adams no. 22)
7. The Magic Ear (Adams no. 40)

Yen also analyzes the Manchurian narrative *Nishan Shaman*, the Japanese tale "The Oni's Laughter" (Adams no. 16), and three Micronesian tales, "Olofat and the Stolen Eyes," "The Life-Restoring Medicine," and "The Island of the Dolphin Women."

Yen discusses the shamanistic element in Japanese folk religion and demonstrates a common shamanistic theme in all 12 tales presented in this study.

54–63. *Works by Lafcadio Hearn*

The writings of Lafcadio Hearn comprise an entire body of work describing Japanese culture during the Meiji era and Hearn's reactions to that culture. Many of his stories and articles deal with fairy tales, legends, ideas of the supernatural, attitudes toward natural phenomena, and miscellaneous customs. He describes many traditional aspects of Japanese folklore, and his work offers a unique glimpse of what life was like for a Westerner residing in Japan during the late nineteenth and early twentieth centuries.

The contents of 10 of Hearn's books are presented in the following pages. For further information and additional titles, see *Lafcadio Hearn: A Bibliography of His Writings* by P. D. and Ione Perkins (Boston: Houghton Mifflin, 1934). This bibliography includes a list of Hearn's articles for English-language newspapers published in Japan and citations on major book reviews and criticisms of Hearn's works by his contemporaries, as well as information on his many essays of literary criticism.

54. *Exotics and Retrospectives.* Boston: Little, Brown, 1898.

Exotics
    Fuji no Yama
    Insect Musicians
    A Question in the Zen Texts
    The Literature of the Dead
    Frogs
    Of Moon Desire
Retrospectives
    First Impressions
    Beauty Is Memory
    Sadness in Beauty
    Parfum de Jeunesse
    Azure Psychology
    A Serenade
    A Red Sunset
    Frisson
    Vespertina Cognitio
    The Eternal Haunter

55. *Gleanings in Buddha Fields: Studies of Hand and Soul in the Far East.* Boston: Houghton Mifflin, 1897.

A Living God
Out of the Street
Notes of a Trip to Kyoto
Dust
About Faces in Japanese Art
Ningyō no Haka
In Osaka
Buddhist Allusions in Japanese Folksong
Nirvana: A Study in Synthetic Buddhism
The Rebirth of Katsugorō
Within the Circle

56. *Glimpses of Unfamiliar Japan,* 2 vols. Boston: Houghton Mifflin, 1894.

Volume I
My First Day in the Orient
The Writings of Kobōdaishi
Jizō
A Pilgrimage to Enoshima
At the Market of the Dead
Bon Odori
The Chief City of the Province of the Gods
Kitzuki: The Most Ancient Shrine of Japan
In the Cave of the Children's Ghosts
At Mionoseki
Notes on Kitzuki
At Hinomisaki
Shinjū
Yaegaki-jinja
Kitsune
Volume II
In a Japanese Garden
The Household Shrine
Of Women's Hair
From the Diary of an English Teacher
Two Strange Festivals
By the Japanese Sea
Of a Dancing Girl
From Hōki to Oki
Of Souls
Of Ghosts and Goblins
The Japanese Smile
Sayōnara!

57. *In Ghostly Japan.* Boston: Little, Brown, 1899, reprint, 1919.

Fragment
Furisode
Incense
A Story of Divination
Silkworms
A Passional Karma
Footprints of the Buddha
Ululation
Bits of Poetry
Japanese Buddhist Proverbs
Suggestion
Ingwa Banashi

Story of a Tengu
At Yaidzu

58. *Japan: An Attempt at Interpretation*. New York: Macmillan, 1920.

Difficulties
Strangeness and Charm
The Ancient Cult
The Religion of the Home
The Japanese Family
The Communal Cult
Developments of Shinto
Worship and Purification
The Rule of the Dead
The Introduction of Buddhism
The Higher Buddhism
The Social Organization
The Rise of the Military Power
The Religion of Loyalty
The Jesuit Peril
Feudal Integration
The Shinto Revival
Survivals
Modern Restraints
Official Education
Industrial Danger
Reflections

59. *A Japanese Miscellany*. Boston: Little, Brown, 1901.

Strange Stories
    Of a Promise Kept
    Of a Promise Broken
    Before the Supreme Court
    The Story of Kwashin Koji
    The Story of Umetsu Chūbei
    The Story of Kōgi the Priest
Folklore Gleanings
    Dragon-flies
    Buddhist Names of Plants and Animals
    Songs of Japanese Children
Studies Here and There
    On a Bridge
    The Case of O-Dai
    Beside the Sea

Drifting
Otokichi's Daruma
In a Japanese Hospital

60. *Kokoro*. Boston: Houghton Mifflin, 1896.
At a Railway Station
The Genius of Japanese Civilization
A Street Singer
From a Travelling Diary
The Nun of the Temple of Amida
After the War
Haru
A Glimpse of Tendencies
By Force of Karma
A Conservative
In the Twilight of the Gods
The Idea of Preexistence
In Cholera Time
Some Thoughts about Ancestor Worship
Kimiko
Appendix: Three Popular Ballads

61. *Kottō*. New York: Macmillan, 1902.
The Legend of Yurei-Daki
In a Cup of Tea
Common Sense
Ikiryō
Shiryō
The Story of O-Kame
Story of a Fly
Story of a Pheasant
The Story of Chūgorō
A Woman's Diary
Heike-Gani
Fireflies
A Drop of Dew
Gaki
A Matter of Custom
Revery
Pathological
In the Dead of the Night
Kusa-Hibari
The Eater of Dreams

62. *Kwaidan*. Boston: Houghton Mifflin, 1904.

The Story of Mimi-nashi Hoichi
Oshidori
The Story of O-Tei
Ubazakura
Diplomacy
Of a Mirror and a Bell
Jikininki
Mujina
Rokuro-Kubi
A Dead Secret
Yuki-Onna
The Story of Aoyagi
Jiu-Roku-Zakura
The Dream of Akinosuke
Riki-Baka
Hi-Mawari
Hōrai
Insect Studies
  Butterflies
  Mosquitoes
  Ants

63. *Shadowings*. Boston: Little, Brown, 1900.

Stories from Strange Books
  The Reconciliation
  A Legend of Fugen-Bosatsu
  The Screen Maiden
  The Corpse Rider
  The Sympathy of Benten
  The Gratitude of the Samebito
Japanese Studies
  Semi
  Japanese Female Names
  Old Japanese Songs
Fantasies
  Noctilucae
  A Mystery of Crowds
  Gothic Horror
  Levitation
  Nightmare Touch
  Reading from a Dream Book
  In a Pair of Eyes

Chapter 2

Japanese Folktale Anthologies

Adams, Robert J. *Folktales of Japan*. See entry 97.

64. Ballard, Susan. *Fairy Tales from Far Japan*. Boston: Religious Tract Society, n.d.

Despite its title, much of this book is concerned with the difficulties of introducing Christianity to Japan. The first part gives a rather inaccurate description of Shinto and Buddhism and discusses the persecution of Christians in Japan. The second part contains a lengthy story of a Japanese girl's conversion to Christianity. The third part contains seven tales:

1. Momotarō: See entry 125.
2. The Old Man Who Made Withered Trees Blossom: See entry 129.
3. Kachi Kachi Mountain: See entry 114.
4. The Man with the Wen: See entry 128.
5. The Magic Mirror: See entry 124(a).
6. The Lucky Hunter and the Skillful Fisher: See entry 122.
7. The Sword of the Assembled Clouds of Heaven: See entry 117.

65. Bang, Garrett. *Men from the Village Deep in the Mountains and Other Japanese Folk Tales*. New York: Macmillan, 1973.

This well-written collection contains stories that are excellent for a storyteller to read aloud to a group or for an older child to read alone.

1. Crafty Yasohichi Climbs to Heaven: Instead of plowing his fields, Yasohichi announces that he will climb to heaven. A large crowd gathers, walking around the fields, but they finally leave when Yasohichi is unable to make good his boast. But because of the crowd's weight on the fields, the ground is completely smooth and no longer needs plowing.

2. Stingy Kichiyomu and the Rice Thieves: Kichiyomu receives two large fish as a gift, but he throws them away rather than let his wife

prepare them. He says that they will require too much rice to go with the meal, and so the fish are nothing more than rice thieves.

3. Dull-Witted Hikoichi, the Mortar and the Worn-out Horse: An old horse is too weak to carry both Hikoichi and a heavy mortar. When Hikoichi is seen holding the mortar in his arms and riding the horse, he says that he is carrying the mortar, while the horse is only carrying him.

4. Crafty Yasohichi and the Flea Medicine: Yasohichi spends a night in an inn whose beds are infested with fleas. By mentioning that a certain shop makes medicine from fleas and pays a good price for them, he is able to guarantee for himself a more pleasant night's stay on his return trip.

5. Dull-Witted Hikoichi and the Duck Soup: The village master invites Hikoichi for a dinner of duck soup, but serves radish soup instead. Later Hikoichi invites the master hunting, saying that he knows a place where there are many ducks. After spending all day there and giving Hikoichi a wonderful meal, the master realizes that the "ducks" are just radishes.

6. Stingy Kichiyomu and the Iron Hammer: Kichiyomu tries to borrow a neighbor's iron hammer so that he can drive in some metal nails. When the neighbor refuses, Kichiyomu accuses him of stinginess; now Kichiyomu will be forced to use his own hammer.

7. Patches: An actor named Patches meets a serpent that has been plaguing a village. The serpent thinks that the man's name is "badger," and since badgers are magic creatures, the serpent asks Patches to do some tricks. By changing his costumes and masks, Patches makes the serpent think that he is actually transforming himself into other beings. Patches "confides" in the serpent that he is afraid of money, and the serpent tells Patches that it is afraid of tobacco tar and persimmon juice. Patches tells this information to the villagers, who drive the serpent away. The snake later returns for revenge and pours a pile of money into Patches's house.

8. The Stone Statue and the Grass Hat: A man is returning home during a storm after being unable to sell any wares and obtain some money for New Year's. He sees a forlorn statue of Jizō and places a sedge hat upon the statue to protect it. Later that night the statue comes to the man's house and leaves him a great deal of money.

9. The Grateful Toad: A girl is inadvertently promised in marriage to a snake. The girl fills some gourds with pins and says that she will marry whoever can sink them in a pond. The snake tries to grab the gourds, but is killed by the sharp needles. A toad whose offspring had been threatened by the snake expresses gratitude. The toad gives the girl an old woman's skin to wear to protect herself during her travels. The girl gets a position as a menial at a rich man's house, but one day the man's son sees her without the old woman's skin on. When he falls ill from love of her, the girl appears before the whole household in her true form, cures the man, and becomes his wife.

10. Raw Monkey Liver: See entry 137.

11. The Crusty Old Badger: A man who has been tricked by a badger says he will obtain his revenge. One day the man sees a beggar, recognizes him as the badger, and kills him. The beggar does not revert to badger form, so the man realizes he is guilty of murder. A Buddhist priest happens along who administers holy orders to the man, shaving off his much prized hair. When he hears people laughing all around him, the man regains his senses and realizes that he has been tricked by the badger once again.

12. The Cloth of a Thousand Feathers: See entry 115.

13. The Old Woman in the Cottage: A man frightens a fox and drives it away. Suddenly the sky grows dark, and the man seeks shelter in an isolated hut where an old woman lives. The man becomes mesmerized by the woman's blackening her teeth, when suddenly the woman jumps up and bites his nose. The man falls back and tumbles into a frozen pond. The hut has vanished, and the man realizes that the old woman was actually the fox.

14. The Two Statues of Kannon: A man meets a mountain witch and offers to carry her on his back. Once he has hold of her, he does not let her down until they reach his house. She manages to escape into a room that houses a statue of Kannon. When the man follows her, he finds two statues in the room. He says aloud that the real statue will smile if he makes an offering and tricks the witch into giving herself away.

15. The Mirror: See entry 124(b).

16. Picking Mountain Pears: Three brothers try to find some mountain pears for their sick mother. The first two boys meet an old woman who tells them how to obtain the pears, but they ignore her instructions and are eaten by a huge serpent. The youngest boy meets the woman, follows her instructions, and obtains the pears. He also manages to kill the serpent and rescue his two brothers.

17. The Strange Folding Screen: A man who has squandered away his family fortune is convinced not to sell off his woodlands and pond by a mysterious old man who is really a frog. One night a blank screen in the man's house is miraculously covered with lifelike paintings of frogs. When the man dies, the ink of the pictures gradually fades from the screen.

66. Brower, Robert H. "The *Koñzyaku monogatarisyū:* An Historical and Critical Introduction, with Annotated Translations of Seventy-eight Tales." Ph.D. dissertation, University of Michigan, 1952.

Brower's dissertation is an important study of this monumental Japanese tale collection. Volume I (pp. i–362) is the literary analysis of the *Koñzyaku*. Volume I is listed in Chapter 1 of this bibliography, entry 4. Volume II (pp. 363–740) gives translations for 78 tales selected from all the extant books of the collection. Volume III (pp. 741–1062) gives the notes to the translations. The contents for Volumes II and III are identical and are listed below. The numbers in the list below refer to the scroll and tale numbers.

67. Davis, F. Hadland. *Myths and Legends of Japan*. New York: Thomas Y. Crowell, 1912; reprint editions Gordon Press, 1976; Arden Library, 1978.

Despite its antiquated writing style, this book remains a valuable and useful collection. It presents a broad spectrum of folk materials, including legends of the founding of the country, animal tales, warrior tales, fairy tales, and Buddhist legends, as well as discussions of Japanese folk religious beliefs and superstitions. The work is divided into 31 chapters according to topic (such as bells, flowers, legends of Mount Fuji, and supernatural beings). There are 32 full-page color illustrations by Evelyn Paul. (The illustrations have more of an Indian or Middle Eastern flavor than Japanese.) The book also contains a glossary of gods and goddesses (both Buddhist and Shinto), a genealogy of the Shinto deities, and a glossary-index.

Chapter 1, The Period of the Gods, relates the legends of the creation of Japan and the descent of the sun-goddess's descendants to the Japanese islands. Based primarily on W. G. Aston's translation of *Nihongi*, this section includes the story of Izanagi and Izanami (entry 119), of Susanō (entry 117), and of the Princes Fire-shine and Fire-fade (entry 122). In this version the princes are reconciled after Fire-fade returns his brother's fishhook.

Chapter 2, Heroes and Warriors, contains stories about historical and fictional heroes. (1) Yorimasa, the great archer, shoots down a fantastic creature that appears within a huge, dark cloud and tries to steal away the life force of the emperor. (2) Yoshitsune, the Minamoto warrior and younger half brother of the Shogun Yoritomo, leads the Minamoto troops in their great victory over the rival Taira clan. Yoshitsune's most faithful retainer is Benkei, a huge, wild warrior-priest renowned for his strength (both physical and supernatural) and for his great knowledge of Buddhist doctrine. Benkei's incantations save Yoshitsune from the spirits of the dead Taira warriors. (For more information on Yoshitsune and Benkei, see *Yoshitsune: A Fifteenth Century Japanese Chronicle* by H. C. McCullough, Stanford University Press, 1971.) (3) Raiko, a warrior during the reign of the Emperor Ichijo, is able to slay a terrible goblin through the use of some magic saké. Raiko also was credited with killing a huge goblin spider. (4) The Tale of Prince Yamato-dake (see entry 138). (5) Momotarō (see entry 125). (6) Hidesato of the Rice Bale (see entry 127).

Chapter 3, The Bamboo-Cutter and the Moon-Maiden, is a version of the complete story of the *Tale of the Shining Princess* (see entry 100).

Chapter 4, Buddha Legends. (1) At the cost of his life, the Buddha learns four great truths from a dragon. (2) A whale hears about the great statue of the Buddha at Kamakura. The whale wishes to learn which of them is the larger. The whale is found to be two inches longer than the Buddha. (3) A young girl who is sent from Japan to become the consort of the Emperor of China sends a crystal back to the Kofuku temple. In its depths is a perfect image of the Buddha. On the sea voyage back to Japan, the crystal is stolen by the Sea God, but it is later recovered through the courage of a fisherwoman.

Chapter 5, Fox Legends, describes the association between the fox and the deity Inari and the various supernatural powers of the fox, including the ability to possess people and to assume human shape. (1) The Lady Tamanomae, who is actually a fox, causes an emperor to fall seriously ill until she is driven from the palace. Her soul enters a stone, which then becomes poisonous to any living creature that touches it. The priest Genno frees the spirit from the stone and its own evilness through his prayers. (2) A skeptic who does not believe in bewitching foxes is tricked into thinking that he has committed a murder and is administered the tonsure by a fox in the guise of a priest. (3) A fox, whose cub had been saved from some children by a certain man, sacrifices the life of that cub when the man's son falls ill and can be cured only by the liver of a fox. (4) Inari grants a woman's wish for a child when the woman shows kindness to a beggar who is really Inari in disguise. (5) Inari assumes the shape of a giant spider to frighten a miser into assuming a more righteous posture of charity.

Chapter 6, Jizō, the God of Children, describes the beliefs of Jizō as a protector of the souls of dead children and as a merciful Buddha who intercedes with the gods of the afterworld on behalf of people who have shown Jizō even the slightest reverence during their lifetimes.

Chapter 7, Legend in Japanese Art, describes the depiction of religious and supernatural motifs in Japanese art and the belief that pictures painted by truly skilled artists can actually come to life. This chapter includes a version of the tale of "The Kakemono Ghost" (see entry 72, tale 37).

Chapter 8, The Star Lovers and the Robe of Feathers (see entries 132(a), 135).

Chapter 9, Legends of Mount Fuji, describes the deities associated with Mount Fuji. This chapter includes a version of the tale about the elixir of life (see entry 68, tale 10) and the story of Visu, a man who goes to Mount Fuji to pray and who becomes entranced watching a pair of fox maidens play *go* for 300 years.

Chapter 10, Bells, gives legends about the bells in various temples in Japan, including the story of Benkei's stealing the bell from Miidera and the story of a woman, who had had a love affair with a priest, turning into a dragon and burning the priest to death when he attempts to hide under the bell of his temple (see entry 73, tales 7 and 16).

Chapter 11, Yuki-Onna, the Lady of the Snow, tells of an old man and his apprentice who take shelter in a hut during a fierce snowstorm. During the night, the young man sees a magnificently beautiful woman, completely clad in white, enter the hut and blow her cold breath on the older man so that he is killed. The Snow Maiden takes pity on the young man and spares his life on the condition that he never tell anyone what happened. Later the man meets a young woman traveler and makes her his wife. After several years have gone by and a number of children are born, the man tells his wife about the Lady of the Snow, whereupon his wife angrily turns into the Yuki-Onna. She says that because of their children she will not kill him for his betrayal and disappears into the snowy night. (The young wife's name was Yuki, the Japanese word for snow.) This chapter also adapts a tale of a snow ghost from the collection of local legends by Gordon-Smith (entry 72, tale 49).

Chapter 12, Flowers and Gardens, describes various aspects of the Japanese gardens and the flowers that are most important in Japanese culture. This chapter includes four tales adapted from Gordon-Smith (entry 72): "The Chrysanthemum Hermit" (tale 45), "The Violet Well" (tale 3), "The Spirit of the Lotus" (tale 42), and "The Spirit of the Peony" (tale 46).

Chapter 13, Trees, discusses the various trees that are important in Japanese culture, such as the cherry, pine, and plum, and includes versions of the tales "The Willow Wife" (entry 68, tale 1), "The Tree of the One-eyed Priest" (entry 72, tale 41), and "The Dwarf Pines" (entry 68, tale 11).

Chapter 14, Mirrors, discusses the importance of mirrors in Shinto. It also contains a version of the "Mirror of Matsuyama," entry 124(a).

Chapter 15, Kwannon and Benten, Daikoku, Ebisu, and Hotei, concerns Kwannon, the goddess of mercy, who is of great importance in Japanese folk religion. This chapter lists the 33 shrines in Japan that are sacred to Kwannon. Benten is the goddess of the sea and one of the deities of good luck and wealth. (Kannon and Benten, also called Benzaiten, are Buddhist deities sometimes depicted as male deities in their original form.) Daikoku is another deity of wealth, often depicted with a magical mallet. His son is Ebisu, a sea-deity who is a patron god of labor. Hotei is the deity of laughter and contentment.

Chapter 16, Dolls and Butterflies—dolls in Japan are sometimes made in such a lifelike way that they can come to life. Butterflies most often were the disembodied souls of human beings who were soon to die. The appearance of a butterfly or butterflies was interpreted both as a good and a bad omen.

Chapter 17, Festivals, discusses the Boys' Festival (Tango no sekku), held on May 5, the Festival of the Dead (Bonmatsuri) from July 13 to 15, and the use of the ritual gateway (torii) in Shinto shrines.

Chapter 18, The Peony Lantern, tells of a young girl who dies of longing when her lover does not keep his promise to visit her. Some time later the man meets the woman and her maid, who is carrying a peony lantern, and they tell him that they had been forced to move away because her family wished to keep the lovers apart. The two lovers resume their affair, but one night the man's servant sees that the woman is really a hideous corpse. The next morning the man goes to the area where the women said that they were living, but he finds their graves at the local temple with the peony lantern marking the place. The man places Buddhist charms all around his house to keep the ghosts from entering again, but the ghost of the maid bribes one of the servants to remove them. The man is found dead the next morning with the bones of a woman beside him.

Chapter 19, Kōbō Daishi, Nichiren, and Shōdō Shonin, concerns Kōbō Daishi, the founder of the Shingon sect of Buddhism and renowned for the many miracles he performed. Nichiren is the founder of the Nichiren sect of Buddhism. He miraculously escaped execution when the sword with which he was to be beheaded broke as it struck his neck. Shōdō Shonin founded the first Buddhist temple at Nikko.

Chapter 20, Fans, describes the importance of the fan in Japanese culture. It also contains a story of two lovers who exchange fans as a symbol of their vows, who then are separated for some time after the girl runs away from her father's house, but who eventually chance upon one another again and happily resume their love.

Chapter 21, Thunder, tells of Raiden, the Thunder God, and the supernatural creatures associated with him. It also concerns Raitaro, the son of the thunder: A poor farmer finds a baby boy in the fields during a storm and brings him home; after that the man's fortunes improve considerably. When Raitaro becomes 18, he reveals that he is the son of the Thunder God, turns into a white dragon, and ascends to the heavens.

Chapter 22, Animal Legends, discusses the hare, badger, cat, and dog. It also contains versions of the tales "The White Hare of Inaba" (entry 136), "Crackling Mountain" (entry 114), "The Badger Tea Kettle" (entry 112), "Shippei Taro" (entry 77, tale 7), "The Old Man Who Made Withered Trees Blossom" (entry 129), and "The Jellyfish and the Monkey" (entry 137).

Chapter 23, Bird and Insect Legends, discusses the Japanese names of several important birds and insects. It also includes versions of the tales "The Tongue-cut Sparrow" (entry 133) and "Human Fireflies" (entry 72, tale 44).

Chapter 24, Concerning Tea, discusses the beverage that is so important in Japanese, Chinese, and English cultures. There is a brief discussion of the tea ceremony.

Chapter 25, Legends of the Weird. (1) The blind priest Hōichi is renowned for his recitation of the *Tales of the Heike*. One night he is summoned to a palace to perform before an audience of nobles. After Hōichi has been going out nightly for some time, the head priest of the temple sends someone to follow him. The man sees that Hōichi has actually been visiting the graveyard of the dead Taira warriors and nobles. The priest paints Buddhist scriptures all over Hōichi's body, so that the ghost of the samurai sent to fetch him will not be able to see him. Unfortunately the priest forgets to paint Hōichi's ears, which are thus visible to the ghost, who tears them off Hōichi's head. Hōichi recovers, but is thereafter called Earless Hōichi. (2) A traveling priest comes to a village that is plagued by a corpse-eating demon. The priest learns that the demon is the reincarnation of a district priest who, during his human lifetime, carried out his priestly functions with a tainted heart. (3) A shopkeeper follows a strange-looking woman who had come to his store for many nights to buy sweets. He discovers that she is the ghost of a woman whose child had been born alive after the mother had been buried. She had been buying the candy for the child, who is found to be safe and sound. (4) An innkeeper purchases a used futon from a secondhand shop, but his guests complain that the bedding is haunted. The man learns that the futon had belonged to two children who had been cruelly turned out into a snowstorm after their parents had died. The haunting voices were the plaintive cries of the children. (5) A poor farmer throws his six children into the river as soon as each is born. When he becomes more prosperous, he welcomes the birth of his seventh child, but one night this child speaks with the voice of the previously murdered children. (6) A suitor sees his would-be bride disinter and eat the corpse of a baby, but he is not frightened by the awful sight. The "corpse" is actually a candy doll, and the scene had been a test of the man's courage.

Chapter 26, Three Maidens. (1) The Maiden of Unai is courted by two equally ardent lovers. A test of skill is proposed to see which is the better marksman, but they both prove to have equal skill. Unable to decide between the two, the maiden throws herself into the river. Her lovers also drown in their attempt to save her. The maiden and the two lovers are buried together, and the lovers continue their rivalry even after death. (2) The Maiden of Katsushika is renowned for her beauty and courted by many suitors, but she refuses to marry because of the shortness of human life. (3) "The Maiden with the Wooden Bowl" (see entry 131).

Chapter 27, Legends of the Sea. (1) During the Festival of the Dead, ghost ships appear on the sea and attempt to sink any vessels they encounter. (2) "Urashima" (see entry 134). (3) Through the use of the Jewels of the Ebb and Flow of the Tide, the Empress Jingo successfully invades Korea. (4) "The Slaughter of the Sea Serpent" (see entry 72, tale 17). (5) "The Spirit of the Sword" (see entry 72, tale 18). (6) "The Love of O Cho San" (see entry 72, tale 27). (7) "The Spirit of the Great Awabi" (see entry 72, tale 43).

Chapter 28, Superstitions, describes beliefs concerning human sacrifice, divination, unlucky years and days, the protection of children, charms, and the God of Poverty.

Chapter 29, Supernatural Beings, describes kappa, tengu, mountain witches, mountain men, and dragons. It also includes the story of the shōjō and its white saké (see entry 72, tale 38).

Chapter 30, The Transformation of Issunboshi, and Kintaro, the Golden Boy (see entries 118, 120).

Chapter 31, Miscellaneous Legends. (1) "Kato Sayemon" (see entry 72, tale 12). (2) "How an Old Man Lost His Wen" (see entry 128). (3) "A Japanese Gulliver"—Shikaiya Wasōbiōye sets out by ship and visits the Island of the Immortals, the 3,000 worlds of the Buddhist scriptures, and a land of giants. (4) "The Jewel Tears of Samebito"—Samebito, a shark-man, is expelled from the sea for some offense. The warrior Tōtarō takes pity on him and builds a pond in his garden where Samebito can live. Later Tōtarō falls in love with a woman whose father is demanding a bride-price of 10,000 jewels. Because Tōtarō is pining for his love, Samebito begins to weep, but as his tears touch the ground, they turn to jewels. Samebito is later pardoned by the Dragon King and returns to the sea.

68. Dolch, Edward W., and Dolch, Marguerite P. *Stories from Japan*. Champaign, Ill.: Garrard Press, 1960.

This collection has 20 entries, but it actually contains only 11 stories. Some of the stories are divided into scenes, each presented as a separate chapter. Each tale has full-page color illustrations by Lucy and John Hawkinson. (In this annotation the chapters are regrouped into complete tales.)

1. The Willow Tree, and The Temple of the Goddess of Mercy. A young farmer prevents the men from his village from cutting down a willow tree to build a bridge. Later the man meets a beautiful woman who becomes his wife. They live happily together, and a son is born. Then an imperial edict is issued, ordering the felling of the willow tree for the construction of a temple. The woman reveals that she is actually the spirit of the tree and disappears when the tree is to be cut down. After the tree is felled, the workmen are unable to move it, but the young son of the willow spirit is able to move it with no difficulty.

2. The Piece of Straw, and The Beautiful Horse: See entry 130.

3. The Girl with the Wooden Bowl: See entry 131.

4. The Two Brothers, and The King of the Sea: See entry 122. (In this version the brothers reconcile with the return of the fishhook.)

5. Momotarō the Peach Boy, The Northeastern Sea, and Momotarō and the Ogre: See entry 125.

6. My Lord Bag-of-Rice: See entry 127.

7. Little One Inch, and The Princess and the Ogre: See entry 118.

8. The Soldier's Sweetheart. A soldier sees the face of a beautiful woman in the water beneath a bridge. One night the woman appears on the bridge and becomes the man's wife. She takes him each night to her magnificent underwater palace. After a while the soldier becomes pale and sickly. An old friend learns what has been happening and realizes that the woman is an evil spirit, but he is too late in his discovery and is unable to help. The soldier dies. The "woman" actually is the spirit of a frog.

9. Urashima, The Princess of the Sea, and the Return of Urashima: See entry 134.

10. The Goddess of Fuji. A young man's mother is stricken by an illness during an epidemic. He learns from a wise magician that he must make an arduous pilgrimage to a shrine on Mount Fuji to obtain the curative water of life. When the boy comes to a place where three paths branch, he meets a woman who shows him the correct path to take. The boy returns to the magic spring every few days for water until the epidemic is over. He cures his mother and the other sick villagers. When he returns to thank the woman, he learns that she is the Goddess of Mount Fuji. She gives him a branch of camellia, which the boy later plants. It grows into a fine tree with curative powers.

11. The Three Dwarf Trees, and The Young Lord. A young lord disguises himself as an itinerant priest to go among his people and learn of any injustices. He finds a samurai and his wife living in abject poverty because they had been wrongfully driven from their home. During the course of the evening, the samurai burns his prized dwarf pine trees to heat the hut for the supposed priest. Later, when the lord issues a summons to all the fighting men in his realm, this samurai answers the call. He is brought before the lord, whom he recognizes as the priest, and he is told that his estates will be restored to him.

69. Dorson, Richard M. *Folk Legends of Japan.* Rutland, Vt.: Charles E. Tuttle, 1962.

This is an excellent book, very well organized and easy to use. The legends are taken from a variety of Japanese sources and are grouped according to topic (priests, temples, and shrines, monsters, spirits, transformations, heroes and strong men, chōjas, knaves, and places). Each section and most of the individual legends have informative introductions. There is a very good general introduction to the entire work. Dorson also gives a list of Japanese sources of the legends and a bibliography of Western-language sources. (Japanese titles and authors are given only in romaji.)

Part One: Priests, Temples, and Shrines

Saint Kōbō's Well: Kōbō Daishi miraculously causes a spring to gush forth in the village of Muramatsu.

The Willow Well of Kōbō: Kōbō Daishi miraculously causes a spring to gush forth in the Zempuku temple.

The Kōbō Chestnut Trees: Kōbō Daishi causes the chestnut trees around Fukiage Pass to bear fruit on the low branches so that little children can reach them.

The Waterless River in Takio: A stream near Ikarijima runs dry when a woman refuses charity to Kōbō Daishi.

The Stream Where Kōbō Washed His Garment: Because the people of Momotomataga criticized Kōbō Daishi for washing his clothes in their river, the river runs dry during the summer. In Suko, where the people allowed him to do his washing, no one has drowned in the river since then.

The Priest's Towel: A young wife who had given a piece of mochi to a priest receives a towel that makes her more and more beautiful when she wipes her face with it. Her evil mother-in-law, who had demanded the return of the mochi, becomes uglier and uglier when she tries to use the towel.

The Kannon Who Substituted: A man becomes suspicious of his wife who goes out every night to worship at a nearby temple of Kannon. He determines to kill her, but although he strikes her with his sword, she remains unharmed. The statue of Kannon is found to have shed blood and to have a scar at the place where the man struck his wife.

The Statue of Buddha at Saiho-ji: When the mistress of a house learns that her maid has been making daily rice offerings to Amida Buddha at the Saiho temple, she burns the girl's face with an iron rod. Through a dream, the master of the house learns that the Buddha statue had substituted itself for the pious maid. The statue is found to have a terrible wound on its face, while the maid is unharmed.

The Earless Jizō of Sendatsuno: A blind biwa-player priest is taken every night by a mysterious warrior to a grand mansion where the priest is told to recite *The Tale of the Heike*. When the chief priest of the temple learns of this, he realizes that the priest has been singing to the spirits of the dead Heike warriors in their graveyard. The chief priest writes Buddhist sutras all over the blind priest's body to ward off the ghosts, but the next day the blind priest is found with his ears torn off; the chief priest had forgotten to write scriptures on his ears. After the blind priest's death, an earless statue of Jizō was erected in his memory.

The Red Nose of the Image: When the priest Ippen is about to die, he says that his spirit will inhabit a stone image. If ever a calamity befalls the area, the image's nose will turn red. In 1597 the image's nose did turn red; the entire area was destroyed and sank into the sea as the result of an earthquake.

The Priest Who Ate the Corpse: A priest accidentally becomes a cannibal and begins digging up the corpses in the temple graveyard. Eventually he is discovered and exiled. Later the priest is torn to pieces by a supernatural creature.

The Monk and the Maid: A monk rebuffs the advances of a woman who has fallen in love with him, but out of sympathy for her he says that he will marry her if she can row across a lake to his temple for 100 consecutive nights. The priest thought that the woman would not try so dangerous a task, but she does, and she is drowned in the lake on March 20. Every year on that date a storm occurs on the lake.

The Shrine of the Vengeful Spirit: An old woman wants to betray the hiding place of a young boy and girl so that she can collect a reward, but she has promised not to say anything. However, she indicates where they are hiding by turning her head. When the two children are killed, the woman's head is suddenly turned to one side forever. An epidemic breaks out, and the children's spirits are propitiated by being enshrined as local deities.

The Shrine Built by Straw Dolls: A carpenter tells a feudal lord that he will build a shrine singlehandedly, but he requests that no one watch him while he is working. One night the lord looks at the construction site and sees many carpenters, all of whom look like the first one. When the shrine is completed, the duplicate carpenters are found to be straw dolls.

Visit to Zenko-ji Driven by a Cow: A cow steals a piece of cloth from an irreligious old woman and leads her to a temple. When the woman reads a saying at the temple, she is converted to Buddhism. One day the woman goes to worship Kannon at a local shrine and finds the piece of cloth on the statue's head.

The Temple of Raikyu Gongen: A feudal lord arranges a marriage between his daughter and his enemy, then treacherously kills his new son-in-law. The wife kills herself and returns as a fire that floats near her father's castle. A temple is built to propitiate the spirits of husband and wife.

The Origin of Enoo-ji: A feudal lord kills a mandarin duck. Later the duck's mate appears to him in a dream as a beautiful woman. The lord kills several more ducks, one being the first duck's mate. Then the lord constructs a temple for the repose of the ducks' souls.

The Origin of Kazo-ji on Mount Wooden Pillow: Mita Genta is caught in a storm at sea and vows to become a priest if he is saved. The ship is guided safely to Kasaura. Genta climbs the mountain and sees the God and Goddess of the Mountain. They ask him to move a statue of the Buddha Yakushi from the valley to the top of the mountain, since Yakushi should be higher than they. The god causes a summit to collapse into a pond, so that there is a place to install the statue. When the statue has been moved, Genta notices that one of its legs is broken, and he places his wooden pillow under the break. The pillow miraculously becomes the missing part of the leg.

Part Two: Monsters

The Kappa of Fukiura: In trying to escape from a farmer, a kappa's arm is pulled from his shoulder. The kappa promises that he will cause no more trouble until the buttocks of a stone Jizō rot away if the farmer will return the arm. Whenever a kappa from another village comes to the pond, the Fukiura kappa calls out a warning to the villagers.

The Kappa of Koda Pond: A kappa is dragged along by a horse so that the fluid on his head spills out. When confronted by the owner of the horse, the kappa asks to be spared, saying that he will lend the man bowls whenever the man has a feast.

The Kappa Who Played "Pull-Finger": A kappa invites people to play "pull-finger," then drags them into a pond and kills them. A man decides to destroy the kappa, and he drags the kappa away from the pond by means of a strong horse. In exchange for his freedom, the kappa teaches the man to set broken bones properly.

The Kappa Bonesetter: When a woman is accosted in her outhouse by a strange creature, she boldly cuts off its hand. The hand proves to be that of a kappa. The hand is returned to the kappa when he promises to teach the woman's husband the secrets of bonesetting.

A Grateful Kappa: A kappa appears to a priest who is a renowned fencer and says that all the kappa children save one have been killed by a huge snake. When the priest kills the snake, the kappa promises that none of the priest's descendants will ever be harmed by kappa.

Wrestling a Kappa: Goro the strong man is weaker than the kappa. After eating the rice offering at a Buddhist temple, Goro is able to defeat the kappa.

Memories of Kappa: A woman tells how one of her girlhood companions was drowned and was thought to be the victim of a kappa.

Tales of Tengu: (1) A tengu jumps off a rock and leaves his footprint in the stone. (2) A fire on a tree top is thought to be the tengu that lives in the trees. (3) A tengu that lived in a pine tree often plagued the villagers nearby, but the tree was eventually felled by a storm.

The Tengu Pine and Takegoro: A man named Takegoro lives near a pine tree where old tengu bring their young children to play. One day Takegoro is abducted by an old tengu, and he remains in the tengu's service for more than 20 years, even after his return to his home.

Burned to Death by a Tengu: A man who has committed various crimes tries to shoot down a bird near a shrine. The bird turns into a tengu who grabs the man and sets him afire. The woods near where the man was burned are thought to be cursed, and if anyone cuts down the trees there, a fire breaks out in the village.

The Tengu of Komine Shrine: The house of Kumagaya the doctor is haunted by an apparition that cannot be exorcised. The apparition proves to be a tengu. The former owner of the house had often arrested people and treated them harshly, and some of these people became ghosts and haunted him in retaliation. In his desperation the officer had asked at the Komine Shrine for a tengu to protect him from the ghosts.

The Tengu's Sword: A man who learns a certain type of magic from a tengu is given a sword by the tengu. The man uses the magic to commit all sorts of crimes. Finally the tengu appears in the guise of a farmer. When the man tries to kill him, thinking he is only a farmer, the tengu breaks the tip off the sword and takes away the man's magic powers.

The Tengu Who Made Rice Cakes: A tengu teaches a poor man to make a special type of rice cake, and the man becomes rich selling them. Every year the family make a special batch of cakes to give to the tengu.

The Demon's Cave: The god Tametomo tries to stop a demon couple from eating people by telling them that they will receive a human sacrifice every day if they can build a stone staircase of 100 steps in one night. When the demons have placed the ninety-ninth step, the god imitates a cock's crow and keeps the demons from completing their task.

The Tooth-Marked Stone: Two tales tell why stones in different parts of Japan are thought to have the marks of a demon's teeth on them.

Great King with Eight Faces: A warrior is sent by the emperor to kill a demon. The warrior prays to Kannon, who tells him he must use an arrow made with a tail feather of a copper pheasant. An old man had saved the life of such a pheasant, and the pheasant had come to the man's house in the guise of a little girl and become his daughter. She gives the man the needed feather and departs.

Mountain Giants: A yamauba eats the baby of a certain family. Later the family give the witch some hot food in which they have placed large stones. When the witch tries to drink from a river, she falls in and is drowned.

The Mountain Man of Mt. Mitsubushi: A hunter leaves his gun with a string attached to the trigger in hopes of shooting a wild boar, but the gun kills a mountain man instead. The hunter comes down with a fever and dies soon after.

The Flute Player and the Shōjō: A female shōjō is lured onto a beach by a young man's exquisite flute playing. In return for his playing, the shōjō gives the young man a strand of her hair and a magical fish-hook; with these the man is able to catch any fish that he desires.

Spider Pool: A huge spider repeatedly comes out of a pool and winds a string around the foot of a man sleeping there. The man wakes up just in time and transfers the accumulated string to a huge tree, which is uprooted when the spider pulls on the strings.

The Bodyless Horse: A strange jingling sound that people might hear when passing a certain field is said to be the bells around the neck of a bodyless horse.

Tales of Zashiki-bokko: Four tales of manifestations by the fairy child that haunts the tatami room (see entry 35, section IV).

Part Three: Spirits

The Ghost That Cared for a Child: For several nights a disheveled young woman comes to a candy shop to buy sweets for a baby. Several people see the strange woman. Finally it is discovered that she is the ghost of a woman who had died during her last month of pregnancy. The child had been born alive in the coffin, and the mother's spirit had returned to care for it.

The Ghost of the First Wife: A man promises his dying wife that he will not remarry, but he soon decides to take a new wife. Whenever the man is not home, the ghost of the first wife comes to haunt the second wife, until she finally returns to her parents' home.

The Mirror Given by a Ghost: The warrior Hayasuke always keeps a small box with him. When his students open the box, they find a small mirror. Hayasuke tells them that he received it from a ghost. A woman had been murdered by her husband's mistress and asked Hayasuke's help in carrying out her revenge. Hayasuke removed a charm from the husband's house so that the spirit of the wife could enter and possess the evil mistress.

The Dish Mansion of Unshu: The evil wife of a samurai breaks one of her husband's ten prize dishes and blames it on a maid. After the maid hangs herself in despair, her ghost appears nightly counting from one to nine until a clever fellow one night calls out "ten" as soon as she says nine. She had been counting the ten dishes, and after the tenth one is "accounted for," the ghost no longer appears.

Fish Salad Mingled with Blood: While preparing fish salad on New Year's Eve, a maid breaks a valuable dish. The maid kills herself. After that the New Year's fish salad at that house always has blood in it.

White Rice on the Pot: A man kills himself after being sentenced to death for losing a single sack of rice. On the anniversary of his death, some rice mysteriously appears on the rice pot near which he had died.

The Seven Blind Minstrels: A man deliberately gives false directions to a group of wandering blind minstrels, so that they all die in the wilderness. After that everyone in the man's family suffers from eye illness. One man tries to cure the curse by carving eyes on the tombstones of the minstrels, but it does not work.

The Revengeful Spirit of Masakado: Because Masakado was killed by Hidesato, his angry spirit causes illness to Hidesato's descendants or to anyone wearing their family crest.

The Evil Spirit of Fusataro: A servant named Fusataro leaves the house every night on unknown business. When a specter tries to kill St. Dengyo, who is visiting the area, it is discovered that the specter is Fusataro.

The Weaving Sound in the Water: A woman carrying a loom falls through a vine bridge and is drowned in the waters below. After that people crossing the bridge hear the sound of weaving in the water.

The Phantom Boat: A fisherman on his boat is approached by a second, swift-moving ship. He sees that the people on that ship are pale and ghostlike.

One Hundred Recited Tales: After a group of boys recite 100 tales, three boys remain behind to spend the night at a shrine. A ghost takes away two of the boys, but dawn comes before the third boy is killed. Sometime later the boy marries a woman who proves to be the same ghost. When he realizes that, the ghost kills him.

Part Four: Transformations

The Serpent Suitor: A girl is visited nightly by an unknown nobleman. Her nurse tells her to stick a threaded needle into the hem of his kimono. When the girl and the nurse follow the thread, they find a huge snake dying in a cave.

The Blind Serpent Wife: A traveling girl is stranded by a storm at a village. She becomes the wife of a man there. After a child is born, the man's mother looks into the wife's room, but she sees a huge snake coiled up with the baby asleep in its coils. The wife leaves her husband, but the man cannot find a nurse for the child. The snake wife gives the man one of her eyeballs with which to nurse the baby. The feudal lord steals the eyeball, which has become a fine jewel. When the snake wife gives her husband her second eye and that too is stolen, she causes a great earthquake in the area.

The Serpent Goddess of Amo-Ga-Ike: A brave samurai descends into a pond to see the Serpent Goddess who lives there. The goddess says that she can no longer remain in the pond since he has seen her. Later the Serpent Goddess comes to the samurai as a beautiful woman, and they marry. The descendants of this couple have three scales under their arms.

The Serpent of Mt. Unzen: A hunting party kills one of two snakes, after which the surviving snake ravishes the area. Some villagers finally wound the snake. Soon a woman appears at the local doctor's office, saying that she wounded herself cutting wood. When the doctor cures her, the woman warns him to leave the area for there will soon be a devastating earthquake. The woman was the snake.

Two Daughters Who Became Serpents: Two girls are transformed into snakes by the evil deeds of their father. Each girl goes to live in a different pond after the transformation.

Hachiro's Transformation: After eating several trout, Hachiro turns into a snake. He is driven away from his original home by an angry deity, but he finally is able to settle in another area after agreeing to make a daily sacrifice to the deity there.

The Marsh of Tatsuko: A girl named Tatsuko drowns in a pond and becomes a dragon.

The Fox Demons: After he frightens some foxes, a man is bewitched into thinking that he is being chased by an animated corpse.

The Fox Wrestler: A farmer returning home from a banquet meets another man who challenges him to a wrestling match. After some time, the two stop to rest. The farmer suddenly realizes that the man has disappeared. Most of the food that the farmer had been carrying also is gone.

The Fox Wife: A man discovers that his wife is really a fox. As she is about to leave him, the wife casts a spell over his rice fields so that the harvest will always be plentiful, but will appear poor to the tax collector.

The Badger That Was a Shamisen Player: A man sees a badger transform itself into a shamisen player. The man follows the badger to a shrine, where he peers through a hole in a paper door, waiting for the badger to be exposed. Suddenly the man realizes that he is looking at the buttocks of a horse.

Dankuro Badger: A badger takes some valuable items from a fallen feudal castle, then lends them to any villagers who need things for special occasions. When one villager does not return the borrowed items, the badger disappears.

Seventy-five Badgers: When the badgers of Otaki-ga-naru kill an old woman, her husband prays to the god of Ashio Shrine for revenge. The god tells the man that he can destroy the badgers with a certain dog. The dog kills 74 of the badgers, but is overcome by the last one.

Koike's Baba: Koike's servant is attacked by wolves who send for a giant cat to help them kill their prey. The servant strikes the cat's forehead with his sword. When he reaches home, he learns that Koike's mother had injured herself during the night. Koike's "mother" is found to be a huge cat, and his real mother's remains are found hidden.

The God Akiba Revealed as a Beggar: A beggar comes to a temple where he is ill-treated. The beggar is later discovered to be the god Akiba.

The Hunters Turned into Rats: A pregnant woman comes to the hut of a group of hunters and asks for shelter, but they refuse her. She goes to a second group, who agree to help her. She proves to be the Mountain Spirit, and she teaches the hunters how to capture bears. She turns the first group of hunters into rats.

The Mystery of the Bull-Trout: A priest appears to some villagers who are planning to drop poison into a lake, warning them not to do so. The people ignore him and discover that the priest had really been a huge bull-trout.

The Blacksmith's Wife: A blacksmith helps a wolf in labor deliver her pups. After that the wolf assumes the shape of a woman and becomes his wife.

The Girl Who Turned into a Stone: A mother whose daughter is always disobedient asks the girl to bury her after her death by the river, thinking that the girl will bury her on a mountain. Overcome with grief, the girl follows her mother's last instructions. For her continual disobedience, the girl is eventually struck by a falling stone and turned into a stone.

The Woman Who Loved a Tree Spirit: The Lady Akoya falls in love with a young man who proves to be the spirit of a pine tree. When the tree is felled to construct a bridge, the tree cannot be moved by anyone except Akoya.

Okesa the Dancer: A cat who belongs to an old man and woman changes itself into a beautiful girl to become a geisha and obtain some money for the poor couple. A boatman who sees the cat's true form is warned not to reveal her secret. When he breaks the taboo, he is killed.

Part Five: Heroes and Strong Men

The Child of the Sun: A child who has no father learns that he is the child of the sun. He later becomes a great prophet.

The Jewel That Grew Golden Flowers: A king drives out his wife for breaking wind in his presence. The woman later gives birth to a son who returns to the king's palace saying that he has a jewel that will grow golden flowers if it is tended by a woman who has never broken wind. When the king says that there is no such woman, the boy reveals his true identity and asks why his mother was sent away.

The Tale of Yuriwaka: After defeating the Mongol force at Tsushima, the warrior Yuriwaka is abandoned on an island by two treacherous retainers who report him killed in the battle. Yuriwaka's wife sends his pet falcon to search for him, and the falcon returns with a note from Yuriwaka. Yuriwaka is rescued by a fishing vessel, returns to his province, and punishes the faithless retainers.

The Story of Kihachi: Instead of handing an arrow to his lord Takeiwatatsu, Kihachi kicks it with his toe. For this terrible breach of etiquette, Takeiwatatsu kills Kihachi, but Kihachi's vengeful spirit sends down a frost that kills the lord's plants. Finally Takeiwatatsu enshrines Kihachi's spirit, whereupon the frost stops.

Koga Saburo: Koga Saburo, his two brothers, and a princess go hunting. The princess suddenly disappears into a deep, strange cavern.

Saburo is lowered into the cavern on a vine by his brothers and saves the princess, but they then learn that the girl has left a book of sutras in the cave. When the brothers lower Saburo the second time, they tire of waiting for him and abandon him. The princess throws herself into Lake Suwa. Meanwhile, Saburo finds a fantastic village in the cavern, marries a woman there, and has a son. But he still grieves for his lost princess. His new wife sends Saburo back to the surface, where he becomes a serpent, enters Lake Suwa, and marries the princess. Saburo's new wife now mourns the loss of her husband. Her son sends her to the surface to join Saburo. She too enters Lake Suwa, and Saburo keeps both serpent-women as his wives.

The Heike Refugees: People in a certain part of Japan believe themselves to be descendants of the vanquished Heike clan, who were supposedly totally destroyed at the Battle of Dan-no-Ura.

The Last of the Aki: During a period of civil war, the lord Aki Kunitora is betrayed to his rival Chosogabe Motochika. Chosogabe captures and burns Aki's castle. Aki has his wife return to her parents and then commits suicide. After the war, his wife comes to his tomb and plants a cedar seedling there. The moat that surrounded the castle becomes a pond, which is thought to be haunted by the ghosts of the noblewomen who drowned themselves to avoid capture by Chosogabe.

Relics of Benkei: Various places in Japan are associated with the legendary warrior-priest Benkei.

Benkei's Stone Mortar: Two stones weighing almost 60 pounds each are said to have been placed in a certain location by Benkei.

The Famous Horse Ikezuki: When the horse Ikezuki sees his own reflection in a pond, he thinks that it is his dead mother and jumps in after her. In this way he learns to swim. He grows into an incredibly strong and swift horse, and eventually he is bought by the shogun Yoritomo.

The Faithful Dog of Tametomo: While on a journey, Minamoto Tametomo is suddenly "attacked" by his pet dog, who springs onto him, barking. Tametomo impulsively cuts off the dog's head, whereupon the head flies up into a tree and kills a snake that was about to attack Tametomo.

Banji and Manji: The lucky hunter Manji meets a woman in labor in the mountains, but he refuses to help her because of ritual taboos. The unlucky hunter Banji later meets the woman, helps her, and delivers 12 children. The woman is actually the Mountain Goddess. After that, Manji's luck comes to an end, and Banji becomes the successful hunter.

Nue the Hunter of Hatoya: (1) Nue kills a snake that is bewitching his daughter. The snake is transformed into a school of strange fish and then into a growth of poisonous grass. (2) Nue kills a phantom creature that appears as a woman by shooting it with a gold bullet. (3) Nue kills a fantastic deer whose eyes are magic treasure balls.

The Strongest Wrestler in Japan: The god Sankichi appears to the wrestler Daihachi in the form of a little boy of great strength. Daihachi goes to the Sankichi shrine for seven nights to pray and endures a test by the god, so that Sankichi grants Daihachi unlimited strength.

The Mighty Wrestler Usodagawa: A wrestler from Awa comes to challenge the renowned wrestler Usodagawa. He meets Usodagawa's mother, who is carrying a heavy brazier that the Awa wrestler is unable to lift. When Usodagawa appears, he is carrying such a large load of firewood that it completely blocks out the sun.

Nasu Kozahara the Strong Man: Nasu once carried two large stones out of a farmer's field, but he discarded one of them, and it still is embedded in the ground where he dropped it.

Part Six: Chōjas

The Charcoal Burner Who Became a Chōja: The daughter of a rich man, who has been unable to arrange a marriage, learns from a fortune-teller that she is destined to marry a poor charcoal-burner. The girl journeys to the man's house and becomes his wife. The wife gives the man some gold coins with which to buy provisions, but he carelessly throws some of them at ducks that are playing by a pond. When the wife chastises him for his foolishness, he says that he had not realized the value of the gold pieces, since the area around his charcoal fire is completely covered with gold. The wife accompanies her husband to his work area and finds that it indeed is covered with gold.

Asahi Chōja: (1) In order to complete rice planting, a chōja promises one of his three daughters to a dragon-god. He also causes the sun to stop so that one day can be extended. The man's youngest daughter is given to the dragon, but she asks that she be placed in a sevenfold tub. The dragon is able to break through the first six tubs and part of the seventh, but he is finally unable to seize his sacrifice. The rice plants all turn into rushes. (2) A chōja sacrilegiously shoots a mochi offering with an arrow, after which his fortunes decline.

Sanya Chōja: Sanya's companion has a dream that tells where a large vein of gold is located. Sanya discovers the gold and becomes very wealthy. Years later, after he and his family have been totally corrupted by wealth, Sanya's son offends the lord of the province, and the family is condemned to death.

The Camellia Tree of Tamaya: The rich man Tamaya Tokubei hides his gold under a camellia tree in his garden, but he still worries so much about theft that he becomes seriously ill. While on a journey, he hears a stranger singing a song about the gold and silver tree of Tamaya. Tokubei rushes home and finds that the tree actually has turned to gold and silver. He becomes even more ill and finally dies. His wife tries to find the gold that he buried, but she discovers that the tree is no longer golden and that the strongbox is no longer under the tree.

The Gold Ox: A servant finds a gold deposit and becomes a chōja.

The main deposit is in the form of a gold ox, but when the workers try to pull the ox out of the ground, the workpit collapses, killing all the men. One man escapes because he hears a mysterious voice calling his name and leaves the pit to see who it is. This sole survivor had always been a totally honest person.

The Poor Farmer and the Rich Farmer: A Buddha disguised as a poor priest asks for lodging at a rich man's house, but he is refused. Instead, he is taken into a poor man's house. The Buddha causes a tree to grow in the poor man's yard, a tree whose magic wood makes the poor man wealthy. The evil rich man tries to use the magic wood, but he becomes poverty-stricken.

The Girl Who Ate a Baby: Three young men wish to marry the daughter of a chōja. They are all good men and pass several tests. Two of the men look into the woman's room, whereupon they see a she-demon eating the corpse of a baby. They flee, but the third man takes a closer look and sees that the "baby" is a doll made of mochi. The woman then takes this brave man as her husband.

The Thief Who Took the Moneybox: A thief determines to steal a moneybox on which a chōja sleeps every night. Although the house is carefully guarded, the man manages to slip inside. When the confusion wakes the chōja, he gets up to see what is happening, whereupon the thief steals the moneybox and escapes.

Part Seven: Knaves

The Origin of Foolish Sajiya Tales: Refugees of the Heike clan flee to the village of Sajiya and begin circulating tales that say only fools live there. Thus the Genji warriors do not pursue them to Sajiya.

The Crow and the Pheasant: A "foolish" man from Sajiya tricks someone into paying a large price for crows by showing off a pheasant.

Kichigo Ascends to the Sky: A large crowd of people comes to a piece of swampland when the owner announces that he is going to climb to the sky. The weight of the crowd on the field compacts it into usable rice fields.

Kitchomu Fools His Neighbor: Kitchomu sees his greedy neighbor burying money in the garden, saying that the gold should appear as snakes to anyone else. Kitchomu steals the gold and replaces it with a number of snakes.

Whew!: Foolish Shuju keeps repeating the word "dumpling" as he is going home so he will not forget the name of this new food, but he passes a dangerous spot and starts to say "whew" instead of "dumpling." When he gets home he asks his wife to make him some whew.

The Wit of Niemonen: In these five short tales, Niemonen tricks other people in various ways so that he becomes quite wealthy. He even tricks the god of a temple into restoring his health.

Boaster's Wit: The young men of a village have a boasting contest.

All of them go to old Ichibei to "borrow his wit." Ichibei tells each of them a great tale to use in the contest, but even he is not sure which will win.

Boasting of One's Own Region: Four men from different regions try to outdo each other by telling tall tales about their home areas.

The Old Man Who Broke Wind: An old man eats a bird, after which the man makes a sound like the bird's song whenever he breaks wind. The feudal lord is so amused by this that he gives the old man some money. A greedy neighbor tries to duplicate the other man's luck, but he is not successful.

Part Eight: Places

Human Sacrifice to the River God: An old woman tricks the villagers into sacrificing her son-in-law whom she dislikes to the River God when a dam breaks. The woman's daughter learns of the mother's plot and goes to die with her husband. When the old woman learns that her daughter also has been killed, she drowns herself in repentance.

The Princess Who Became a Human Sacrifice: A feudal lord orders one of the forks of a river dammed, but the villagers are unable to complete an effective dam. They decide to sacrifice a maiden, who will be chosen by lot. The village headman's daughter is chosen, whereupon the daughter of the lord, a cripple, asks to be substituted. When the princess drowns herself, the currents of the river slacken, and the dam is completed.

A Mystery at Motomachi Bridge: During the reconstruction of Motomachi Bridge over the Oyodo River, two of the soldiers working on the project are killed when a scaffold collapses. After the bridge is completed, people say that the bridge is haunted by the spirits of the soldiers.

A Human Sacrifice at Kono Strand: When the villagers are unable to complete construction of a harbor at Kono Strand, a pilgrim agrees to be a sacrifice for the villagers.

The Bridge Where Brides Were Taken Away: A young messenger vows to remain celibate for three years, but a woman tries to seduce him. He runs to a large pine tree overhanging a pond. The girl sees his reflection, jumps into the pond, and becomes a serpent. After that the serpent seizes any woman who passes by. Once a bride is taken when she is going past the pond, and thereafter no bride is allowed to cross that bridge over the stream.

Gojo Bridge in Kyoto: A farmer has a dream telling him to go to Gojo Bridge. When he gets there, he meets a man who says that he had a dream about some gold buried beneath a certain tree. The farmer realizes that the man is speaking about the tree in the farmer's garden. The farmer finds the gold and becomes wealthy.

The Mountain of Abandoned Old People: Although the law of their district decrees that people over age 60 must be left in the mountains, two brothers hide their elderly father in their house. When the lord of the area asks that someone make a rope of ashes, the old father tells his sons what to do. The lord praises the men for their knowledge, but they inform him that the wisdom is actually that of their father. The lord decrees that old people should no longer be abandoned.

Feather-Robe Mountain: See entry 132 (in this version the man foolishly takes out the robe for a festival).

Contest of Height between Two Mountains: When Mount Yatsu-ga-take is found to be taller than Mount Fuji, the Goddess of Fuji angrily strikes the summit of her rival and causes it to break into eight peaks.

The Mounds of the Master Singers: Two men from neighboring villages engage so vigorously in a singing contest that they both become ill and die.

The Village Boundary Mound: A clever man from Nagura obtains a favorable boundary decision for his village at the expense of a lazy man from Kamitsugu.

Oka Castle: The inhabitants of Oka Castle make it seem as if a river is full during a season of drought by filling the riverbed with rice. However, because the lord of the castle slights a foot soldier, the soldier goes to the enemy camp and exposes the deception.

The Laughter of the Maidenhair Tree: A villager who is cruelly executed near a certain maidenhair tree curses the village headman. The headman goes insane, his family dies out, and the tree is said to be haunted by the executed man's spirit.

The Discovery of Yudaira Hot Spring: A man finds a spring of cura-tive waters when he sees a monkey with a healed wound.

The Spring of Saké: See entry 104, tale 2.

Blood-Red Pool: A pool is stained red by the blood of a pilgrim who is murdered nearby.

Otowa Pond: A woman inadvertently pollutes the sacred waters of a pond. Thereupon the former guardian-deity is freed to ascend to the heavens, and the woman is compelled to become the new deity.

70. Edmonds, I. G. *Ooka the Wise: Tales of Old Japan*. Indianapolis, Ind.: Bobbs-Merrill, 1961.

This well-written collection contains stories that are excellent for a storyteller to read aloud or for an older child to read alone. The central character is the clever judge Ooka Tadasuke, who was an actual histori-cal person. In each tale Ooka is presented with a seemingly insoluble problem, but he always manages to discover the truth and solve the dilemma somehow. Each story has an illustration by Sanae Yamazaki. These tales are very amusing and entertaining, as are those in Ed-monds's collection about the priest Ikkyu (entry 71).

Ooka and the Stolen Smell: A greedy tempura dealer accuses a student of theft because the student smells the broiling fish while eating plain rice. Ooka finds the student guilty and orders to him to jingle some coins in front of the shopkeeper. The price for the smell of food is the sound of money.

Ooka and the Pup's Punishment: A merchant demands that a boy's puppy be killed for attacking him. Ooka learns that the man had been wearing a brand new kimono and had struck the boy just before the puppy attacked. Thus the puppy had taken the merchant for a robber. Ooka orders the man to pet the puppy each time he sees it and to treat the little boy kindly.

Ooka and the Shattering Solution: A poor boy wishes to buy a fine china dog for his grandfather, but he has only a small amount of money. The shopkeeper scornfully says that he can have three dogs for the small amount, if he can carry one dog home by himself, knowing full well that the boy cannot possibly lift such a heavy object. Ooka tells the boy to pay the amount and smash one of the dogs. Then he can carry it home in pieces and still have two dogs left. The chagrined merchant agrees to sell the boy one dog for the small amount and to have a porter carry it to the boy's home. Ooka warns the shopkeeper not to hurt people's feelings again.

Ooka and the Marble Monster: Ooka's grandson boasts that Ooka can bring a marble lion to life. Not wanting to contradict the boy in front of his friends, Ooka takes the boys to the base of the statue and tells them to say goodbye to one another, since the lion will surely eat all of them if he is brought to life. The nervous boys say that there is no reason for Ooka actually to perform the trick; they will accept the possibility on faith.

Ooka and the Honest Thief: Small amounts of rice begin to disappear from a rice shop every night. Ooka learns that the thief is a laborer who has been unable to find work. The laborer intends to repay the stolen rice as soon as he is employed. Ooka discreetly secures the man a job, and the rice begins to be repaid the same night.

Ooka and the Terrible Tempered Tradesman: A young boy is apprenticed to his bad-tempered uncle. Ooka demands to read the apprenticeship papers and sees that the boy agreed to work hard in exchange for his room, board, and whatever gifts the uncle wishes to give him. Ooka decrees that anything the man throws at the boy in a fit of anger is a "gift" and belongs to the boy. The uncle gradually learns to control his temper.

Ooka and Tosuke's Tax: When an orphanage is destroyed in a typhoon, Ooka levies a special tax of one ryō per door on each house. Stingy Tosuke does not wish to pay, so he seals up five of his six doors. When he still protests that he should not have to pay anything, Ooka excuses him from the tax, then orders the last door of Tosuke's house be sealed up. Ooka does not allow the house to be unsealed until Tosuke agrees to take in all the orphans and care for them himself.

Ooka and the Willow Witness: Mompei recognizes that the man Gohei is the thief who robbed him, but he is unable to prove his accusation since there were no witnesses. The crime took place near a willow tree. Ooka says that the tree is a witness and orders Mompei to bring the tree to court. He orders Gohei to wait at court until Mompei returns, and in the ensuing conversation Gohei inadvertently describes the willow tree, thus proving his own guilt.

Ooka and the Wonderful Wishes: When Ooka's grandson says that he wants to be the son of a higher ranking nobleman, Ooka says that he has three magic wishes that can grant the boy's desire. He, of course, must leave his present family (and his pet puppy), and he will still have to bow to people like the emperor. They boy finally decides that he is satisfied with his own status.

Ooka and the Wasted Wisdom: Two women both claim to be the mother of a baby boy. Ooka sends for various items so that he can perform a divination about the boy's future. When Ooka predicts that the boy will be in an accident, become an invalid, and be dependent on his mother, the false mother reveals herself, while the real mother says that she will gladly take care of her son no matter what. Ooka then completes the prophecy, saying that the boy will recover and become very prosperous (which he does).

Ooka and the Suspect Statue: A bolt of silk is stolen from an old man who was sleeping near a statue of Jizō. Ooka orders the Jizō arrested. When the assembled crowd sees the statue bound with ropes, the people start to laugh. Ooka levies a large fine for contempt of court. Since the people are unable to pay, Ooka orders each person to bring a swatch of cloth as a token. The man who stole the silk foolishly brings a piece of that as his token and is discovered.

Ooka and the Two First Sons: After their father dies, identical twin sons argue about who should become the new family head. One man is good and dutiful, the other evil and greedy, but no one can tell the two apart by appearance. Ooka picks one and tells him to divide the property between himself and his brother. The man claims everything for himself, proving that he is the evil twin. Ooka awards the estate to the good twin.

Ooka and the Barbered Beast: The barber Zenroku offers to pay a woodcutter one ryō plus a shave for himself and his helper in exchange for all the wood that the woodcutter's ox is pulling. When the woodcutter agrees, Zenroku demands the wood in the cart and the wooden cart itself. Ooka decrees that the woodcutter's helper was his ox, not another man who had been riding in the cart, and he orders Zenroku to shave the ox. After several futile attempts at the task, Zenroku agrees to cancel the unfair bargain.

Ooka and the Stronger Stick: Ooka's two grandsons quarrel incessantly. Ooka hires a neighborhood youth to play the bully and stop either grandson when he goes out on an errand. The only way the boys can succeed is by cooperating and helping each other against the bully. Thus the grandsons learn the importance of family harmony.

Ooka and the Halved Horse: Two daimyo demand an equal division of 13 horses. Ooka's rival, Judge Kiyo, wagers his own horse that Ooka will be unable to solve the case. Ooka adds his own horse to the 13 and tells each daimyo to take 7 horses. When they protest that a judge cannot solve a case by causing himself any financial loss, Ooka says that he has suffered none, since he will now take Kiyo's horse.

Ooka and the Cleanest Case: An old man's savings are stolen, and there are eight suspects. Ooka orders each man to write an oath swearing his innocence and finalize it by touching the head of a roadside statue of Jizō. Each man must rinse his hands with water before touching the sacred statue. Only one of the eight men returns with clean hands, and Ooka charges him with being the thief. The statue had been covered with dust from being by the roadside; this man had not dared to touch the statue, since he was making a false oath.

Ooka and the Death Decree: When a maid is ordered put to death for breaking the shogun's vase, Ooka points out that people will say that the shogun values a piece of clay more than a human life. The shogun is placed in an embarrassing position, since he cannot rescind his decree. Ooka says that the maid's death will pay for the embarrassment, but not for the vase. She will have to pay back one mon a year, at which rate it will take her several hundred years to pay off the debt. After that she can be put to death. Thus the maid's life is spared.

71. Edmonds, I. G. *The Possible Impossibles of Ikkyu the Wise*. Philadelphia: Macrae Smith, 1971.

Like the collection of tales about Judge Ooka (entry 70), this collection is well written and the stories are suitable for a storyteller to read aloud or for an older child to read alone. The central character is the Buddhist priest Ikkyu, a trickster. Like Ooka, Ikkyu was an actual historical person. Ikkyu's tricks are meant to help people out of trouble, secure aid for the poor, and teach basic ideals. Each story has a full-page black-and-white illustration by Robert Byrd. The introduction includes a short biographical sketch of Ikkyu.

Punishment Worse than Death: The merchant Chōbei is condemned to death for delivering inferior quality rice to an imperial minister. Ikkyu convinces the minister that banishing Chōbei to Kamakura would be a punishment even worse than death, while tricking Chōbei into making a sizable contribution to the poor. After Chōbei is assured of his reprieve, Ikkyu gets him to donate several months' profit to the poor fund, a punishment that Chōbei indeed finds worse than death.

The Sweet Punishment: An old woman brings a tiny bit of honey for a priest and his eight acolytes, one of whom is Ikkyu. The priest decides to keep all the honey for himself, saying that it would probably be poisonous to young boys. Ikkyu determines to see that the honey is divided among everyone as the woman intended. While the priest is away, Ikkyu breaks a rice bowl, eats his honey, and gives each of the other boys his share of honey. When the priest returns, Ikkyu says that he had broken a rice bowl and was so filled with remorse that he wished to kill himself, so he ate the "poison." The next time the old woman brings honey, the priest shares it with the boys.

The Wrongdoer's Reward: Jirobei, the son of a silk merchant, is about to be expelled from his temple school for stealing. After a long discussion between Ikkyu and the boy's teacher Okubo, Ikkyu decrees that the thief should remain at the temple, while the only other student, a virtuous boy named Goheji, is sent away. After several months of further training, Jirobei is cured of his evil ways, while Goheji establishes a splendid reputation for his pastoral work among the poor. Ikkyu explains that Goheji no longer needed instruction, while Jirobei needed it desperately. Ikkyu convinces the silk merchant to pay for a new temple roof and to support old Okubo for the rest of his life in gratitude for Jirobei's reform.

The Doubled Treasure: A jar of 50 copper coins is found in the stream separating the lands of two feudal lords. Although it is a trivial sum, each man obstinately claims the total amount. Ikkyu had just stopped a fight between the two men, and once again he is called upon to mediate. He tells each man that he will receive the 50 coins, has 50 people make a contribution of one copper coin to the temple, then gives each lord 50 coppers. Ikkyu then tricks each lord into making a huge donation to the poor fund. The two lords never argue again for fear that Ikkyu will extract even larger donations from them.

The Payment in Kind: In the town of Otsu, Ikkyu tricks the mayor, the magistrate, and the innkeeper into making large contributions. The three men decide to embarrass the priest in turn. When Ikkyu and his companion Shinzaemon are unable to pay for a simple meal of two eggs, the innkeeper eagerly extends them credit for a few weeks. The two priests presently return from their journey and wish to settle the account, but the innkeeper gives them a huge bill, based on the value of the eggs and chickens that would have been produced in the past few weeks from those eaten eggs. Ikkyu presents the innkeeper with a plum seed, then demands his change, since the value of the fruit will eventually be far greater than the price of the bill.

The Losing Winner: While spending the night at an inn, Ikkyu and Shinzaemon hear the most pitiful wailing. It is Kitahachi, a wealthy man and a renowned complainer. Kitahachi tells Ikkyu all of his troubles. Ikkyu tries to convince Kitahachi that his problems are not really very serious, but is unsuccessful. Kitahachi even bewails his fate so loudly in his sleep that no one in the town is able to sleep. Finally Ikkyu steals the bag of Kitahachi's gold, gets the man to admit that his former troubles were trivial, and tricks him into promising that he will donate half of his wealth to the poor if he ever complains again after the gold has been returned. Unfortunately, Kitahachi begins to shout about his blessings as loudly as he formerly had complained!

Ikkyu's Treasure: The thief Hanzo decides to rob Ikkyu, since Ikkyu surely must have taken large amounts of money from the donations that he collects. When Hanzo confronts Ikkyu, the priest tells him that his treasures are the moon and the stars. Through Ikkyu's intruction, Hanzo renounces his life of crime and becomes Ikkyu's student.

The Reward for Greed: Ikkyu and Shinzaemon find a splendid jeweled treasure that was lost by the daimyo of Kii. When they try to return it, the lord's guard demands half of their reward for writing their names on the day's audience list. The lord's chamberlain demands the other half for approving the list. As expected, the relieved daimyo offers the priests a reward. Ikkyu demands that each of them receive 25 blows with a split bamboo whip. Then he reveals the bribery that was required to enter the daimyo's audience chamber. The two corrupt officials receive their just rewards.

A Bag of Rice: The rich rice merchant Goto tricks Ikkyu into accepting a single bag of rice as a donation. Ikkyu tells all his friends to bring a pad of writing paper, some water, and some rice flour to Goto's shop. All the sheets of paper are pasted together with the wet rice flour to make a huge paper bag that covers Goto's entire shop. Goto admits defeat and gives his usual donation of three bags of rice.

The Life Saver: The Lord of Kii has a beautiful vase painted by the renowned artist Sesshu. Then the lord decrees that any servant who damages the vase while dusting it will be put to death. To teach Kii to stop making such rash statements, Ikkyu deliberately cracks the vase himself. After Kii admits his error, Sesshu modifies the painting to incorporate the crack, producing an even finer painting. The daimyo then places the vase on permanent open exhibition so that all people can enjoy it.

72. Gordon-Smith, Richard. *Ancient Tales and Folklore of Japan*. London: A. and C. Black, 1908.

This book contains 57 local legends that Gordon-Smith rewrote from tales recorded in the diary he kept during 20 years of travels. An immediacy and attention to detail enrich the stories. They are all quite spellbinding; many deal with ghosts or other supernatural phenomena. The

62 full-page color illustrations by Mo-no-Yuki are appropriately eerie. (The tales in this collection may be considered by some to be inappropriate for children, since many of them deal with the macabre, especially with suicide.)

1. The Golden Hairpin: A young man returns to the home of his fiancée, only to learn that she has died during his long absence. Later he has an affair with a woman he thinks is his fiancée's younger sister. When the man discusses the matter with the girl's parents, he brings with him the woman's gold comb. The girls' astonished mother reveals that the younger daughter has been ill for many months and that the golden comb is the one that had been buried with the older daughter.

2. The Spirit of the Willow Tree: See entry 68, tale 1.

3. Ghost of the Violet Well: The daughter of a samurai falls in love with a young doctor who has saved her life, but they are unable to marry because the man is of the outcast class. The daughter drowns herself in the Violet Well, and later the doctor drowns himself in the same well.

4. Ghost Story of the Flute's Tomb: A young woman takes advantage of her husband's blindness to have an affair with an actor. When the husband discovers what is going on and tries to confront the couple, he accidentally falls and is killed. His ghost appears to a friend in a distant village, explaining what has happened and leaving the blind man's prized flute. The friend carries the flute back to the blind man's house, whereupon the man's ghost materializes from the flute and exacts its revenge on the couple. The friend then buries the flute in a special tomb.

5. A Haunted Temple in Inaba Province: A priest who hears that a particular temple is haunted tries to exorcise the place, but when he sees the spirits he is paralyzed with fear. He is found by the villagers, but he dies shortly thereafter. The temple remains abandoned until it is destroyed by a bolt of lightning.

6. A Carp Gives a Lesson in Perseverance: A man named Rosetsu studies painting from the master Okyo, but in spite of his hard work, he makes little progress. Rosetsu finally leaves the school, but on his way home he sees a carp that struggles for more than three hours to reach a piece of food. Inspired by the carp's perseverance, Rosetsu returns to the school and becomes Okyo's finest student.

7. Legends Told by a Fisherman on Lake Biwa, at Zeze: (1) During storms on the lake, a fireball appears in the sky and attacks fishing vessels. This is the soul of the daimyo Akechi Mitsuhide whose castle was defeated through the treachery of a fisherman. (2) Every year on February 25, a storm is caused on the lake by the restless spirit of a young girl who was drowned while trying to cross the lake in a washtub. She had been going to the opposite shore to see a young monk whom she loved. (3) A clerk runs away with a geisha whom he loves. They reach the Ishiyama temple, where they write out their prayers on strips

of paper and hang them from the rocks, and then commit suicide. Because it is believed that the lovers were granted happiness in the afterlife, people still tie their prayer papers to the rocks at this temple.

8. A Miraculous Sword: See entry 138.

9. The Procession of Ghosts: A priest who spends a night in a ruined temple sees a procession of 100 ghosts. The painter Tosa Mitsunobu hears of this and decides to draw the procession. He spends a night at the temple, but he discovers that the "ghosts" are designs formed on the walls by luminous fungi that had grown there during the period of the temple's neglect. This incident was the inspiration for Mitsunobu's famous painting.

10. A Faithful Servant: When the scholar-official Sugawara no Michizane is falsely accused of treason and exiled, his enemy tries to kill his young son Kanshusai. Michizane's faithful servant learns of the plot and substitutes his own son for Kanshusai, thus saving the life of his master's child.

11. Prince Hosokawa's Most Valuable Title Deeds: When a fire breaks out in the home of Prince Hosokawa, a faithful retainer saves the prince's title deeds by cutting open his own torso and shielding the papers inside his body.

12. The Story of Kato Sayemon: Kato Sayemon's wife and favorite concubine are playing a game of go. Suddenly Sayemon sees a snake coming out of each woman's head. This is the embodiment of the women's jealousy. Sayemon instantly renounces the world and becomes a priest. Years later his son comes in search of him, but Sayemon denies his identity and sends the boy away.

13. Great Fire Caused by a Lady's Dress: A young girl dies from her love for a priest. Her father donates the girl's dress to a temple, but the head priest sells the dress. On the anniversary of the girl's death, the new owner of the dress dies. Again the priest sells the dress, and again the new owner dies. The priest decides to release the girl's spirit from the dress by burning it. As soon as the dress is set afire, a great wind arises, scattering the flames and setting the temple on fire. The fire spreads through a great part of Edo (Tokyo).

14. History of Awoto Fujitsuna: A god appears to the regent Hojo Tokiyori telling him to take a man named Awoto Fujitsuna into government service. Fujitsuna proves to be an exemplary honest public servant, as demonstrated by an incident in which he called out an entire village to search for a single half-cent piece because the money belonged to the government.

15. A Life Saved by a Spider and Two Doves: When the Minamoto warrior Yoritomo is defeated in battle by Oba Kage-chika, he flees with six retainers and hides in the hollow of a tree. Before Kage-chika reaches the tree, a spider spins its web across the opening, leading the pursuers to believe that no one is there. Nevertheless, they stick a bow into the opening, whereupon two doves fly out of the tree. This proves to them

that Yoritomo and his warriors cannot be nearby, and so Yoritomo and his men are able to escape.

16. Murakami Yoshiteru's Faithfulness: While fleeing from the regent Hojo Takatoki, Prince Morinaga is forced to leave an imperial flag as a hostage at a border crossing. When the prince's retainer, Murakami Yoshiteru, reaches the border, he is so angered that the flag is being handled by commoners that he takes it back single-handedly. Later, in a climactic battle between the forces of the prince and the regent, Murakami dramatically commits suicide while posing as the prince.

17. A Story of Oki Islands: O Tokoyo, the daughter of the warrior Oribe Shima, travels to the Oki Islands when her father is banished there. She meets a young girl who is about to be thrown into the sea as a sacrifice to the god Yofune-nushi and offers to take her place. O Tokoyo jumps into the sea and encounters a huge dragon, which she manages to kill after a fierce battle. O Tokoyo also discovers an image of the regent Hojo Takatoki, which had been used to place a curse on him.

18. Cape of a Woman's Sword: Around Fudo's Cape in the Amakusa Sea, the fishermen notice that the catch of fish has ceased and realize that the God of the Sea has somehow been offended. Then the spirit of a young woman appears on a fishing vessel. A man dives into the sea to find the woman's body, but he finds instead a sacred sword that had been sunk. The sword is installed in a shrine and the cape is renamed Cape of a Woman's Sword.

19. How Yogodayu Won a Battle: The warrior Yogodayu is treacherously attacked by his brother-in-law. While hiding in the forest, he sees a bee trapped in a spider's web and sets it free. The bee appears to Yogodayu in a dream and tells him to build a wooden hut with hundreds of jars in it. All the bees from miles around hide in the jars and attack the brother-in-law's army when they come to kill Yogodayu.

20. The Isolated or Desolated Island: The strong man Makino Heinei is driven out to sea during a storm and cast ashore on an unknown island. The only inhabitant proves to be a giant named Tomaru. Tomaru gives Heinei an old boat and some seaweed that cures sword cuts and sends him back to Japan with the request that Heinei not mention the giant's existence. Later Heinei returns to the island, but Tomaru is gone.

21. Chikubu Island, Lake Biwa: When O Tsuru becomes ill, her sister rows out to the sacred island of Chikubu to pray to Kannon for her recovery. However, on the return journey her boat is capsized, and she is eaten by a huge carp that lives in the lake. O Tsuru tries to drown herself in the lake, but is prevented by a mysterious Buddhist priest, who tells her to pray for her sister's salvation. The carp is later found dead upon the shore of Lake Biwa.

22. Reincarnation: Two monkeys come to the priest of Kinoto Temple and ask him to copy the Buddhist scriptures. They bring the priest food from the forest every day, but after the priest has finished

five books, the monkeys mysteriously disappear. The priest finds them dead in the forest. Forty years later, the governor of Echigo Province comes to Kinoto and reveals that he is the reincarnation of one of the monkeys for whom the priest had prayed.

23. The Diving-Woman of Oiso Bay: While recuperating from an illness at Oiso Bay, the warrior Takadai Jiro falls in love with a diving girl named O Kinu. She refuses to marry him because of the great discrepancy in their social positions. In despair, Takadai drowns himself. O Kinu vows never to marry, and from that time until her death, a flock of seagulls hovers over the place where Takadai drowned.

24. Theft and Recovery of a Golden Kannon: When a golden statue of Kannon is stolen from the castle of the Lord of Kii, he sends his retainer Iganosuke to find the robber and recover the statue. Iganosuke is traveling on a ship when he sees an old samurai drop a golden pipe, borrowed from a young samurai, into the sea. Both men are about to commit suicide because of their shame when Iganosuke offers to dive and recover the pipe. He does so, and he also finds the gold Kannon on the seafloor. The robber who had stolen it had been shipwrecked in a storm.

25. Saigyo Hoshi's Rock: Emperor Shutoku is exiled to Naoshima, but a faithful retainer substitutes his own son for the emperor. The man is befriended by a fisher couple on the island. Later the emperor is ordered executed, and the substitute dies in his place. The real emperor then flees to Naoshima and lives out the rest of his life there. Both the ex-emperor and his substitute had spent time at a favorite rock on the island, which was later visited by the priest-poet Saigyo.

26. How Masakuni Regained His Sight: When the celebrated swordsmith Masakuni loses his eyesight, his daughter engages in extreme Buddhist austerities until the god Fudō sends a doctor who can cure her father.

27. Sagami Bay: A young woman on an isolated island is so beautiful that all the men of the community wish to marry her. When she finally chooses the man she wants, dissention erupts among the rejected suitors. To maintain the harmony of the community, the girl drowns herself. A festival is held on the anniversary of her death on Hatsushima.

28. The King of Torijima: A retainer escapes to an uninhabited island to await a chance to avenge his master's death. Later he travels to a second island, where the inhabitants tell him that the first island is called Torijima (Bird Island) because it is controlled by a huge eagle that will kill any man who goes there. The retainer returns to Torijima, kills the eagle, and is declared king of both islands.

29. The Perpetual Life-Giving Wine: A girl returning from a prayer vigil at a mountain shrine is attacked by a wild man. She is saved by the Goddess of the Mountain, after which she returns daily to pray to the goddess. When the girl is about to leave her home to marry, the goddess gives her a gourd containing the wine of perpetual youth for herself and her husband.

30. The Hermit's Cave: Three deformed children are miraculously cured by an old man in the mountains. When two adults follow the children to learn who the man is, the hermit returns to his mountain cave. The men and children reach the cave, only to see the old man ascending to heaven.

31. Yosoji's Camellia Tree: See entry 68, tale 10.

32. Whales: (1) A man whose ship is destroyed in a storm is saved by a whale, which carries him on its back until a second ship comes along to rescue him. Later, when the man becomes mayor of his island, he issues an edict forbidding the hunting of whales in the area. (2) Whale and Whaler: A wealthy whaler who cruelly kills a mother whale and her baby falls into misfortune until he is bankrupt.

33. The Holy Cherry Tree of Musubi-no-Kami Temple: A young woman goes to a shrine to pray for a fine husband; she meets a handsome young man and falls in love with him. Later she learns that he is the spirit of the sacred cherry tree at the shrine, so she becomes a nun and spends the rest of her life as a caretaker at the shrine.

34. A Story of Mount Kanzanrei: A young Korean woman is saved from a band of robbers by a young woodcutter. After she has visited him for several months trying to win his love, the man reveals that he is really a Japanese samurai and must return to Japan.

35. White Bone Mountain: A priest goes mad and becomes a cannibal when the woman he loves dies. A visiting priest reads a passage from a Buddhist scripture in an attempt to save the mad priest's soul. Weeks later the visiting priest returns to find the mad priest dead, but his corpse is still sitting and reciting the passage.

36. A Stormy Night's Tragedy: A retainer of the Tokugawa shogunate is captured while trying to assassinate an imperial leader. The imperial leader, swayed by the man's intense loyalty, asks him to join the emperor's cause, but the man refuses, choosing instead to be executed as a loyal Tokugawa supporter.

37. The Kakemono Ghost of Ake Province: A young woman who is engaged to a painter runs away from home when she is falsely told that the man has decided to marry another woman. Years later the two lovers meet, but by then the painter has indeed married. The woman kills herself. The painter draws her picture on a hanging scroll, but the dead woman's spirit emerges from the scroll every night until the man divorces his wife and donates the scroll to a temple.

38. White Saké: A young boy who is searching for some saké for his sick father meets a shōjō couple on a beach. They give him some excellent white saké. An evil neighbor steals the saké, but to him it tastes bitter. The man forces the boy to take him to the shōjō. They tell him that the saké is sweet and beneficial to those of pure heart, but bitter and poisonous to those who are evil.

39. The Blind Beauty: A shop clerk who is loved by the shop-owner's daughter is falsely accused of embezzlement by his rival. The

daughter still refuses to marry the rival, whereupon he burns the shop, ruining the shopowner's fortune. When the vindicated shopclerk returns, he finds that the shopowner has died and the daughter has become blind. The clerk and the daughter marry despite her handicap.

40. The Secret of Iidamachi Pond: The ghost of a drowned woman appears nightly to the wife of a samurai and his little daughter. The man's grandmother finally admits that years before she had accidentally caused a maid to drown in the pond outside the house because the maid was having an affair with the man's grandfather.

41. The Spirit of Yenoki: The priest Yenoki becomes blind in one eye because he looked upon a secret image of the god Fudō. After Yenoki's death his spirit passes into a cryptomeria tree. Yenoki begins to appear to young girls from a nearby village as a handsome youth, and he lures them to a cave in the mountains. A man climbs the mountain and confronts the cryptomeria, asking why the girls have been kidnapped, whereupon the spirit of Yenoki reveals that the girls are unharmed, but were taken to punish themselves and the villagers for their licentiousness. The girls are returned, and the villagers repent.

42. The Spirit of the Lotus Lily: When the Lord of Koriyama and his family are stricken during an epidemic, they learn that the spirits of illness were able to enter the castle because the lord had neglected to plant sacred lilies in the northern moat to ward off evil spirits. The moats are then filled with fresh water and lilies, and the lord and his family recover. Years later a samurai sees some young boys playing in the moat at night. Thinking that they are kappa, he attacks them with his sword, but in the daylight he sees that he has cut down the stalks of the lilies. Realizing that the boys were the spirits of the sacred lilies that had saved his lord's life, the samurai commits suicide.

43. The Temple of the Awabi: An earthquake causes a rock island to form in the sea near Nanao. The villagers suddenly see a tremendous light emanating from the bottom of the sea near the island. A fisherman and his son go to investigate. The father accidentally falls into the sea and is killed, but when the son tries to rescue him, he learns that the light is due to a large number of pearls from a colony of awabi (earshells). The boy returns to land and arranges a memorial service for his father. The spirit of the largest awabi appears to the priest in a dream, saying that he had killed the father, but in repentance he will kill himself and send away his followers. That is why there are no awabi near Nanao any longer. A temple is constructed for the spirit of the awabi.

44. Human Fireflies: An old man who is taken ill on a pilgrimage to Ise is robbed of his offering-money by an unscrupulous innkeeper. When the old man dies, a stream of fireflies pours out of his grave and attacks the innkeeper, until they finally kill him.

45. The Chrysanthemum Hermit: A feudal lord and his retainer are forced to flee to the mountains. Because the lord had loved chrysanthemums, the retainer grows a huge bed of them, and when the lord dies,

the retainer grows the flowers around the lord's grave. Many years later the old retainer grows ill, whereupon the spirits of the flowers appear to him and say that he will die in 30 days and that they will die with him.

46. The Princess Peony: Princess Aya is prevented from stumbling by a strange, handsome samurai who mysteriously appears near her peony bed. After the youth has appeared several times while the princess is pining from illness, it is discovered that the youth is really the spirit of a large peony. The princess recovers from her illness and marries, whereupon the peony instantly withers and dies. After this the princess is called the Princess Peony.

47. The Memorial Cherry Tree: A man kills the spirit of a cherry tree. The spirit causes a picture of a beautiful woman that the man owns to turn into a terrifying sight of a woman being murdered. The man finally throws the picture and himself into a fire. A cherry tree is planted near the site as a memorial to what happened.

48. The "Jirohei" Cherry Tree, Kyoto: A man named Jirohei erects a teahouse at the Hirano Temple near a beautiful cherry tree. He reveres the tree and will let no one harm it. One day a brash samurai demands a branch from the tree, but Jirohei refuses. In the resultant fight, a huge branch is cut from the tree and Jirohei is fatally wounded, but he continues to cling to the tree even in death. The tree also dies as a result of this. The samurai later returns to see if the tree is haunted by the spirits of Jirohei and his wife. At midnight the samurai sees the tree come into full bloom, and he madly attacks it with his sword, but in the morning he learns that he actually killed his own father, who had followed him to the temple.

49. The Snow Ghost: A man is awakened on a snowy night by a young woman asking for shelter. She proves to be the spirit of a woman who had died in a snowstorm the year before. She is going to her husband's home, for her husband, who had been an adopted son-in-law, had abandoned her father upon her death. After the wind dies down, she does indeed go to her former husband, who promises to care for her father in his old age.

50. The Snow Tomb: While returning home after a night of telling ghost stories, the sword master Rokugo sees several female ghosts. He finally realizes that they must be the manifestations of a bewitching animal. He kills the beast, which proves to be an otter. A tomb is constructed for the otter, known as the Snow Tomb, because all of this happened on a snowy night.

51. The Dragon-Shaped Plum Tree: An old gardener has a plum tree shaped liked a lying dragon. So beautiful is the tree that word of it reaches a high court noble, who demands the tree for his own garden. When the samurai sent to get the tree begins to fight the gardener, the spirit of the tree appears as a young girl. She is struck by the sword instead, and the tree soon withers and dies.

52. The Chessboard Cherry Tree: A bad-tempered daimyo strikes

and abuses anyone who beats him at *go*. Finally one of his retainers beats him three games and then gives the lord a stern lecture about his conduct. When the lord goes to kill the retainer in his anger, the retainer reveals that he has already committed the ritual for suicide. The retainer dies and the lord buries him, along with the *go* board that the lord had accidentally cut. A cherry tree grows out of the retainer's grave, and the bark at the base of the tree cracks into the pattern of the squares on a *go* board.

53. The Precious Sword "Natori no Hoto": When the oldest son is denied his inheritance by his stepmother and driven from his house, his old nurse steals the precious sword that is the family's most valued heirloom to give to the wronged son. The stepmother starves the old woman to death in her attempt to retrieve the sword, whereupon the nurse's ghost takes the sword from its hiding place and brings it to the oldest son, who is the rightful owner.

54. The White Serpent God: When the rival of a fencing master treacherously kills him and steals his golden statue of Kannon, the master's son sets out to revenge his father's death. After disguising himself as a servant and obtaining work in the rival's household, the boy pines away and dies. His spirit becomes a white snake, which ultimately manages to strangle the murderer and show the members of the household who had been the rightful owner of the statue.

55. A Festival of the Awabi Fish: After a man is drowned in a bay, the harvest of fish steadily decreases. The villagers hold a ceremony for the repose of the man's soul two years after his death. During the ceremony, a great light bursts forth from the floor of the sea and the Goddess of the Bay appears. Two young girls dive into the water, hoping to find the body of the drowned man, but they find instead a large number of pearl-bearing awabi. Thereafter a festival is held every year.

56. The Spirit of a Willow Tree Saves Family Honor: A man who inherits a large family fortune spends his time painting rather than attending to the household accounts. When he has brought the house to the verge of bankruptcy, the spirit of the old willow tree in his garden appears and tells him that an ancient ancestor buried a large sum of gold at the base of the tree for just such an emergency. The man recovers the gold, clears his debts, and takes proper charge of his finances. He later paints a kakemono of the beautiful woman who was the spirit of the willow tree.

57. The Camphor Tree Tomb: A lumber contractor forges a document allowing him to cut down a huge, ancient, and sacred camphor tree. The tree's caretaker commits suicide, and his spirit immediately passes into the tree, causing the branches to struggle with the contractor's workmen. Although the tree has been felled, it is never moved from the place. A shrine is later built for the tree.

73. Griffis, William Elliot. *The Fire-fly's Lovers and Other Fairy Tales of Old Japan*. New York: Thomas Y. Crowell, 1908.

Fourteen of the stories in this collection are Griffis's versions of Japanese tales; six are by Griffis himself (designated by asterisks). The first 17 tales are reprinted from Griffis's earlier collection, *Japanese Fairy World* (entry 74), but they are annotated in this entry because of the greater availability of the 1908 anthology. Griffis was one of the first to render Japanese tales into English, so this anthology and *Japanese Fairy World* are very important for historical study. *The Fire-fly's Lovers* has eight full-page partial color illustrations.

1. *The Fire-fly's Lovers: The Fire-fly Princess is courted by many suitors, but she declares that she will marry only the one who can bring her fire. Many insects lose their life in the attempt. Finally a Fire-fly Prince courts the princess, bringing his own natural fire, and he succeeds in winning her. But each generation of male insects wishes to gain a fire-fly princess for his bride, and their attempt to capture fire is the reason why insects are drawn to lights.

2. The Travels of the Two Frogs: A frog from Osaka sets out to see Kyoto on the same day that a frog from Kyoto sets out to see Osaka. The two frogs meet at the top of a hill halfway between the two cities. They decide to prop each other up and look at the city of their destination, whereupon each declares that the city to which he is are traveling looks exactly like his hometown. Each frog instantly ends the journey and returns home. The frogs, however, had forgotten that their eyes are on the back of their heads when they are upright, and so each had actually been looking back on his original city.

3. *The Child of the Thunder: A poor farmer finds a baby boy in the fields during a storm. The man and his wife take the child in, naming him Raitaro, the child of the thunder. From that day on the couple's fortunes steadily improve. When Raitaro becomes 18, he announces that he is indeed the child of the Thunder God, turns into a white dragon, and ascends to the heavens.

4. The Tongue-cut Sparrow: See entry 133.

5. The Ape and the Crab: See entry 113.

6. The Wonderful Tea Kettle: See entry 112.

7. Benkei and the Bell: While the warrior-priest Benkei is living at a rival monastery, he steals the great bell from the temple of Miidera. After he hangs it in his own monastery, the bell rings with a sound of "I want to return to Miidera" whenever it is struck, so Benkei is eventually forced to return the bell to its rightful owner.

8. *Little Silver's Dream: Little Silver dreams of ghosts trying to swamp boats, of shōjō drinking saké, and of the great storehouse of wealth and happiness that the demon king has amassed by giving saké to foolish drunkards.

9. The Magic Frog: A man who has learned magic from a frog, his wife who has learned magic from a snail, and his young retainer who has learned magic from a tengu join forces to vanquish a terrible robber who is the son of a snake.

10. How the Jellyfish Lost Its Shell: See entry 137.

11. *Lord Cuttlefish's Concert (sequel to tale 10): After the Queen of the Sea has somewhat recovered from her illness, she is resting in her apartments when she hears a wonderful concert at the cuttlefish's mansion. She discreetly hides behind a rock to have a look, and the sight of the fish orchestra is so ludicrous, as is the behavior of the various guests, that the queen is thoroughly amused and recovers even further from her malady.

12. Raiko and His Guards: (1) Raiko the archer shoots a fantastic beast that hovered in a cloud over the Imperial Palace and was draining away the emperor's soul. (2) Raiko's retainer Tsuna cuts an arm off a demon. The demon comes to Tsuna's house in the guise of Tsuna's aunt, steals back the arm, and magically reattaches it to his body. (The hero of (1) is usually the warrior Yorimasa, and Tsuna is usually called Watanabe.)

13. Raiko Slays the Demons (sequel to tale 12): (1) Tsuna kills a gigantic spider that had been haunting Raiko. (2) Raiko and his men enter the lair of the demons, trick them into drinking some drugged wine, and slay them.

14. The Ambitious Carp: A carp of unusual determination could struggle up the rapids of the Yellow River to a section called the Dragon's Gate. If the carp could succeed in reaching the still pond beyond, it would be turned into a great white dragon. For this reason kites shaped like carp are given to young boys to remind them that they must be indefatigably studious if they wish to succeed.

15. *Lord Long-legs' Procession: The Insect Lord and his many insect retainers make an annual journey between their rice field and Edo.

16. The Power of Love: A priest falls in love with a young woman, and they carry on an affair for several months, but the priest finally repents of his sinful actions and terminates the relationship. In her anger at being spurned, the woman turns into a huge dragon. The terrified priest hides under the bell of his temple, but the serpent-woman finds him, winds herself around the bell, and heats the bell until the priest is reduced to ashes.

17. The Tide Jewels: Empress Jingu manages to destroy the Korean fleet and conquer the country through the use of the Jewels of the Ebb and Flow of the Tide, which she obtains from the Dragon King of the sea. The Dragon King later presents the tide jewels to Jingu's son, Ojin.

18. The Grateful Crane: See entry 115.

19. The Idol and the Whale: The vain whale is convinced that he is the largest creature in the world until he hears of the great statue of

Buddha at Kamakura. The whale travels to the city to examine the statue, and it is discovered that the whale is two inches longer than the statue.

20. *The Gift of Gold Lacquer: The spirit of the lacquer tree appears as a white bird to an honest old man and reveals the secret of making lacquer from the tree's sap. Later the spirit teaches the man's son how to use colors and gold leaf.

74. Griffis, William Elliot. *Japanese Fairy World: Stories from the Wonder-Lore of Japan*. Schenectady, N.Y.: James H. Barhyte, 1880.

This is one of the first collections of Japanese fairy tales to be printed in English and consequently is of historical importance. Twenty of the tales from this collection were reprinted in Griffis's later anthology (entry 73); these stories are marked by asterisks. Tales 19 and 20, 21 and 22, and 32 and 33 were merged into single stories in the later anthology. *Japanese Fairy World* has 12 full-page black-and-white illustrations by Ozawa Nankoku.

1. The Meeting of the Star Lovers: See entry 135.
2. *The Travels of the Two Frogs: See entry 73, tale 2.
3. *The Child of the Thunder: See entry 73, tale 3.
4. *The Tongue-cut Sparrow: See entry 133.
5. *The Fire-fly's Lovers: See entry 73, tale 1.
6. The Battle of the Ape and the Crab: See entry 113.
7. *The Wonderful Tea Kettle: See entry 112.
8. The Peach Prince and the Treasure Island: See entry 125.
9. The Fox and the Badger: A badger pretends to be dead so that a fox in human guise can sell him for some food. After the badger escapes, the fox pretends to be dead so that she can be sold. But the greedy badger warns the buyer that the fox is still alive, and she is killed. The fox's cub tells the badger to watch on the bridge for a procession of nobles, for that will be the cub in disguise. The badger runs up to the procession, but it really is a group of humans, and they kill the badger.
10. The Seven Patrons of Happiness: The seven are Fukoruku Jin, patron of long life, Daikoku, patron of wealth, Ebisu, patron of daily food, Hotei, patron of contentment, Toshitoku, patron of talents, Bishamon, patron of fame, and Benten, patron of love.
11. Daikoku and the Oni: Because the Buddhist deities are jealous of Daikoku's great popularity, Emma-sama sends one of his demons to destroy Daikoku. Daikoku's rat chases the demon away with a sprig of holly. This is why holly sprigs are placed over doorways at New Year's to keep the house safe from demons.
12. *Benkei and the Bell: See entry 73, tale 7.
13. *Little Silver's Dream of the Shōjō: See entry 73, tale 8.
14. The Tengu, or the Elves with Long Noses: Describes the natures and habits of tengu.

15. Kintaro, the Wild Baby: See entry 120.
16. *Jiraiya, or the Magic Frog: See entry 73, tale 9.
17. *How the Jellyfish Lost Its Shell: See entry 137.
18. *Lord Cuttlefish Gives a Concert: See entry 73, tale 11.
19. *Yorimasa the Brave Archer, and 20.*Watanabe Cuts Off the Oni's Arm: See entry 73, tale 12.
21. *Watanabe Kills the Great Spider, and 22.*Raiko and the Shi Ten Doji: See entry 73, tale 13.
23. The Sazaye and the Tai: The sazaye shellfish is very proud of its shell, which protects it from predators, but it is unable to protect the shellfish from a diving fisherman.
24. Smells and Jingles: A stingy merchant saves money by eating plain rice while smelling the fish from the neighboring shop. The fish merchant charges the merchant for smelling his fish, whereupon the merchant "pays" by jingling some coins.
25. The Lake of the Lute and the Matchless Mountain: Describes Lake Biwa and Mount Fuji.
26. The Waterfall of Yoro, or the Fountain of Youth: A young wood-cutter whose old father is very fond of saké finds a magic waterfall of it. This magic saké causes his father to live for many more years in good health.
27. The Earthquake Fish: The Japanese islands are held on the top of a great fish, the earthquake fish. When there is an earthquake in the country, it is due to the movements of the fish.
28. *The Dream Story of Gojiro: See entry 73, tale 14.
29. *The Procession of Lord Long-legs: See entry 73, tale 15.
30. *Kiyohime or the Power of Love: See entry 73, tale 16.
31. The Fisherman and the Moon Maiden: See entry 132(a).
32. *The Tide Jewels, and 33.*Kai Riu O or the Dragon King of the World under the Sea: See entry 73, tale 17.
34. The Creation of Heaven and Earth: See entries 116, 119.
35. How the Sun Goddess Was Enticed Out of Her Cave: See entry 117.

75. Harris, Omori. *Japanese Tales of All Ages*. Tokyo: Hokuseido Press, 1937.

Most of the tales in this collection are myths and historical legends of the period from the founding of the country through the medieval era. About the first third of the book gives versions of stories from the *Kojiki, Nihongi,* and *Tales of the Heike*. Because Harris did not attempt to maintain historical accuracy in all details, this work should be used with caution by researchers not already familiar with the history and historical legends of Japan. There are four full-page illustrations by Shu-jaku Suzuki.

The stories include:

1, 2. The Beginning of Things and The Land of Death: See entry 119.

3. The Rabbit of Inaba: See entry 136. This section also tells of the later adventures of Okuninushi.

4. The Dawn of Japan's History: See entry 117. This section also tells of the descent to earth of Ninigi, the grandson of Amaterasu.

5. The Robe of Feathers: See entry 132(a).

6. Shotoku Taishi: Describes Shotoku's promotion of Buddhism in Japan and his Seventeen-Article Constitution.

7. The Nightingale Princess: A man follows a mysterious woman to her cottage in the hills. She tells him he can stay with her, but he must not look inside her chest of drawers. He violates this taboo and sees in each drawer a landscape of rice fields in different stages of cultivation. The woman turns into a nightingale and flies away, and the man discovers that he has been away from his village for a year and a day, not just a single night and day as he had supposed.

8. Ishido-maru: When Kato Sayemon falls out of favor at court, he leaves his family and becomes a priest. Years later, his son Ishido-maru goes to search for him and finds him on Mount Koya, but the old man denies his identity and says that the boy's father has died.

9. Ushiwaka-maru: The young Yoshitsune, after he, his brother, and his mother surrender to Kiyomori, is sent to become a Buddhist priest, but when he learns of his family history, he leaves the monastery to join the fight against the Heike clan. One night while crossing the Gojo Bridge, he encounters the warrior-priest Benkei, defeats him in combat, and makes him his retainer.

10. How Two Warriors Swam the Ujigawa: During one of the battles of the Gempei wars, the Genji warriors reach the banks of the Ujigawa (or Yodogawa), which is swollen by floodwaters. Two fearless warriors drive their horses across the river; the rest of the Genji troops are inspired by this example and successfully cross the treacherous river.

11. How They Came Down Hiyodorigoe: Yoshitsune and his small band of followers win the Battle of Ichi-no-tani for the Genji by riding their horses down a treacherous slope at the rear of the Heike warriors.

12. How Nasu no Yoichi Shot the Fan: During the Battle of Dan no Ura, Heike warriors set up a fan with a red sun on a white background on the imperial ship, which is out to sea. Nasu no Yoichi shoots the fan from a very great distance.

13. Kanjincho: After his fall from grace with Yoritomo, Yoshitsune flees to Ōshu with Benkei and his other retainers, all of them dressed as monks from Tōdaiji who are soliciting contributions for the reconstruction of the temple. (*Kanjincho* is the name for the scroll on which the list of contributors was recorded.)

14. Issunboshi: See entry 118.

15. The Defense of Chihaya Castle: Emperor Godaigo rebels against the Hojo regents with the help of the warrior Masashige.

16. Masashige Dies at Minatogawa: Although he knows that the battle will be lost, Masashige follows the emperor's order to engage the enemy.

17. Ikkyu the Priest: Because Ikkyu is the son of an emperor, he is able to chastise properly the Lord of Harima and teach him to have more concern for the feelings of the common people.

18. Ikkyu, the Wizard and the Innkeeper: Ikkyu admonishes a charlatan wizard to stop duping poor people. Later he tricks a dishonest innkeeper into returning some money that he had stolen from a lodger.

19. The Story of Uyesugi Kenshin: Kagetora comes to be daimyo over his older brother. Later he is a very successful general, but in one of his battles, he fights against his older brother, who is forced to kill himself. After he has brought peace to his realm, Kagetora Uyesugi takes Buddhist orders, adopting the priestly name of Kenshin.

20. Takeda Shingen and Kawanakajima: On the eve of a battle, a bird flies into the war camp of Takeda Harunobu, a renowned general, and is hailed by his soldiers as a good omen. Takeda instantly shoots the bird dead, warning his men to rely on their own abilities and not on superstitions. At the Battle of Kawanakajima, Takeda is defeated by Uyesugi Kenshin, but when another daimyo later tries to detroy Takeda by cutting off his supply of salt, Kenshin sends Takeda the much-needed salt on the grounds that this sort of blockade is unbefitting the dignity of a warrior.

21. Fukuden-maru: A young boy, Fukuden-maru, learns to read and write and studies Buddhist scripture so that he can become a servant in the home of a rich man whose daughter he loves, but when he returns home after his studies, he finds that the girl has died during his absence. He then becomes a renowned priest.

22. Little Monkey-face: The clever son of a farmer leaves home to find his fortune. He becomes an apprentice to a mercenary, a priest's companion, and later the student of a renowned sword master. He eventually becomes a samurai in the service of Oda Nobunaga.

23. Hideyoshi among the Priests: After Lord Nobunaga is killed by a rebellious retainer, Hideyoshi leads an army to punish the rebels. At one point Hideyoshi is driven alone by the enemy into a temple. There he disguises himself as a priest so successfully that his pursuers cannot find him among the other priests at the temple.

24. The Taiko Hideyoshi: Hideyoshi, the son of a farmer, rises to the highest pinnacle of political power in Japan.

25. Ōkubo Hikozayemon: Instead of accepting a position as a great daimyo, Ōkubo Hikozayemon asks that he remain a hatamoto, but that he be able to ridicule Ieyasu's daimyos when they become too arrogant.

26. Hikozayemon and the Plum Tree: When the shogun decrees that any person who breaks a branch off the lord's favorite plum tree will

be put to death, Hikozayemon deliberately ravishes the tree and chastises the lord for placing the life of a tree above that of a human.

27. Isshin Tasuke: Tasuke, an outspoken farmer, impresses Hikozayemon with his honesty and good sense, so he is taken as a retainer into Hikozayemon's house. When Tasuke learns that Hikozayemon has a set of ten plates he regards so highly that he will kill anyone who breaks one of them, Tasuke destoys them and reminds his master of the shogun's plum tree.

28. Shiobara Tasuke: After the son of a samurai is driven from his home by his stepmother, he is taken in by a kindly charcoal merchant. Eventually the young man starts a successful shop of his own, is reconciled with his family, and marries the daughter of a chōja.

29. Hidari Jingoro: A young man becomes the most skilled woodcarver in Japan. When a rival attacks him and cuts off his right arm, Jingoro is still able to work because he had always trained himself to use his right and left hands equally. But because of this incident, he was named Hidari, meaning "left-handed."

30. Chushingura: The Revenge of the Forty-seven: When Lord Asano refuses to pay a bribe to Lord Kira, Kira refuses to teach Asano the formalities necessary for the proper reception of an imperial envoy. In his frustration at being shamed before the envoy, Asano draws his sword against Kira within the palace of the shogun. For this offense, Asano is ordered to commit suicide, but Kira's offense goes unpunished. Over the course of many months, a number of Asano's loyal retainers plot to avenge their master's death. They finally storm Kira's mansion, capture Kira, and put him to death. The number of loyal retainers involved in this final assault is 47. The 47 retainers are ordered to commit suicide, since their attack had not been sanctioned by the government.

31. The Rolling Potatoes: The people of an isolated village build a new mansion for their mayor, whereupon he invites them all to a banquet. The people are afraid that their ignorance of proper manners will cause them to commit some grave mistake, but the local doctor tells them all simply to do exactly as he does. At the banquet the doctor accidentally drops a potato, whereupon all the villagers drop a potato. The doctor hastily takes his leave, followed immediately by the host of dull-witted villagers.

32. Ninomiya Sontoku and Hanawa Hokiichi: Ninomiya Sontoku, a poor farmer who restored his house to great wealth through his hard work, is called upon to give advice to others in financial distress, even high-ranking samurai. Hanawa Hokiichi, a blind boy with an excellent memory, becomes renowned for memorizing classical Japanese texts and delivering lectures on them.

33. Byakkotai: The Young Heroes of Aizu: Twenty boys who are fighting in a battle between the forces of the shogun and the emperor commit suicide when they mistakenly think that their castle has fallen to the enemy.

34. Fukuzawa Yukichi: The son of a samurai casts off the customs and restrictions of his class, studies Western learning, and becomes a driving force in the Westernization of Japan during the early Meiji era.

35. Two Modern Heroes: Nogi and Togo: General Nogi, who led the Meiji armies to great victories, commits suicide upon the death of the Meiji emperor. Admiral Togo commanded the Japanese navy during the Russo-Japanese War.

76. Haviland, Virginia. *Favorite Fairy Tales Told in Japan*. Boston: Little, Brown, 1967.

This collection contains Haviland's rewritten versions of five tales. Each story has black-and-white illustrations and partial color illustrations by George Suyeoka.

One Inch Fellow: See entry 118.
The Good Fortune Kettle: See entry 112.
The Tongue-cut Sparrow: See entry 133.
Momotarō, or The Story of the Son of a Peach: See entry 125.
The White Hare and the Crocodiles: See entry 136.

77. Hearn, Lafcadio. *Japanese Fairy Tales*. New York: Boni and Liveright, 1918, 1924; Great Neck, N. Y.: Core Collection Books, 1979.

Hearn was associated with at least three books of this title. The most important is *Japanese Fairy Tales by Lafcadio Hearn and Others*, published by Boni and Liveright in 1918. That edition and the Core Collection Books 1979 edition contain 20 tales; the 1924 edition contains 16 tales. The four tales deleted in the 1924 edition are marked by asterisks in the following list.

1. Chin Chin Kobakama: A young girl is so lazy that she does not even discard her used toothpicks properly, but slips them into the spaces between the floor mats. One night hundreds of tiny warriors begin to menace her. They prove to be the animated toothpicks who are chastising her for her lazy habits.

2. The Goblin Spider: A samurai goes to a haunted temple to rid it of its demons. A priest appears who is playing a shamisen, but when the samurai takes hold of the instrument, it turns into a huge spiderweb and the priest turns into a goblin spider. The samurai manages to strike the spider with his sword and drive it away. Later the spider is tracked to its lair and killed.

3. The Old Woman Who Lost Her Dumpling: An old woman accidentally drops a dumpling down a hole and then falls in after it. She meets three Jizō statues who warn her of a man-eating demon, but she does not heed their warning to flee. She is taken home by the demon

and made his cook. She runs away, taking the demon's magic rice-producing paddle. As she is crossing a river, the demons try to stop her by drinking up the water, but the old woman makes funny faces at them and makes them laugh.

4. The Boy Who Drew Cats: An acolyte who spends all his time drawing is sent away from his temple to become an artist. The boy spends a night in an abandoned temple, but before going to sleep he draws a number of lifelike cats on a screen. During the night a goblin rat appears, but the cats come to life and destroy the monster.

5. The Silly Jellyfish: See entry 137.

6. The Hare of Inaba: See entry 136.

7. *Shippei Taro: A warrior spends a night in an abandoned temple and overhears some cats saying that they fear only Shippei Taro. In the morning the warrior comes to a nearby village and learns that a young woman is to be sacrificed to the creatures that night. He also learns that Shippei Taro is a dog. The warrior and the dog take the girl's place and destroy the cats.

8. The Matsuyama Mirror: See entry 124(a).

9. My Lord Bag-o'-Rice: See entry 127.

10. *The Serpent with Eight Heads: See entry 117.

11. The Old Man and the Devils: See entry 128.

12. The Tongue-cut Sparrow: See entry 133.

13. The Wooden Bowl: See entry 131.

14. The Tea Kettle: See entry 112.

15. Urashima: See entry 134.

16. Green Willow: A retainer who is carrying an urgent message for his lord is caught in a storm and spends a night at an isolated hut. He falls in love with the daughter there, and casts aside his former allegiance to run away with her. Some years later the woman, who is named Green Willow, reveals that she is a tree spirit and that she is dying because the tree has been cut down.

17. *The Flute: A young girl is murdered by her stepmother while her father is away on business. When the father tries to play a flute that the girl had given to him, it reveals the murder and the place of the girl's grave.

18. Reflections: See entry 124(b).

19. *The Spring Lover and the Autumn Lover: The God of Autumn and the God of Spring are brothers. They both court the same princess, but she chooses the God of Spring and spurns the elder brother. The God of Autumn in his anger threatens to kill the two young lovers, but the gods' mother casts a spell that causes autumn to die away.

20. Momotarō: See entry 125.

78. Henderson, Bernard, and Calvert C. Henderson. *Wonder Tales of Old Japan*. New York: Frederick A. Stokes, 1924.

The tales in this collection were composed from Japanese originals and previously published English versions, but the collection seems to be based mostly on the previous English anthologies.

1. The Sparrow Whose Tongue Was Clipped: See entry 133.
2. The Foxes' Gratitude: A fox, whose cub has been saved from some children by a man, sacrifices the life of the cub when the man's son falls ill and can be cured only by the liver of a fox.
3. Kurage: See entry 137.
4. Benkei and the Bell of Miidera: See entry 73, tale 7.
5. The Hare and the Badger: See entry 114.
6. The Goddess of Fuji-san: See entry 68, tale 10.
7. Urashima: See entry 134.
8. Lord Sack-of-Rice: See entry 127.
9. The Buddha and the Kujira: See entry 73, tale 19.
10. The Two Frogs: See entry 73, tale 2.
11. Tanabata-matsuri, or the Festival of the Weaver and the Herdsman: See entry 135.
12. Samebito, or The Jewel Tears: See entry 67, chapter 31, tale 4.
13. Issunboshi: See entry 118.
14. Yanagi
15. Tokutaro san
16. The Story of Visu: Visu goes to Mount Fuji to pray, but he becomes entranced watching two fox-maidens play *go*. When the maidens finally run off, Visu learns that he has been there for 300 years.

79. Iwaya, Sueo. *Japanese Fairy Tales*. Tokyo: Hokuseido Press, 1951.

Japanese Fairy Tales was originally translated by Ume Tsuda and Hannah Riddle in 1914. Hokuseido reissued the stories as a set of 12 booklets in 1938 under the editorship of G. Craiger. This 1951 edition is a selection of six tales from the 1938 edition.

Momotarō: See entry 125.
The Crab's Revenge: See entry 113.
The Old Man Who Made Trees to Blossom: See entry 129.
The Tongue-cut Sparrow: See entry 133.
The Tea Kettle of Good Fortune: See entry 112.
The Story of Kachi Kachi Mountain: See entry 114.

80. James, Grace. *Green Willow and Other Japanese Fairy Tales*. London: Macmillan, 1912; reprint 1923; New York: Mayflower Books, 1979.

Despite its age, this work remains a very good anthology of Japanese tales. The original edition contains 38 tales; the reprint editions contain 30. The eight tales omitted in the reprint editions are marked by asterisks in the list below. This anthology is also one of the most beautifully illustrated collections of Japanese tales, containing full-page color illustrations by Warwick Goble. The Macmillan editions contain one illustration for each tale; the Mayflower edition contains only 16 illustrations.

1. Green Willow: See entry 77, tale 16.
2. The Flute: See entry 77, tale 17.
3. The Tea Kettle: See entry 112.
4. The Peony Lantern: See entry 67, chapter 18.
5. The Sea King and the Magic Jewels: See entry 122.
6. The Good Thunder: See entry 73, tale 3.
7. The Black Bowl: See entry 131.
8. The Star Lovers: See entry 135.
9. Horaizan: A wise man from China sails to Horaizan, the Island of Immortality. He remains there happily for eternity. A wise man from Japan also sails to Horaizan, but he determines to return to his native land, even though it means his death from old age.
10. Reflections: See entry 124(b).
11. The Story of Susa the Impetuous: See entry 117.
12. The Wind in the Pine Tree: A traveler meets a woman weaving beneath the sacred pine tree that was planted by a heavenly divinity. They become man and wife and live together in harmony for many years. When they finally are about to die of old age, they go to the base of the pine tree to spend their last moments together. Their spirits ascend through the branches of the tree. When the myriad spirits that live in the pine tree sing, lovers say that it is the wind in the pine tree.
13. Flower of the Peony: See entry 72, tale 46.
14. *The Mallet
15. The Bell of Dōjōji: See entry 73, tale 16.
16. The Maiden of Unai: See entry 67, chapter 26, tale 1.
17. *The Robe of Feathers
18. The Singing Bird of Heaven: Amaterasu sends a heavenly deity down to subdue the earth, but the deity falls in love with an earthly goddess and gives up his quest. When Amaterasu sends the singing bird of heaven to question him, the god shoots the bird, and his arrow continues to ascend to the heavens until it arrives at the Celestial Palace. The heavenly deities cast the arrow back to earth, saying that if the god's heart is false, the arrow will strike him. The god is instantly killed by the returning arrow.
19. The Cold Lady: See entry 67, chapter 11.
20. The Fire Quest: See entry 73, tale 1.
21. A Legend of Kwannon: A pious priest is about to die of starvation during a great snowstorm when he finds the carcass of a deer. Taking this as a gift from the gods, the man eats the meat, even though it is in violation of strict Buddhist law. When the storm is over and the villagers come to see if the priest has survived, they find the man alive

and well, but they also find that the meat left over from the priest's meal has turned into gold gilted wood. The "meat" fits into a hole that is discovered in the nearby statue of Kwannon. The deer had actually been a manifestation of the goddess.

22. The Espousal of the Rat's Daughter: See entry 126.
23. The Land of Yomi: See entry 119.
24. The Spring Lover and the Autumn Lover: See entry 77, tale 19.
25. The Strange Story of the Golden Comb: See entry 72, tale 1.
26. The Jellyfish Takes a Journey: See entry 137.
27. Urashima: See entry 134.
28. Tamammo, the Fox Maiden: See entry 67, chapter 5, tale 1.
29. *Momotarō
30. *The Matsuyama Mirror
31. *Broken Images
32. *The Tongue-cut Sparrow
33. The Nurse: See entry 72, tale 53.
34. The Beautiful Dancer of Yedo: A geisha has two lovers, but she sends them both away. She then meets a fine young man who also falls in love with her, but she refuses him also, although she is in love with him. Many years later, after she happens by the third lover's house, it is learned that she had run away to become a nun.
35. *The Old Man Who Made Withered Trees Blossom
36. The Moon Maiden: See entry 100.
37. Karma: A traveler meets a woman in a desolate area and makes her his wife. Later he discovers that she was a spirit that had returned for the festival of the dead. He remains faithful to her and waits to meet her again. After their second meeting he is found dead because he had loved a spirit.
38. *The Sad Story of Yaoya's Daughter

81. *Japanese Fairy Tale Series*. London: Griffith Farran, 1886.

This is a set of 16 richly and colorfully illustrated booklets published by Kobunsha in Tokyo for the London company. Each booklet contains a single tale. The style of the booklets is very much like that of a comic book, with full-page pictures and small amounts of text. This series is important for historical reasons. The style of printing is reminiscent of the style of Japanese-language fairy tale booklets that were popular during the Meiji era and that would have inspired some of the early English anthologizers.

1. Momotarō
2. The Tongue-cut Sparrow
3. The Battle of the Monkey and the Crab
4. The Old Man Who Made the Dead Trees Blossom
5. Kachi Kachi Mountain
6. The Mouse's Wedding

7. The Old Man and the Devils
8. Urashima, the Fisher Boy
9. The Eight-headed Serpent
10. The Matsuyama Mirror
11. The Hare of Inaba
12. The Cub's Triumph
13. The Silly Jellyfish
14. The Princes Fire-flash and Fire-fade
15. My Lord Bag-o'-Rice
16. The Wooden Bowl

82. Jones, S. W. *Ages Ago: Thirty-seven Tales from the "Konjaku monogatari Collection."* Cambridge, Mass.: Harvard University Press, 1959.

This work has a brief foreword that discusses the *Konjaku monogatari* and its place in Japanese literature. In addition each tale is accompanied by extensive background notes that give information on such things as religious terminology and historical persons. The ten Tales of India were chosen mainly to illustrate the effects of transmission from India through China to Japan on tales that contain motifs resembling those found in Western folktales. The eight Tales of China were chosen from the stories about the introduction of Buddhism to China and from the tales about renowned Chinese "heroes" such as Confucius and Chuang-tzu. The 19 Tales of Japan were chosen mainly for their narrative technique.

Tales of India

1. Vakkula's Good Deed
2. King Prasenajit's Daughter, Vajra the Deformed
3. How Preceptor Bodhidharma Toured India Observing the Acts of Monks
4. How a Poor Woman in India Got the Lotus Sutra Copied
5. How Three Beasts Practiced the Bodhisattva Discipline and the Hare Roasted Itself
6. How Lion's Pity for Monkey's Young Made Him Cut a Chunk off Himself for Eagle
7. How in India a Fox Passed for Beast King and Died of Riding a Lion
8. How Tortoise, Heedless of Crane's Warning, Fell to Earth and Got a Cracked Shell
9. How Tortoise Was Outwitted by Monkey
10. Where Persons over Seventy Were Deported

Tales of China

11. How under Emperor Ming of the Later-Han Dynasty Buddhism Crossed to China

12. How under Emperor Wu of the Liang Dynasty Bodhidharma Crossed to China
13. How Chinese Meng Tsung's Filial Piety Got His Old Mother Bamboo Shoots in Winter
14. How Chinese Han Po-yü when Beaten by His Mother Wept for Grief
15. How T'ang Emperor Hsüan-tsung's Yang Kuei-fei Was Killed by His Majesty's Favor
16. How Knight Confucius while Traveling Met Boys Who Quizzed Him
17. When Chuang-tzu Observed the Doings of Animals and Took to His Heels
18. How a Woman of Ch'ang-an Changed Pillows with Her Husband and Was Killed by His Enemy

Tales of Japan

19. The Might of Assistant High Priest Jitsu-in of Heizan
20. Wrestler Umi Tsuneyo's Match with a Snake
21. How Wrestler Kisaichi Munehira Tossed a Blue Shark
22. How a Man Tossed His Sword-Sheath Rod on a Fingernail and a Woman Her Needle
23. When Kudara Kawanari and Hida Takumi Competed
24. How a Lady Went to a Master of Medicine, Was Cured of a Boil, and Slipped Off
25. How a Man's Wife Became a Vengeful Ghost and How Her Malignity Was Diverted by a Master of Divination
26. When Emperor Murakami and Sugawara Fumitoki Each Composed a Chinese Poem
27. How Taira Koremochi Had a Retainer Killed on Him
28. How an East-Bound Traveler Fathered a Child by a Turnip
29. How in Mimasaka Province a God Was Trapped by a Hunter and Living Sacrifice Stopped
30. How Mikawa Province Originated Dog's Head Silk
31. How the Reizei-in Water Spirit Assumed Human Form and Was Caught
32. How Ki Tōsuke's Meeting with a Ghost-Woman in Mino Province Ended in His Death
33. How Ex-Emperor En-yū's Rat-Day Was Attended by Sone Yoshitada
34. When Chikuzen-Governor Fujiwara Akiie's Samurai Forgot Himself
35. How in Mutsu Province a Dog-and-Mountain Dog Bit to Death a Big Snake
36. Tsunekiyo Yasunaga's Fuha-Barrier Dream about His Wife at the Capital
37. Two Brothers Plant Day-Lilies and Asters

83. McAlpine, Helen, and McAlpine, William. *Japanese Tales and Legends*. New York: Henry Z. Walck, 1958; reprint edition Oxford University Press, 1980.

The book is generally well written, and it presents a wide variety of folk materials. It contains legends of the creation of Japan, medieval warrior tales, classic fairy tales, and a complete version of the *Tale of the Shining Princess*. This work is a very good introduction to Japanese tales for older students (junior high school or high school age).

1. The Birth of Japan: See entries 116, 119.
2. The Luck of the Sea and the Luck of the Mountains: See entry 122.
3. Tales of the Heike: Contains four tales. (1) "The Secret Meeting at Shishi no Tani": The courtier-warrior Narichika plots to overthrow the rule of the Heike with the consent of the ex-emperor Goshirakawa, but the plot is discovered by the Heike premier Kiyomori and thwarted. Narichika is exiled, and Kiyomori learns that Goshirakawa is sympathetic to the rebels. (2) "The Poem from the Sea": Naritsune, Narichika's son, and two other rebels, Yasuyori and Shunkan, are banished to a wilderness on southern Kyushu. Yasuyori, who had been forced to leave without saying farewell to his aged mother, carves a poem on a piece of wood and sets it adrift on the sea, hoping that someone will find it and deliver it to the old woman. This indeed happens, and when word of Yasuyori's filial concern becomes known, Kiyomori is forced to pardon him. He also pardons Naritsune, but he refuses to allow Shunkan to return to the mainland, so he is left in solitary exile on Kyushu. (3) "The Battle of Ichi-no-Tani": During the war between the Heike and the Genji, the Heike take refuge in a fortress at Ichi-no-Tani, whose rear walls press against a treacherous mountain that cannot be descended. During the battle, Yoshitsune and a handful of his followers manage to ride their horses down the terrible slope and attack the Heike from the rear, sending the troops into complete chaos. The Heike warriors attempt to escape by sea, but one warrior, a 16-year-old boy named Atsumori, is stopped by the Genji general Kumagai. When Kumagai sees how young Atsumori is, he wishes to allow him to escape to his ships, but the arrival of the main Genji forces makes this impossible. Kumagai kills Atsumori quickly, then immediately leaves the battlefield and takes religious orders. (4) "The Fall of the Heike": At the Battle of Dan-no-Ura, the Heike clan is totally obliterated. The Lady Nii, seeing that the battle is lost, leaps into the sea with the infant emperor Antoku. Most of the court ladies also drown themselves. The handful of women who are dragged from the waters by the Genji warriors take religious orders and become Buddhist nuns.
4. The Peach Boy: See entry 125.
5. The Old Man Who Made the Trees Blossom: See entry 129.
6. The Young Urashima: See entry 134.

7. The Vanishing Rice-straw Coat: A man tricks a tengu into giving
him the creature's magic coat of invisibility by claiming that a piece of
bamboo is really a telescope and presenting it to the tengu. The man
puts on the coat and performs all sorts of pranks in his village. When the
man returns home and goes to sleep, his mother finds the garment and
thinks that it is just a dirty old coat that he has picked up from some-
where, so she burns it. When the man learns what has happened, he
tries rubbing the ashes on himself and indeed becomes invisible. But
when the man goes into the village and steals a drink of saké, the ashes
wash off his mouth, and he becomes partially visible. In the resultant
chaos, the villagers drive the man into the river, so that all the ash is
washed off and they learn who the culprit is.

8. The Tale of the Princess Kaguya: See entry 100.

9. The Tongue-cut Sparrow: See entry 133.

10. The Lucky Tea Kettle: See entry 112.

Mayer, Fanny Hagin. *Japanese Folk Tales*. See entry 109.

84. Mills, D. E. *A Collection of Tales from Uji*. Cambridge, England: Cambridge University Press, 1970.

This is a translation of the complete *Uji shūi monogatari* accompanied by Mills's excellent seven-chapter introduction. In the course of his
discussion of the *Uji shūi*, Mills examines nearly 50 additional Japanese
tale collections. Although few of the 197 tales in the *Uji shūi* are classic
folktales, the stories in this collection are still of great importance in the
study of Japanese folklore.

Introduction

1. An outline of the development of tale literature in Japan to the
end of the Kamakura period (1333)
2. Problems and aspects of tale literature
3. *Uji shūi monogatari*
   I. Content, style and literary qualities
   II. A description of parallels with other works
   III. A survey of Japanese views on its date
   IV. A survey of Japanese views on its relationship with other
   works
   V. Some personal observations on its date, structure, and position

The Translation

1. How the Holy Teacher Dōmyō Recited the Sutra at the Home
of Izumi Shikibu and the Roadside Deity from Fifth Avenue
Came to Listen

2. How Mushrooms Grew at Shinomura in the Province of Tamba
3. How Someone Had a Wen Removed by Demons
4. About the Ban Major Counsellor
5. How a Priest Put the Magic Incantation of the Bodhisattva Zuigu into His Forehead
6. How the Middle Counsellor Morotoki Investigated a Priest's Penis
7. How the Holy Man of Ryōmon Tried to Take the Place of a Stag
8. How Gold Was Found by Divination
9. How Lord Uji Fell from His Horse and the High Priest from Jissōbō Was Summoned to Exorcise Him
10. How Hata Kanehisa Called on Michitoshi and Criticized Him
11. How the Minamoto Major Counsellor Had the Bell of Lifelong Chastity Rung
12. How a Young Lad Pretended to Be Asleep When They Were Preparing a Feast of Rice Balls
13. How a Young Lad from the Country Wept on Seeing the Cherry Blossoms Falling
14. How Kotōda Was Startled by His Son-in-Law
15. How a Big Apprentice-Lad Stole Some Salmon
16. How a Nun Saw Jizō
17. How an Itinerant Priest Encountered a Nocturnal Procession of Demons
18. About Toshihito and the Yam Gruel
19. About the Supernatural Powers of the Holy Man Seitoku
20. How the High Priest Jōkan Succeeded in Making Rain by Magic
21. How This Same High Priest by His Prayers Destroyed a Rock on the Great Peak
22. About Mt. Kimbu and the Gold-beater
23. About Mochitsune and the Parcel of Fish
24. How Atsuyuki Let a Corpse Be Taken Out through His House
25. About the Priest with the Long Nose
26. How Seimei Used His Magic Powers to Protect an Archivist Minor Captain
27. How Suemichi Nearly Met Disaster
28. How Hakamadare Encountered Yasumasa
29. How Akihira Nearly Met Disaster
30. How a Stūpa in China Became Smeared with Blood
31. How Narimura Met a Student of Herculean Strength
32. How a Buddha Appeared on a Persimmon Tree
33. About the Thief Daitarō
34. How the Mistress of Fujiwara Major Counsellor Tadaie Broke Wind

85. Mitford, A. B. (Lord Redesdale). *Tales of Old Japan*. London: Richard Clay and Sons, 1871; reprint editions New York: Macmillan, 1893, and Rutland, Vt.: Charles E. Tuttle, 1966.

This collection contains folktales, historical legends, ghost stories, Buddhist sermons, and essays explaining some aspects of Japanese culture. It is one of the earliest anthologies of Japanese tales in English, and it had a great effect on many later anthologies. This book was extremely popular at the turn of the century, going into ten printings between 1871 and 1908. Lord Redesdale lived in Japan for some time as a British diplomat and studied the Japanese language himself. He used actual Japanese sources, both written and oral, as the basis for his work. Considering the age of the work and its ethnocentric attitudes, the book is surprisingly well written and scholarly, with many informative notes and explanations. The book also contains 31 full-page black-and-white illustrations by a number of Japanese artists.

1. The Forty-seven Ronin: See entry 75, tale 30.

2. The Lovers of Gompachi and Komurasaki: Tells of a young ronin who embarks on a career of murder and theft in an attempt to raise money to ransom his love from a geisha house. This section also discusses traditional Japanese attitudes toward chastity of women and toward prostitution.

3. Kazuma's Revenge: Describes a young boy's struggle to avenge his father's brutal and treacherous murder, as well as the rank of hatamoto, which could be held by a samurai.

4. A Story of the Otokodate of Yedo: Tells about the bands of fighting men that tried to maintain honor and order within the capital city.

5. The Wonderful Adventures of Funakoshi Jiuyemon: In addition to Jiuyemon's numerous exploits, this section describes the Japanese laws concerning adultery and discusses the history of sumo wrestling.

6. The Eta Maiden and the Hatamoto: Tells of a samurai who is stripped of his rank and banished for having an affair with a woman of the outcast class.

7. The Tongue-cut Sparrow: See entry 133.

8. The Accomplished and Lucky Tea Kettle: See entry 112.

9. The Crackling Mountain: See entry 114.

10. The Story of the Old Man Who Made Withered Trees to Blossom: See entry 129.

11. The Battle of the Ape and the Crab: See entry 113.

12. The Adventures of Little Peachling: See entry 125.

13. The Foxes' Wedding

14. The History of Sakata Kintoki: A samurai chances upon a strong, brave boy in the wilderness, learns of his parentage, and takes the boy as his retainer.

15. The Elves and the Envious Neighbor: See entry 128.

16. The Ghost of Sakura: A man who is put to death brutally along with his wife and three young sons returns to haunt the evil official who decreed the terrible punishment.

17. How TajimaShume Was Tormented by a Devil of His Own Creation: A ronin who kills a wandering priest and steals his collection money is haunted by the priest's ghost.

18. Concerning Certain Superstitions: Gives several tales about beliefs concerning cats, foxes, and badgers.

19. Japanese Sermons: Gives translations of three sermons preached by the priest Kiu-ō of the Shingaku sect of Buddhism.

20. An Account of Hara-kiri

21. The Marriage Ceremony

22. The Birth and Rearing of Children

23. Funeral Rites

86. Naito, Hiroshi. *Legends of Japan*. Rutland, Vt.: Charles E. Tuttle, 1972.

This is a collection of 22 tales. Most of them are from the *Konjaku monogatari;* two tales, "The Iron Hat" and "The Lost Dinner," are from *Essays in Idleness* by the priest Kenko. Each story has a black-and-white woodblock print by Masahiko Nishino. The stories and the illustrations originally were published in the *Mainichi Daily News* in Japan.

1. The Fisherman's Battle: A group of fishermen who always carry arms for protection are driven to a deserted island by a mysterious storm. The god of the island appears to them as a handsome young man and asks their help in fighting a giant centipede that is trying to take over the island. During the battle the god is seen to be a huge serpent. With the fishermen's help, the centipede is defeated. The god invites the men to bring their families and settle on the island, which they do after going to pray to the god of Kumata Shrine, who is the serpent-deity's brother.

2. Wrestling a Serpent: The wrestler Tsuneyo, renowned for his great strength, is attacked by a huge serpent, which wraps itself around his leg. Tsuneyo is victorious, but later wishes to learn just how strong the serpent was. It takes 60 villagers pulling on a rope tied around Tsuneyo's leg to equal the strength of the snake.

3. The Lost Chance: A young man wishes to learn magic from a renowned sorcerer-priest. The priest takes the man to his old magic teacher, but warns the man not to bring anything made of metal with him. The man brings a dagger, which is detected by the magic teacher as soon as the man and the priest reach the temple. The temple and the magic teacher instantly disappear, and the sorcerer-priest loses his powers.

4. The Reed Mower and the Lady: A poverty-stricken husband

and wife divorce so that each can try to seek a fortune alone. The woman eventually becomes the wife of the provincial governor of Settsu, but the husband sinks to the level of a reed-cutter. The two happen to meet some years later, and after an exchange of poems, take their leave of each other forever.

5. The Iron Hat: During a banquet for an acolyte who is to become a priest the next day, the drunk acolyte forces an iron pot onto his head. When the party ends, no one is able to remove the pot. Finally the pot is removed by sheer force, but the acolyte's face is badly ripped and he barely survives the ordeal.

6. The Demon's Spittle: A man becomes invisible when a demon spits in his face. After he prays to Kannon to restore him, the goddess reveals the manner in which the man can become visible again.

7. A Piece of Straw: See entry 130.

8. The Hunter's Trick: A hunter and his dogs substitute themselves for a young maiden who is to be sacrificed to the monkey-god. After the dogs have defeated the monkeys, the chief monkey vows that they will never again demand human sacrifices.

9. No Melon to Spare: An old man asks for a watermelon from some men who have a large number, but they refuse. The man then takes some of the watermelon seeds, plants them, and causes them miraculously to grow and fruit in a matter of minutes. After all the melons on the new vine have been given to passersby, the old man disappears, and the men discover that their watermelons are also gone.

10. A Water Sprite: A mysterious old man begins to appear at night to the people who live around a certain pond. A samurai captures the old man, who refuses to answer any questions, but who asks that a basin of water be brought to him. The old man then says that he is the Water Sprite, jumps into the basin, and dissolves in the water.

11. The Ogre's Horses: Three itinerant priests come to a house of an ogre who turns people into horses. One of the priests manages to escape, but his two companions are transformed and are never released.

12. The Dragon King's Palace: A young man who saves the life of a snake is brought to the palace of the Dragon King and given a magic rice cake that always regenerates itself. The snake had been the Dragon King's daughter. When the man dies, the rice cake disappears.

13. The Bishop's Kick: When Bishop Kancho is attacked by a robber, he kicks the man so hard that the man is sent flying to the top of the scaffolding by the temple. The acolytes rescue the man, and the bishop gives him a stern lecture on giving up his life of crime.

14. The Long-nosed Goblins: A Chinese tengu visits a Japanese tengu and boasts that he can overcome several Japanese holy men. He is unsuccessful and finally admits the great spiritual powers of the Japanese.

15. Bewitched by a Boar: A pious but uneducated priest sees a vision of the Buddha. A hunter also sees the vision and realizes that since he is not an ascetic, he should not be able to see it. He shoots the

vision with an arrow, and the Buddha turns out to have been a bewitching badger.

16. A Cat Hater: When Fujiwara Kiyokado, a renowned cat hater, refuses to pay his taxes, the local governor locks him in a room with five cats until he signs an order releasing some money for payment.

17. The Flying Water Jars: A young priest is very proud of his magic ability to make water jars fetch water by themselves until he sees a different water jar doing the same thing. He follows the jar to the hut of an old priest and decides to test him, but the old priest proves more than a match, and the young priest's trick backfires.

18. Grave of a Chopstick: A princess is visited nightly by an unknown suitor. When she says she wishes to see him during the day, he tells her to look into her comb box in the morning, but he warns her not to be afraid of what she sees. She finds a small snake and cries out. The man takes his leave of her because she has shamed him. The princess stabs herself with a chopstick and dies.

19. The Bell Thieves: A traveler dies in the bell tower of Koyadera, and except for his relatives who come to claim the body one night, no one enters the belfry until the period of mourning is over. The death is discovered to be a ruse by a band of robbers who had actually stolen the great bell and melted it down for scrap metal.

20. The Monkey's Gratitude: A farmer's wife helps a monkey to escape from a shell that has caught its hand. Later when the woman's baby is threatened by some eagles, the monkey protects the baby.

21. The Lost Dinner: Some priests bury a picnic lunch, then later pretend to a young page that they are magically divining where some food is hidden. However, they are unable to find the lunchbox, because someone had seen them burying it and had stolen it during their absence.

22. Reunion with Death: A poor samurai marries a wealthy woman without divorcing his first wife. After several years, the man goes to find his first wife and spends the night with her, but in the morning he finds that he is sleeping beside a decayed corpse. His first wife had died of longing some time before.

87. Newman, Shirlee P. *Folk Tales of Japan*. Indianapolis, Ind.: Bobbs-Merrill, 1963.

This collection contains Newman's rewritten versions of 13 tales. Each includes a black-and-white illustration on the title page.

1. The Magic Mortar: See entry 123.
2. The Leak: See entry 121.
3. Happy Hunter and Good Fisher: See entry 122.
4. The Girl with the Bowl on Her Head: See entry 131.
5. The Mirror: See entry 124(a).
6. Keepers of the Mats: See entry 77, tale 1.

7. The Princess of Hase: The princess is beautiful and accomplished, but she is hated by her evil stepmother. The stepmother orders a servant to kill the girl in the mountains, but the faithful servant and his wife build a cottage for the girl and care for her until her father comes to find her. The stepmother is then banished for her wickedness.

8. The Cap that Heard: A man receives a magic cap from a deity by means of which he can understand the language of animals. He overhears some birds speaking, who state why a certain rich man is sick. The man goes to the rich man's house in the guise of a faith healer, announces the reason for the illness, and cures the victim. The man is given a large reward for his cure, and becomes a rich man through the use of the magic cap.

9. The Sparrow Who Drank Starch: See entry 133.

10. Kintaro, the Golden Boy: See entry 120.

11. Urashima, the Fisherman: See entry 134.

12. Momotarō, the Apricot's Son: See entry 125.

13. Faces in the Mirror: See entry 124(b).

88. O'Donnell, James E. *Japanese Folk Tales*. Caldwell, Idaho: Caxton Press, 1958.

A collection of 8 stories with 31 color illustrations by Kasumi Nagao. The stories contain some Japanese names and words that may be difficult for young children.

1. The Monkey and the Crab: See entry 113.

2. The Grandfather of the Cherry Blossoms: See entry 129.

3. The Beautiful Mouse Girl: See entry 126.

4. The Shining Princess: See entry 100.

5. The Gift of the Sparrow: See entry 133.

6. Tiny Finger: See entry 118.

7. Momotarō: See entry 125.

8. Urashima Tarō: See entry 134.

89. Ozaki, Yei Theodora. *Japanese Fairy Tales*. New York: A. L. Burt, 1903; reprint editions E. P. Dutton, 1903, 1922; Dover, 1967.

This book has also been entitled *The Japanese Fairy Book*. Ozaki's work is very well written and has been popular and influential since its first publication. The stories flow very well. There are black-and-white illustrations by various Japanese artists throughout the book.

1. My Lord Bag-of-Rice: See entry 127.

2. The Tongue-cut Sparrow: See entry 133.

3. The Story of Urashima Tarō, the Fisher Lad: See entry 134.

4. The Farmer and the Badger: See entry 114.

5. The Shinansha, or the South-Pointing Carriage: When a mythical emperor of China must fight against a rebel magician, the magician causes a thick fog to settle on the battlefield, so that the emperor's troops cannot tell direction. The emperor invents a compass, which is shaped like a man riding in a carriage; the tiny figure has one outstretched hand that always points to the south. In this way the emperor's troops cannot become confused in their movements and are able to defeat the enemy.

6. The Adventures of Kintaro, the Golden Boy: See entry 120.

7. The Story of Princess Hase: See entry 87, tale 7.

8. The Story of the Man Who Did Not Wish to Die: A man prays that he will be able to obtain the elixir of immortality. He is allowed a vision of what life would be like on Horaizan, the island of immortality, and he sees that he would eventually grow weary of perpetual youth and would wish to return to his native land. He gives up all vain desires to obtain immortality.

9. The Bamboo Cutter and the Moon Child: See entry 100.

10. The Mirror of Matsuyama: See entry 124(a).

11. The Goblin of Adachigahara: A priest crossing the plain of Adachigahara asks to spend the night in a lonely hut. The old woman who lives there goes out to fetch some wood, but she tells the man not to look into a certain room. The priest's curiosity is aroused, and he sees that the inner room is filled with human bones and blood. Realizing that the old woman is really a goblin, the priest runs out of the house, but the goblin pursues him across the plain until the dawn breaks and the goblin vanishes.

12. The Sagacious Monkey and the Boar: A man decides to sell his dancing monkey to a butcher because the animal is too old to perform tricks any longer. The monkey engages the boar's help. The boar kidnaps the man's young baby, and while the frantic parents are still wondering what to do, the monkey gives chase and rescues the child. In gratitude, the man decides to keep the faithful monkey as a pet.

13. The Happy Hunter and the Skillful Fisher: See entry 122.

14. The Story of the Old Man Who Made Withered Trees to Flower: See entry 129.

15. The Jellyfish and the Monkey: See entry 137.

16. The Quarrel of the Monkey and the Crab: See entry 113.

17. The White Hare and the Crocodiles: See entry 136.

18. The Story of Prince Yamato-dake: See entry 138.

19. Momotarō, or The Story of the Son of a Peach: See entry 125.

20. The Ogre of Rashomon: The warrior Watanabe cuts off the arm of the ogre that has been haunting the Gate of Rashomon. He must keep it for seven days, or else the ogre will be able to reattach the arm to its body. On the seventh night after the struggle, Watanabe's aged aunt comes to his house and asks to be shown the ogre's arm. Watanabe takes

the arm out of its hiding place, whereupon the "aunt" turns into the ogre, seizes the arm, and escapes.

21. How an Old Man Lost His Wen: See entry 128.

22. The Stones of Five Colors and the Empress Jokwa (An Old Chinese Story): When a pillar holding the sky above the earth is damaged by a rebellious wizard, Empress Jokwa is able to repair the sky with a porcelain made from stones of five colors. She then replaces the broken pillar with the legs of a great turtle.

90. Ozaki, Yei Theodora. *Warriors of Old Japan and Other Stories*. Boston: Houghton Mifflin, 1909.

This is a well-written collection of historical legends and tales. It includes ten full-page black-and-white illustrations by various Japanese artists.

1. Hachiro Tametomo, the Archer: Tells of the exploits of this renowned archer, the uncle of Yoritomo and Yoshitsune.

2. Gen Sanmi Yorimasa, the Knight: Recounts the exploits of this renowned warrior who shot a fantastic vampire creature that was attempting to drain the life force from the emperor.

3. The Story of Yoshitsune: See entry 91, tale 6.

4. The Story of Benkei: Tells of the wild warrior-priest who was Yoshitsune's most loyal retainer.

5. The Goblin of Oyeyama: The warrior Raiko manages to slay a terrible goblin that has been plaguing the capital through the use of some magic wine.

6. Kidomaru the Robber, Raiko the Brave, and the Goblin Spider: An entertaining adventure.

7. The Story of Pots of Plum, Cherry and Pine: The regent Tokiyori disguises himself as an itinerant priest to go among his people and learn of any injustices. He finds a samurai and his wife living in abject poverty because their lands had been stolen from them. During the course of the evening the samurai burns his three dwarf trees to heat the hut for the supposed priest. Later Tokiyori issues a summons to all samurai, which this wronged samurai answers. He is brought before Tokiyori and told that his estates will be restored to him.

8. Shiragiku, or White Chrysanthemum: After many trials and tribulations, a young adopted daughter finds her lost father and brother.

9. The Princess of the Bowl: See entry 131.

10. The Story of Lazy Taro: A man is so lazy that he will not even pick up a rice cake he has dropped. The governor of the province happens along and learns of the man's laziness. Through the governor's patience and kindness, Lazy Taro is cared for until he actually becomes a retainer in the governor's house, applies himself diligently to his work, and ends up a great success.

91. Pasteur, Violet M. *Gods and Heroes of Old Japan*. London: Kegan Paul, Trench, Trubner, 1906.

This collection contains legends about the founding of Japan and early Japanese history, based in part on Basil Hall Chamberin's *Kojiki* and W. G. Aston's *Nihongi*. The book is lavishly printed and physically beautiful. Each page has the text at the center surrounded by a wide illustrated border in pale shades of grey. The stories unfortunately suffer from an antiquated writing style that can be rather tedious for modern readers.

Prologue: The Way of the Gods: See entries 116, 119.

1. The Story of the Making of the Mirror, and 2. The Story of the Finding of the Sword: See entry 117.

3. The Story of Fire-shine and Fire-fade: See entry 122.

4. The Story of Yamato-dake the Hero: See entry 138.

5. The Story of the Good Emperor: Emperor Ojin names his youngest son crown prince, but the people wish his second son, Prince Sazaki, to be the next emperor. Upon Ojin's death, each son defers to the other, and neither will accept the crown. The country is plunged into chaos until the younger son commits suicide and Prince Sazaki is crowned Emperor Nintoku. At one point during his reign, Nintoku notices that no smoke rises from the hearths of the peasants' houses. Realizing that this means the rice harvest has been poor, Nintoku suspends all taxes to ease the peasants' burden. He also halts work on the construction of the Imperial Palace so that the workers can return to their fields and improve the harvest. (Nintoku was revered in Japanese history as an exemplary emperor.)

6. The Story of the Perfect Knight: Tells of the Genji warrior Yoshitsune. After Yoshitsune's mother Tokiwa is forced to surrender to the Taira leader Kiyomori in order to save her own mother's life, Kiyomori sends the young Yoshitsune to a temple to become a priest. In the wilds of Mount Kurama, Yoshitsune meets a tengu who teaches him martial arts and some magical powers. Yoshitsune then flees to the northern province of Ōshu where he receives sanctuary from the lord Hidehira. When Yoshitsune next returns to the capital, he meets the warrior-priest Benkei. Benkei had vowed to steal 1,000 fine swords and has already captured 999. Seeing Yoshitsune's fine sword, Benkei attacks him on the Gojo Bridge, but Yoshitsune is able to defeat the huge monk in the struggle. Benkei then vows to become Yoshitsune's retainer. Meanwhile, Yoritomo, Yoshitsune's older half brother who had been living in exile, gathers together the Genji forces to revolt against the Taira clan. Yoshitsune gladly joins his brother's revolt, and eventually becomes the military leader of the rebellion. Yoshitsune masterminds the Genji's defeat of the Taira. After the victory, however, Yoritomo becomes increasingly suspicious and jealous of Yoshitsune and decides to have his popular brother killed. Yoshitsune and his followers escape

back to Ōshu, where they again are welcomed by Hidehira. But upon Hidehira's death, Hidehira's sons treacherously betray Yoshitsune to Yoritomo, forcing Yoshitsune to commit suicide after killing his wife and children.

7. The Story of the Loyal Samurai: The warrior Masashige leads a rebellion against the Hojo regents in an attempt to restore real power to Emperor Go Daigo. Although the rebellion is initially successful, Go Daigo's own excesses as ruler cause another outbreak of civil war. Masashige is ordered to give battle at a certain place, despite Masashige's warnings that the imperial troops will be defeated. Masashige nevertheless obeys the emperor's orders and is killed in the ensuing battle.

92. Piggott, Juliet. *Japanese Fairy Tales*. Chicago: Follett, 1967.

The stories in this collection were composed by Piggott from her memories of tales told to her during her childhood in Japan and from previously published collections of tales in English. The book includes 20 black-and-white illustrations.

1. The White Hare of Oki: See entry 136.
2. The Dragon with the Sword in Its Tail: See entry 117.
3. The Fight between the Crab and the Monkey: See entry 113.
4. How Prince Yamato Used the Dragon Sword: See entry 138.
5. The Fisherboy and the Turtle: See entry 134.
6. Kintaro: See entry 120.
7. The Crane Who Said Thank You: See entry 115.
8. The Men with the Lumps on Their Faces: See entry 128.
9. The Straw Cape: See entry 83, tale 7.
10. The Burning Mountain: See entry 114.
11. The Old Man of the Cherry Blossoms: See entry 129.
12. The Bamboo Princess: See entry 100.
13. The Wedding of the Mice: See entry 126.

Redesdale, Lord. *Tales of Old Japan*. See Mitford, A. B., entry 85.

93. Rinder, Frank. *Old World Japan: Legends of the Land of the Gods*. New York: Macmillan, 1896.

This collection contains 13 tales that Rinder composed primarily from previously published anthologies of Japanese tales in English and French. It contains 20 full-page black-and-white illustrations by T. H. Robinson.

The Birth Time of the Gods: See entries 116, 119.
The Sun Goddess: See entry 117 (this version only goes as far as the enticement of the Sun Goddess out of the cave).

The Heavenly Messengers: See entry 80, tale 18.

Prince Ruddy Plenty: Tells of the descent to earth of Ninigi, the grandson of the Sun Goddess.

The Palace of the Ocean Bed: See entry 122.

Autumn and Spring: See entry 77, tale 19.

The Star Lovers: See entry 135.

The Island of Eternal Youth: See entry 80, tale 9.

Raitaro, the Son of the Thunder God: See entry 73, tale 3.

The Souls of the Children: There was once a river that took the souls of good people to Paradise, but it was dammed up by demons. Now people's souls must make their way unaided down the dry riverbed. The souls of children are unable to make the journey and so they gather in the dry riverbed of souls, where they are protected from the demons by the Buddha Jizō.

The Moon Maiden: See entry 132(a).

The Great Fir Tree of Takasago: See entry 80, tale 12.

The Willow of Mukochima: A young boy is kidnapped by a band of robbers. His mother follows after them, but she learns that her son has died at a certain village. The mother goes to the boy's grave every night. The boy's spirit speaks to her as a wind that passes through a sacred pine tree growing beside the grave.

The Child of the Forest: See entry 120.

The Vision of Tsunu: See entry 78, tale 16.

Princess Fire-fly: See entry 73, tale 1.

The Sparrow's Wedding

The Love of the Snow-White Fox: A prince saves a white fox from some hunters, but in the struggle the prince's father is killed. The fox takes the form of a beautiful woman, becomes the prince's wife, and bears him a son. She then is forced to leave him by the order of the god Inari.

Nedzumi: See entry 126.

Koma and Gon: Two cats fall in love, but they belong to different people, neither of whom is willing to give up ownership. The cats run away, and after some trials and tribulations, they find a new owner who takes them both in as pets.

94. Sakade, Florence. *Japanese Children's Stories*. Rutland, Vt.: Charles E. Tuttle, 1952; revised edition 1959.

The stories in this collection are simply written and suitable for reading aloud. There are 12 full-page color illustrations. In addition, almost every page of text contains a black-and-white illustration. Two of the stories in the collection—marked by asterisks in the following list— are by modern writers.

1. Urashima Tarō: See entry 134.

2. The Fairy Crane: See entry 115.

3. *The Dragon's Tears: A boy who is not afraid of the local dragon invites the dragon to his birthday party. Overcome by the boy's kindness, the dragon weeps until a river is formed by its tears. The boy rides home on the back of the dragon down the new river.

4. The Sandal Seller: A poor but honest sandal seller trades his sandals for some charcoal. The charcoal turns out to be magical, and every spark it produces turns to gold. The charcoal seller had really been an elf who had been touched by the sandal seller's honesty.

5. The Robe of Feathers: See entry 132(a).

6. The Old Man with a Wen: See entry 128.

7. The Flying Farmer: A greedy farmer tries to capture an entire flock of ducks at once. The ducks all fly away, and the farmer, who is holding the end of the traps, is carried into the sky. He lands on the top of a high pagoda and is forced to jump into a huge "safety net" to get down. In the end it proves to be a dream, but he is nevertheless cured of his greed.

8. The Magic Mortar: See entry 123.

9. The Biggest in the World: The lobster thinks that he is the biggest creature in the world until he is blown into the sky by a whale. When the lobster falls back into the sea, his back is broken; that is why lobsters have curved backs.

10. *Why the Red Elf Cried: The Blue Elf helps his friend the Red Elf to make friends of the nearby villagers by causing all sorts of mischief and letting the Red Elf be the hero. When the Red Elf goes to thank the Blue Elf, he learns that the Blue Elf has gone away so as not to jeopardize the Red Elf's new friendships.

11. Mountain-Lucky and Sea-Lucky: See entry 122.

12. The Magic Spring: An old man becomes young again when he drinks some water from a magic spring. His wife drinks too much of the water and becomes a baby again.

13. The Rolling Rice Cakes: An old man loses his rice cakes down a hole. When he goes after them, he meets some mice who thank him for the cakes and give him a magic rice sack that is always full.

14. How to Fool a Cat: A lord commissions two artists to carve a mouse. The carving that is skillful enough to trick a cat into pouncing on it will be paid for with gold. One man carves a fine mouse from wood, but the other artist carves a rough mouse from dried fish. Both artists are paid, the one for his skill and the other for his cleverness.

15. The Princess and the Herdboy: See entry 135.

16. Saburo the Eel-Catcher: Through a series of accidents, Saburo obtains a huge eel, a wild boar, some yams, a pheasant, and the pheasant's eggs. He manages very ingeniously to carry everything home.

17. The Singing Turtle: An industrious man finds a singing turtle and makes some money showing it to the villagers. His lazy brother

steals the turtle and tries to make a fortune, but the turtle refuses to sing for him. The evil brother is driven from the village.

18. Kintaro's Adventures: See entry 120.

95. Scofield, Elizabeth. *A Fox in One Bite and Other Tasty Tales from Japan*. Tokyo: Kodansha International, 1965.

This is a collection of six marvelously written tales about foxes and badgers. These stories are excellent for a storyteller to read aloud to a group or for an older child to read alone. Each story has one full-page color and one full-page black-and-white illustration by K. Wakana. There is also a small black-and-white illustration by each story title. See also entry 96 by Scofield.

A Fox in One Bite: A little boy tricks a fox that has been haunting the village into turning itself into a rice dumpling. The boy eats the dumpling, and that is the end of the haunting fox.

The Badger Priest: A man who has set out to capture a badger is tricked by the badger into thinking that his house is on fire, then into thinking that his house is threatened by a flood. Realizing that he is no match for the clever badger, the man gives up trying to catch the animal.

The Fox and the Shrike: The fox and the shrike steal some fish from a fish merchant, but the fox eats all the fish before the shrike can get any. The shrike then sees to it that the merchant gives the fox a good beating.

The Yamabushi and the Badger: A mountain priest startles a sleeping badger. Suddenly night falls and a funeral procession approaches. The priest climbs up a tree, but a ghost emerges from the coffin and pursues the priest. The priest is terrified until he is brought out of his delusion by a group of villagers who are standing around the tree in broad daylight. It had all been a trick by the badger.

Zuiten and the Fox: An acolyte named Zuiten hears someone calling him. He learns that it is a fox. The fox brushes its tail against the temple door to make the sound "zui," then hits the door with its tail to make the sound "ten." The clever acolyte manages to trap the fox and forces it to promise not to bother people any more with its pranks.

The Old Tea Kettle: See entry 112.

96. Scofield, Elizabeth. *Hold Tight, Stick Tight*. Tokyo: Kodansha International, 1966.

Like Scofield's collection of tales about foxes and badgers (entry 95), this collection is marvelously written, and the stories are excellent for a storyteller to read aloud to a group or for an older child to read alone. Each tale is about an honest old man who is rewarded and an evil old man who is punished. Each story has one full-page color and one full-page black-and-white illustration by K. Wakana. There is also a small black-and-white illustration by each story title.

1. The Singing Turtle: An old man helps a turtle that has fallen on its back. The turtle returns the kindness by singing before a crowd of people so that the old man can make some money. An evil neighbor steals the turtle, but the turtle refuses to sing for him. The neighbor kills the turtle, and the kind man buries it in his garden. A magic tree grows that gives the kind man gold. When the neighbor tries to get some gold, he falls out of the tree.

2. The Magic Geta: An old woodcutter offers some wood to the local god. The god rewards the man with a pair of geta that produce a gold coin every time the wearer takes a step. A greedy neighbor steals the geta and does get some gold from them, but each time he takes a step he grows smaller until he is no larger than an insect.

3. Heavenly Treasure: An old man dreams of getting treasure from heaven. He finds some buried treasure, but he leaves it, thinking that it was not meant for him. A greedy neighbor, who had seen the man digging, unearths the pot, which he finds to be full of snakes and centipedes. In anger he throws them down the good man's chimney, but as they fall "from heaven" they turn into gold pieces.

4. The Monkeys and the Jizō: Some monkeys find an old man sitting in a field and, thinking that he is a Jizō statue, they carry him to a shrine and make him offerings. During the whole time, the old man does not make a sound. A greedy neighbor tries to duplicate the good man's fortune, but he is unable to keep quiet while the monkeys are carrying him, and they drop him in a river.

5. Hold Tight, Stick Tight: A man in a field hears a voice say "Hold tight or stick tight?" The man replies that either is fine, whereupon he is covered from head to toe with gold coins. A greedy neighbor tries to duplicate the good man's fortune, but he winds up covered with pitch instead of gold.

6. The Roly Poly Dumpling: A man drops his dumplings down a hole. When he goes after them, he meets some mice who thank him for his gift and give him a magic hammer that shakes out food. An evil neighbor tries to steal all the mice's gold by meowing like a cat, but the mice realize his deception and drive him away empty-handed.

97. Seki, Keigo. *Folktales of Japan*. Translated by Robert J. Adams. Chicago: University of Chicago Press, 1963.

This book contains 63 tales selected from Seki's *Nihon no mukashi-banashi* (see Appendix A). It includes a glossary, a bibliography, a motif index, and a tale type index. This is a very good source book of Japanese tales. (*Folktales of Japan* is one volume in the series Folktales of the

rld, published by the University of Chicago Press under the general
torship of Richard M. Dorson.)

Animal Tales

1. The Fish Thief: The fox steals some fish from a fisherman.
When the bear asks where the fish came from, the fox says that he
caught them by using his tail as a fishing line. The bear puts his tail
through a hole in the ice on the frozen lake, but his tail freezes and is
torn off.

2. The Hare, Badger, Monkey, and Otter: The hare divides some
goods that the animals have stolen from a person. The hare keeps the
beans for himself, and he gives the worthless items to the other animals.
When they come to rebuke him, the hare pretends that he has become
sick from the beans.

3a. Kachi Kachi Mountain: A farmer traps a mischievous badger,
but the badger escapes and kills the man's wife.

3b. The Rabbit and the Bear: The rabbit tricks the bear into getting
badly hurt three times, then he tricks the bear into going out onto a lake
in a mud boat. After the bear drowns, the rabbit makes him into bear
soup. He tricks some farmers into chewing on the bones and breaking
their teeth. The farmers try to kill the rabbit, but he escapes. As the
rabbit is running away, one of the farmers throws a knife at him, cutting
off his tail. That is why rabbits have short tails.

4. The Quail and the Badger: After the quail tricks the badger into
getting a beating, the badger catches the pheasant by the tail. The
pheasant escapes, but his tail is pulled off. That is why pheasants have
no tails.

5. The Monkey and the Crab: Monkey cheats crab, but crab manages to grab monkey's bottom in his pincers. Crab releases monkey in
exchange for three hairs. This is why the crab has hair on its legs.

6. The Monkey and the Pheasant: After pheasant has done all the
work raising rice and making mochi, monkey tries to steal all the mochi
for himself, but he fails. Pheasant will not give monkey any, so monkey
threatens to exact revenge the next night. When the monkey comes to
pheasant's house, the egg, needle, dung, and mortar help the pheasant
overcome the monkey.

7. The Wolf's Reward: A man helps a wolf who has a bone stuck in
its throat. The wolf then brings the man a huge pheasant.

8. The Greedy Hawk: A hawk tries to kill two boars at the same
time. As a result, the hawk's legs are broken.

9. The Whale and the Sea Slug: The whale and the sea slug swim a
race. The sea slug has all its friends wait for the whale at various
beaches, so it always seems as if the sea slug has beaten the whale.

10. The Cat and the Crab: The cat and the crab run a race. The
crab hangs onto the cat's tail, and when the cat turns around at the finish
line to look for the crab, the crab jumps down and claims the victory.

11. The Monkey's Liver: See entry 137.

12. The Rain Leak in an Old House: See entry 121.

13. The Mole's Bridegroom: See entry 126, except that in this version the mole is the main character, not the mouse.

14. An Endless Story: A large number of rats jump into the sea; the first goes splash, the second goes splash, etc.

Ogres

15. Shippei Taro: See entry 77, tale 7, except that in this version the hero is a priest and the "gods" are monkeys.

16. The Oni's Laughter: A woman goes to search for her daughter who has been kidnapped by an oni. Through the help of a goddess, the mother finds her daughter. They are escaping from the demon by ship when the demon tries to drink up all the water to stop their flight. The women uncover themselves, which causes the oni to laugh and release the water.

17. Momotarō, the Peach Boy: See entry 125.

18. The Dirt Boy: An old couple fashion a boy from the dirt on their bodies. The boy grows up to be an incredibly strong warrior. He meets two other strong men who become his retainers. Together the three men save three girls from a haunting spirit that has kidnapped them.

19. The Three Lucky Charms: An acolyte is captured by a female oni, but he manages to escape by using three magic charms. When the boy reaches his temple, the priest confronts the oni, tricks her into shrinking to the size of a bean, and eats her.

20. The Oni and the Three Children: Three children who have been abandoned in the woods come to the house of an oni. The old woman there hides them and tells the oni that they have run away. The oni chases after them, wearing his magic boots. The children follow later, steal the boots while the demon is sleeping, and make good their escape.

21. The Golden Chain from Heaven: Three children who have been left alone are tricked into thinking that a mountain witch is their mother returning from visiting their father's grave. The witch eats one of the children, but the other two manage to flee from the house and climb a tree. When the witch starts to climb after them, they call upon the Heavenly Deity to help them. A chain descends from the sky, and the children escape. When the witch calls out, a rotten rope descends from the sky. The witch falls when she tries to climb the rope.

22. The Swamp Nushi's Messenger: A swamp spirit gives a farmer some money for a pilgrimage to Ise in exchange for his carrying a letter to the spirit of another swamp. While the farmer is on his journey, he meets a priest who reads the letter and learns that it instructs the second spirit to eat the man. The priest rewrites the note to say that the spirit should give the man a reward for his hard work. The spirit gives the man a horse, which produces a piece of gold each time it is fed a cup of rice.

Supernatural Husbands or Wives

23. The Woman Who Came Down from Heaven: See entry 132(c).

24. The Fire Boy: A boy is driven from his father's house because of the slanders of his stepmother. He gains employment as a fire attendant in a rich man's house. He always looks dirty and unkempt. When a three-day festival is held, the boy secretly dresses himself in his fine kimono and rides his fine horse, which he keeps hidden. The people all think that he is a god, except for the rich man's daughter, who recognizes him. She finally takes him for her husband. The Fire Boy goes back to visit his father's house, but on the road he dies from eating some poisoned berries. His wife searches for him and restores him to life with some magic life-giving water.

25. The Crane Wife: See entry 115.

26. The Snow Wife: A man finds a beautiful woman in a snowstorm. He makes her his wife, but as the spring comes, she begins to get thinner. One day he finds that she has melted to a pool of water in front of the stove.

27. The Snail Chōja: An old couple pray to the water-deity for a son, even if it is only a snail. The woman soon gives birth to a snail. After 20 years, the chōja learns of the snail boy and decides to marry one of his daughters to the boy, since he is really the son of the water-deity. The chōja's youngest daughter agrees to marry the snail boy. In time she comes to love him in spite of his appearance because of his great kindness. When the girl goes to worship the Buddhist god Yakushi, she takes her husband with her but leaves him just outside the shrine. She is unable to find him when she returns and is about to drown herself in a pond when a fine young man stops her. He is the snail boy, who has been transformed into a real man.

28. Little One Inch: See entry 118.

29. The White Bird Sister: A girl who is betrothed to a great lord is killed by her stepmother, who substitutes her own daughter to be the man's bride. The spirit of the dead girl is transformed into a white bird. The bird weaves a fine kimono for her younger brother, through which the lord comes to know what happened to his true fiancée. The white bird bathes in two basins of water that are placed up on posts and is thus able to resume her human shape. The false wife is killed and her head is given to her evil mother as a gift. The mother dies when she sees her daughter's head. The lord and his true bride are married.

30. The Girl without Arms: Through the instigation of her stepmother, a girl's arms are cut off by her father and she is left alone in the wilderness. The girl is found by a young nobleman who takes her as his wife. While the man is in Edo, a son is born, so a letter is sent informing him. But the letter is intercepted by the girl's stepmother, who changes it to say that a monster has been born. When the man reads the letter,

he orders that the mother and child be well cared for nonetheless, but this letter is also intercepted, and it is changed to say that the mother and child must be driven from the man's house. As the armless girl is traveling along, she stops to take a drink from a stream. The baby begins to slip off her back into the water, and in her desperation to catch the child, the girl miraculously grows her arms back again. When her husband learns what has happened, he searches for her, restores her to his house, and has the evil stepmother and the father punished.

Kindness Rewarded and Evil Punished

31. The Good Fortune Kettle: A man saves a fox from some children. The fox turns itself into a kettle to be sold to a temple, into a girl to be sold to a house of prostitution, and into a horse to be sold to a nobleman so that the man can make some money.

32. Urashima Tarō: See entry 134, except that in this version there is no injunction against opening the box, and Urashima becomes a white crane, while the daughter of the Dragon King comes to meet him in the form of a turtle.

33. The Tongue-cut Sparrow: See entry 133.

34. The Old Man Who Cut Bamboo: A man eats a bird, but the bird's legs protrude from the man's body. When the man pulls on the bird's legs, a bird song sounds from his stomach. While cutting bamboo in the daimyo's field, the man is confronted by the angry landowner, but he pulls the bird's legs and thus amuses the daimyo. He is given a reward. A greedy neighbor tries to imitate the first man's fortune, but he fails and is punished.

35. The Old Man Who Made Flowers Bloom: See entry 129.

36. The Old Men Who Had Wens: See entry 128.

37. The Monkey's Jizō-sama: See entry 96, tale 4.

38. Benizara and Kakezara: Benizara, the stepdaughter, is given a broken sack to fill with chestnuts, while Kakezara, the real daughter, is given a good sack. Benizara stays in the mountain until it is dark, then she happens upon the house of some oni. The old woman there tells Benizara how to return home safely and gives her a magic box that will give the girl anything she asks for. The next day the mother takes Kakezara to a festival, leaving Benizara home with a great deal of work to do. Benizara's friends come and help her do her work. Benizara gets a fine kimono from the magic box and goes to the festival, where she is seen by the lord. He comes to her house the next day, but the mother tries to have him take Kakezara. The lord asks the girls to compose a poem. Kakezara composes a very poor poem, while Benizara composes a fine poem.

39. The Salt-grinding Millstones: See entry 123.

40. The Magic Ear: A man who saves the life of a fish is given a magic ear that can understand animal languages by the Dragon King.

The man learns from listening to some crows the cause of the illness of a rich man's daughter. He is able to cure her and eventually becomes her husband.

41. The Chōja Who Became a Monkey: The Sun Deity comes to the house of a rich man in the guise of a traveling priest. The rich man drives him away. Then the priest goes to the house of the rich man's poor neighbors, where he is well received. In gratitude, the god has them set up a magic bath that makes them young again. When the rich man hears what has happened, he asks the priest to come back and make him young again also. The priest tells him to set up a bath, but instead of becoming young, the man and his wife turn into monkeys.

42. The Skeleton's Song: While crossing an isolated mountain pass, a man kills his friend and steals his money. Three years later the man is again crossing the pass, when he hears someone calling him. It is his friend's skeleton. The skeleton proposes that the man take him around and let the skeleton dance for people, and in this way they can make a great deal of money. When the man is asked to bring his dancing skeleton before the lord, the skeleton reveals how the man had murdered and robbed him.

Good Fortune

43. The Charcoal Burner Chōja: A man overhears a local deity saying that the man's son who was born that day has poor luck, while the girl who has been born the same day to the man's friend is fated to be very wealthy. The man arranges a betrothal between the two children. When the children grow up, they are married, but the husband finally drives his wife from the house. As she is leaving, she overhears the storehouse-deities saying that they will no longer remain with her husband, but will go to the house of a certain charcoal maker. The woman finds the charcoal maker and becomes his wife. They go to look at the charcoal stoves and find that they contain gold. Meanwhile the woman's first husband becomes very poor. He happens to come to his former wife's new house, and when he recognizes her, he runs to the storehouse and dies. The woman offers a small amount of grain for his soul and makes him a guardian of the storehouse.

44. Luck from Heaven and Luck from the Earth: See entry 96, tale 3.

45. The Man Who Bought a Dream: Two merchants who are traveling together stop to rest. One has a dream that some money is buried at the base of a particular tree. The second man buys the dream, locates the tree, and actually does find a fortune buried beneath the tree.

46. The Advice that Cost a Thousand Ryō: A poor man works in the capital for a year and saves 30 yen. On the journey home, he meets a mysterious man on three consecutive nights who demands 10 yen each night for some advice. The first two pieces of advice save the traveler's life, while the last piece of advice causes him to obtain 500 yen.

Cleverness and Stupidity

47. The Monkey Bridegroom: A man rashly promises one of his daughters to a monkey who helps him dig some roots. The man's youngest daughter agrees to become the monkey's bride if she is given certain heavy objects which the monkey must carry on his back. When the girl and the monkey come to a cherry tree that is blooming on top of a cliff overhanging a river, the girl tricks the monkey into climbing the tree with his heavy load. The tree branch breaks, and the monkey falls into the river far below.

48. The Wife's Portrait: A poor farmer has a wife who is so beautiful that he cannot take his eyes off her long enough to work in the fields. She has a portrait drawn so that the man can hang it in the fields and look at it while he is working. The portrait gets blown away in the wind and is found by the lord of the province. He takes the woman for himself, but before she leaves, the wife tells her husband to come to the castle on New Year's selling pine branches. For the entire time that the woman is kept in the castle she does not smile until she hears her husband's voice selling the pine branches. The lord, who has been trying to get her to smile the entire time, exchanges clothes with the husband and goes outside the castle selling pine branches so that he can make her smile too. As soon as her husband is inside the castle, the woman has the gates closed. The lord is locked outside, and the farmer becomes the new lord.

49. The Golden Eggplant: The pregnant wife of a lord is set adrift in a hollow log for breaking wind in the lord's presence. She is rescued by an old couple and gives birth to a son. When the son learns about his father, he travels to the lord's province and claims to have the seeds of a plant that will produce golden eggplants if it is tended by a woman who has never broken wind. When the lord says that there is no such woman, the boy demands to know why his mother was banished. The lord realizes that this is his son.

50. The Bundle of Straw and the King's Son: A boy learns that his mother had been the wife of a king, but had been driven from her palace with nothing but three bundles of rice straw for committing a trivial offense. Through several clever exchanges, the boy manages to trade the straw for all the water rights in his father's kingdom. When the people complain of the inconvenience of having to pay a tithe each time they want to use any water, the king tries to regain the water rights, but the boy refuses and finally reveals his true identity. The king then abdicates in favor of his son.

51. The Boy Who Told Tall Tales: A renowned teller of tall tales comes to challenge a second man who is also a fine tale teller, but the second man's son proves to be cleverer than either of them.

52. A Tall Tale Contest: Three men hold a tall tale contest to see who should sit in the place of honor during dinner. The first two men tell good tales, but the third man tells a tale so wild that he is able to use the other men's tales as a small part of it.

53. The Mountain Where Old People Were Abandoned: Instead of abandoning his old father in the mountains as the law of the province commands, a man hides the old man under his house. When the lord of the province asks his subjects to weave a rope of ashes and to thread a conch shell, the man is able to do the tasks through the wisdom of his old father. When the lord asks how he knew to perform such difficult tasks, the man reveals that he had hidden his old father who was the one who really had the wisdom. The lord then decrees that old people should no longer be abandoned.

54. The Three Year Sleeping Boy: The son of a poor widow does nothing but eat and sleep. One day he disguises himself as the local deity, appears at the house of a rich man, and orders that the rich man marry his daughter to the son of the poor widow. In this way he and his mother become wealthy.

55. The Nun as Judge: See entry 124(b).

56. The Clever Lord: A man accidentally kills the master of the village. He goes to the clever lord for help. The clever lord agrees to help, and in the course of the evening he manages to make a number of other people think that they have killed the master and that the lord will help them. Finally the lord makes it seem as if the master has died of a fever, but in the end he receives payments from all the "murderers."

57. The Hawk Fledgling: A man invites the lord of his province to come to the village to obtain a hawk fledgling. Then the man learns that the village is unable to entertain the lord. The man then tricks the lord into thinking that the man had mistaken a kite for a hawk, so the lord cancels his trip.

58. Stinginess: A man tries to use his neighbor's hammer to pound in some metal nails, but the neighbor refuses to lend his hammer. The man is then forced to use his own hammer.

59. It's Been Well Used: An old woman accidentally exposes her private parts while she is washing a jar by a stream. A young man obliquely tries to inform her, but she thinks that he is talking about her jar, and the conversation becomes more and more suggestive.

60. The Pillow: A man who has never used a pillow asks his wife what it is, but she thinks that he is asking her her name. The next day the man tells his new in-laws about his nocturnal exploits with the pillow, but he uses the girl's name instead of the word "pillow."

61. There's No Deity There: An acolyte needs to relieve himself, but wherever he tries to do it, the priest stops him, saying that there is a deity there. Finally the acolyte relieves himself on the priest's head.

62. The Sweet Mochi's Parents: A priest tells several lies to his acolyte, then he chastises the acolyte about his behavior. In retaliation, the acolyte begins following all of the priest's orders more and more literally with the expected comical result.

63. Bedding in One's Ear: A priest warns his acolyte not to mention to any guest that they must sleep on straw instead of bedding. One day

when the priest has a guest, the acolyte sees a piece of straw in the priest's ear and says that the man has a piece of bedding in his ear.

98. Steinberg, Barbara H. *The Magic Millstones and Other Japanese Folk Stories*. London: Oxford University Press, 1969.

This collection contains Steinberg's rewritten versions of nine tales. There are partial color illustrations on almost every page of text and four full-page illustrations by Esme Eve.

The Magic Millstones: See entry 123.
The Mouse Lord Chooses a Bridegroom: See entry 126.
Urashima Tarō: See entry 134.
The Grateful Crane: See entry 115.
The Pheasant's Revenge: See entry 97, tale 6.
The Tongue-cut Sparrow: See entry 133.
The Monkey's Liver: See entry 137.
Momotarō, the Peach Boy: See entry 125.
The Badger Tea Kettle: See entry 112.

99. Suzuki, Yoshimatsu. *Japanese Legends and Folk-Tales*. Tokyo: Sakurai Shoten, 1949.

This collection contains 43 tales, most of which are short local legends.

The Quarrel between the Mountains: In an argument over whether Mount Fuji or Hakusan is taller, Fuji proves to be taller by the width of a straw sandal. This is why visitors to the summit of Hakusan traditionally left one sandal behind.

The Seven Wonders of Tōkai-ji Temple: (1) A sea bass with one side cut off returns to life. (2) Frogs in the temple pond do not croak. (3) A ginkgo tree bears fruit only on one side. (4) A stone cistern indicates whether the tide is at ebb or flow. (5) A sacred tree sheds blood when it is cut. (6) A tree in the temple courtyard puts out a fire in China. (7) A mosquito net is large enough for a 100-mat room.

Kanewaka and His Pictures: Kanewaka's picture of a colt comes to life and eats the barley in nearby fields, while his picture of the Fire God starts a fire in the temple.

The Fox and the Roast Mouse: A fox that was a messenger for a feudal lord ate a mouse that was attached to a snare and was killed. The fox's spirit was later enshrined.

The Twice-Born Man: A man who had been born stupid because of his sins from former lives is reincarnated rich and intelligent through his faith in Buddha.

The Well that Kōbō Daishi Dug: When an old woman from a village that is perpetually drought-stricken travels a great distance to fetch some water from him, Kōbō Daishi causes a pure spring to gush forth miraculously.

The Bald-Headed Cat of Kowashi: A man's mother begins to act strangely, and it is discovered that the mother is really an evil cat that had previously killed the old woman and taken her place.

The Priest and the Boar: See entry 86, tale 15.

Kichiji, the Charcoal Burner: A rich woman receives a prophesy to marry a certain poor charcoal burner. When the new husband treats the wife's gold carelessly, she rebukes him, but he tells her that the area around his kiln is covered with gold. Thus the charcoal burner becomes a rich man.

The Kannon of Shido: A mysterious wandering monk offers to carve a statue of Kannon in one night from a huge log if he can do so unobserved. The lord of the province is unable to restrain his curiosity, whereupon the monk disappears, and the statue is left half finished.

Shakusi Jima: Ghost women appear to sailors on the ocean and ask for dippers. If they are given one, they use it to fill the ship with water and sink it.

The Clever Cook: When the servant of a certain house spies on its mysterious cook, the woman takes her leave of the household and predicts its ultimate ruin.

A Strange Case of Vicarious Sacrifice: Two girls with the same name live in neighboring villages. One is fated to die, but the demon sent to fetch her soul kills the wrong girl. When she is sent back to earth, she learns that her body has already been cremated. Her soul then is placed into the body of the second girl who really was supposed to die.

The Unseen Bell: A bell cannot be cast to give the right tone until an apprentice bell maker is accidentally killed in the bell forge. Later, when the forged bell is rung at night, an unseen bell echoes from the grave of the apprentice.

The Cistern of Yuka: A drought could be ended if the cisterns in the area are rinsed out, but the man who performs the ritual would shortly be killed by the wrath of the white serpents that live in the cisterns.

The Talking Image of Jizō: A man who waylays a traveler before a Jizō statue is shocked into repentance when the statue says it will not reveal the man's crime.

The Ponds and the Love-Knots: A traveler cures a girl of a serious illness and is given the girl as his bride. The girl runs away and drowns herself in one of a pair of ponds. The traveler follows her and drowns himself too, but he jumps into the wrong pond.

The Uneatable Pears: The priest Kūkai asks a man for some pears from his orchard, but the man says that the pears are not fit to eat. After that the pears in the orchard indeed grow hard as stones and cannot be eaten.

The Original Home of the Finny Tribe: When the animals of the world become too numerous, the god of animals kills all the worthless beasts and throws them into a lake. The lake becomes a fertile plain, and because of this a tribe of people migrate to the area.

The Serpent Grove: A young woman is visited nightly by an unknown suitor until she becomes pregnant. Her mother tells her to stick a threaded needle into the hem of the man's kimono. The next morning a servant follows the thread to a cave where some snakes are living. The male snake is dying because the needle has been stuck into him, but he boasts that he has made the girl pregnant. The other snake then inadvertently reveals how the girl can abort the unnatural pregnancy.

The Gold Image of Daikoku: A man accidentally drops his gold statue of Daikoku into the sea, but when he later attends a banquet, he finds the statue inside a fish.

The Mystery of the Missing Treasure: A ghost appears to a man and gives him a sword. The man soon falls into a delirium. Later it is discovered that the sword has been stolen from the house of the lord, and the man is ordered to commit suicide.

The Frog Stones: A girl tries to swim across a river to meet her lover, but she drowns and turns into a frog-shaped stone. Her lover on the other bank also turns into a frog stone where he is standing.

History of the Yuka Shrine: A fisherman takes a demon mask from a floating boat. Because the mask had been tormented by the Sea God, it restores the eyesight of the man's blind mother out of gratitude. The mask is later enshrined deep in the mountains.

Shiratori Jinja: A rainstorm starts during a festival, and the shrine bearers leave the portable shrine uncovered in the middle of the road. A man passing by covers the shrine with the wood that he had been carrying. After the storm, the shrine will not move unless it is carried by the man who had covered it during the storm.

The Living Headless Priest: A robber and his wife cut off the head of a priest while he is sleeping and steal his money. In the morning the priest is found alive and well, but the statue of Kannon that the priest always carries with him has sword marks in its neck.

The Doomed Noble Princess: A noblewoman who contracts leprosy is set adrift on Naniwa Bay in a wooden tub.

The Petrified Furies of the Adonis: A young girl's lover is killed by a serpent who wants the girl for himself. Later a huge stone falls out of the heavens and crushes the serpent. The stone was the petrified fury of the young man whom the serpent had killed.

The Horse Stone: A bewitching horse turns into a stone and causes accidents to happen in the area around it.

The Giant and the Tobacco Pouch: A man successfully fights against a giant until the giant convinces him to remove his tobacco pouch, which contains numerous talismans.

The Dog Stone: A man receives a magic dog that will produce one gold coin a day if fed one bowl of sand. The man overfeeds the dog to get more gold, and the dog dies. The man throws the dog into a river, and the dog turns into a dog-shaped stone.

Kuro, the Faithful Dog: A man thinks that his dog is attacking him and kills it, not realizing that the dog is trying to protect him from an evil snake. The man shoots the snake, but it turns into a huge serpent. The man dies from being possessed by the serpent's evil spirit.

The Sweating Bell: A bell of unknown manufacture is pulled from the sea. It sheds drops of water during the heat of summer.

The Whispering Cats: A mysterious cat comes to visit the cat of the temple priest, and the priest hears the cats whispering together. Later the strange cat appears as an apparition during a funeral. The cat also appears as a maiden who lures travelers into a pond.

The Blind Serpent: (1) A man learns that his wife is really a snake, and she leaves his house. She gives him one of her eyes to use in nursing their baby, but the local lord hears of the rare treasure and confiscates it. The snake gives the man her other eye, but this too is taken by the lord. The serpent then causes a huge volcanic explosion in the province. (2) A hunter who is not mindful of Buddha's teachings is turned into a snake. He gives one of his eyes to his brother to use in making excellent saké.

The Ageless Nun: A woman who eats the flesh of a mermaid obtains virtual immortality, but she soon learns that it is a mixed blessing. After many decades, the woman does finally die.

Hanako Zuka: A young woman falls in love with an itinerant priest who is an excellent flute player. When her parents drive the priest from the house, the woman goes mad and hangs herself. The ghost of the woman haunts her grave, lured out by the sound of any young man who passes by playing a bamboo flute.

The Sacred Calabash: A single calabash remains on a tree for several seasons until the exact moment of the birth of the Prince Shōtoku, when it is removed from the tree by a supernatural dragon-horse. The infant prince never opens his right hand until the calabash is presented to him, whereupon the stone of the gourd is found in his clenched fist.

Motoshichi Koroshichi: An old hunter's two sons are lost in the forest, and the old man searches for them until he dies from exposure. His soul becomes a bird with one white wing and one black wing whose song is thought to sound like the old man calling out his sons' names.

Shirahage Daimyōjin: A badger turns itself into a kettle so that an old couple can sell it and obtain some money. The badger becomes bald on the spot where the purchaser of the kettle rubbed it to make it shine.

The Sea Palace: See entry 122.

Kaguyahime: See entry 100.

The Tunnel of Ao: A retainer who kills his lord becomes a bandit, but later he repents of his evil life and becomes a priest. On his travels he comes to a treacherous mountain pass and vows to dig a tunnel through the rock. Years later the priest is confronted by the grown son of the murdered lord, but he convinces the son to delay his revenge until the tunnel is completed. As the son watches the priest at his labors, he realizes that the man has repented of his former ways and has actually become a saint.

100. *The Tale of the Shining Princess.* New York: Metropolitan Museum of Art/Viking Press, 1980.

    Taketori monogatari 竹取物語, which has been translated into English under the titles "The Tale of the Shining Princess," "The Tale of the Bamboo Cutter," "The Moon Maiden," and "Kaguyahime," かぐや姫, is a very important work in the folklore of Japan. This version was adapted by Salley Fisher from the translation by Donald Keene. (Keene's original translation, "The Tale of the Bamboo Cutter," appeared in *Monumenta Nipponica* 11, no. 4 [1956]: 1–27.) This Metropolitan Museum publication is a sumptuous book, with full-page color illustrations reproduced from an eighteenth-century Japanese scroll of the tale.

    An old bamboo cutter finds a tiny luminescent girl in a stalk of bamboo. He brings her home, and he and his wife raise the girl as their own child. They name her Kaguyahime, the Shining Princess. She rapidly grows into a beautiful young woman. Five noble suitors try to obtain Kaguyahime's hand in marriage, but she assigns each of them an impossible task to perform before she will consider their proposals. The tasks are to find the begging bowl of the Buddha, to obtain a branch from the jewel-bearing tree of paradise, to make a robe from the magic fire-resistant fur of the Chinese fire rats, to secure a five-colored jewel from the head of a dragon, and to bring the magical charm from the body of a sparrow, which ensures easy childbirth. Each of the suitors fails at his assigned task. Kaguyahime is then courted by the emperor himself. She demonstrates to him that she is a supernatural being from the moon. Later she announces to her human parents that she must soon return to her celestial home. Despite the emperor's attempts to keep Kaguyahime on earth, she is taken away by an escort of men from the moon. Kaguyahime writes her farewell poem to the emperor and sends it to him with a jar of the elixir of immortality. The emperor decides that he does not wish to become immortal, since he must spend his entire life without Kaguyahime. He writes his own farewell poem to her, sends the poem and the elixir to the top of Mount Fuji, and has them set afire. The smoke from this supernatural fire is said to be still rising from the top of the mountain.

101. Tomita, Kumasaku, and Lee, G. Ambrose. *Japanese Treasure Tales.* London: Yamanaka, 1906.

The stories in this collection are meant to explain folklore motifs that often appear in Japanese art. Each tale has a corresponding photograph of a sword guard and/or netsuke.

Rochishin: Rochishin is an ex-priest who joins a very successful band of robbers.

Tadamori and the Oil Thief: At a certain temple, Tadamori sees a sinister creature stealing lamp oil, but on closer inspection it proves to be a strangely done-up priest who is filling the lamps on his regular rounds.

Kikujido, or The Chrysanthemum Boy: The emperor's favorite page is banished for accidentally kicking the emperor's pillow. The emperor gives the boy two Buddhist verses of great power, which the boy later writes onto the leaves of a chrysanthemum plant.

Ono Tofu and the Frog: A man who has very poor penmanship sees a frog struggle for a long time to jump onto a tree. Inspired by the frog's example, the man continues to work on his writing and becomes a renowned calligrapher.

Shoki and the Demon: A man who is unable to attain the position to which he aspires kills himself in despair, but he is posthumously awarded the desired titles by the emperor. Generations later, when the descendant emperor is haunted by a demon, the man's spirit returns to protect the emperor.

Rosei: A poor man who wishes to become wealthy has a dream in which he becomes a great king. He realizes that any man's life is really just a dream that will soon end, so he returns to his poor house, contented.

Shiro and the Boar: When a wild boar rushes upon the shogun Yoritomo, his retainer Shiro tackles the beast and kills it.

Koufu and the Saké Shop: A poor man dreams that he will become rich if he starts a saké shop. The man's shop is visited often by a mysterious patron who proves to be a shōjō.

The Lady Yokihi: The emperor is so infatuated with Lady Yokihi that he ignores his duties. His subjects rise up in rebellion and kill Yokihi. Later the emperor speaks with the lady through a medium and then kills himself.

Saburo and the Fisherman: The Genji general Saburo is informed of a place on a certain river that is shallow enough for the Genji army to ford without ships. Saburo kills the informant, but after the war he returns to the site and enshrines the man's spirit.

A Kamakura Judge: The judge Fujitsuna is renowned for his honesty.

Tenaga and Ashinaga: Tenaga is the land of long-armed people, and Ashinaga is the land of long-legged people.

Tsuna and the Beautiful Lady: Watanabe Tsuna meets a young woman late at night, but she proves to be a demon in disguise.

Choun and Ato: The warrior Choun saves the emperor's son Ato from the enemy when the boy is separated from his father during a battle.

The Sennin and the Lady Sendara: A magician traps all the dragons in a rock, causing a great drought. Lady Sendara is sent to seduce the magician, thus robbing him of his magic powers and freeing the dragons.

Sennin: Sennin were mountain ascetics who possessed magic powers.

Omori Hikohichi: Hikohichi meets a beautiful young woman late at night, but she proves to be a demon.

The Ama and the Jewel: When a jewel is stolen by the Dragon King of the Sea, a diving woman agrees to recover it for the emperor on the condition that her child be made the heir of a certain lord who was the boy's father.

Chorio: The faithful minister Chorio helps a certain warlord become emperor, defeating a rival who had killed Chorio's previous lord.

Yorimasa's Lucky Shot: The archer Yorimasa shoots a fantastic creature that had hovered in a black cloud over the Imperial Palace and caused the emperor to fall ill.

Soga Goro and Asashina Saburo: During a somewhat raucous party, two samurai engage in a tug-of-war, which results in the armor of one man being torn asunder.

Kojima Takanori: A warrior disguises himself as a peasant and writes a poem for the imprisoned Emperor Godaigo on a tree outside the emperor's rooms.

Kidomaru: Kidomaru is a very strong robber. He is captured by the brother of the warrior Raiko, and Raiko warns his brother not to let the man escape. Kidomaru does escape and bears a grudge against Raiko, trying to kill him in an ambush, but Kidomaru is killed by Raiko's guards.

The Blind Tortoise: A miraculous turtle has a single eye on its underside and can see the sun only under very special conditions once every 3,000 years.

Manzai: Certain singers perform songs called Manzai, which end with words meaning "ten thousand years' comfort."

Takeda Shingen and Uyesugi Kenshin: See entry 75, tale 20.

Ujigawa: See entry 75, tale 10.

Yojo: Although he is captured several times, the retainer Yojo continues to try to kill the victorious daimyo who had killed Yojo's previous lord.

Gentoku's Ride: When he realizes that he has stumbled into an ambush, Gentoku drives his horse into a swollen river and manages to escape.

Nitta Yoshisada at Inamuraga Saki Harbor: During a battle to save Emperor Godaigo, Yoshisada comes to the bay near Kamakura, but has no boats with which to cross the water. He prays to the gods for help, and during the night the tide recedes so far that the sand of the ocean floor is exposed and the troops are able to cross by foot.

Shun Kwan: See entry 83, chapter 3 (Tales of the Heike), tale 2.

Kioyu and Sofu: The emperor offers to make the ascetic Kioyu his successor, but the ascetic refuses. He goes to a waterfall to wash the evil left by what he heard out of his ears. He meets his friend Sofu, also an ascetic, who has brought his ox to drink from the stream. He refuses to let the animal drink the water that had been contaminated by the earthly temptation.

Ono-no-Komachi: Komachi was a brilliant poetess of the Heian era who was also renowned for her great beauty.

102. Uchida, Yoshiko. *The Dancing Kettle and Other Japanese Folk Tales*. New York: Harcourt, Brace, 1949.

This is a collection of 14 beautifully written tales. The stories are wonderful for a storyteller to read aloud to a group or for an older student to read alone. Each tale has one full-page black-and-white illustration by Richard C. Jones.

Uchida's other two anthologies (entries 103 and 104) are also excellent.

1. The Dancing Kettle: See entry 112.
2. Urashima Tarō and the Princess of the Sea: See entry 134.
3. The Eight Headed Dragon: See entry 117.
4. The Old Man with the Bump: See entry 128.
5. The Rabbit and the Crocodiles: See entry 136.
6. The Jewels of the Sea: See entry 122.
7. The Princess of Light: See entry 100.
8. The Wedding of the Mouse: See entry 126.
9. Momotarō: Boy-of-the-Peach: See entry 125.
10. The Piece of Straw: See entry 130.
11. The Tongue-cut Sparrow: See entry 133.
12. The Princess and the Fisherman: A fisherman catches a clam that mysteriously grows very large, then opens to reveal a beautiful maiden. She goes to live with the fisherman and his mother, who become wealthy from all the presents given to them by people who want to see the maiden. Finally the maiden weaves a rich cloth that the fisherman sells to a celestial being. The maiden then reveals that she had been sent to bring fortune to these two people who had always been so honest. She ascends to the heavens.
13. The Old Man of the Flowers: See entry 129.
14. Isunboshi, the One-Inch Lad: See entry 118.

103. Uchida, Yoshiko. *The Magic Listening Cap*. New York: Harcourt, Brace, 1955.

This is a collection of 14 beautifully written tales. The stories are wonderful for a storyteller to read aloud to a group or for an older student to read alone. Each tale has one full-page black-and-white illustration by Uchida.

Uchida's other two anthologies (entries 102 and 104) are also excellent.

1. The Magic Listening Cap: See entry 87, tale 8.

2. The Terrible Leak: See entry 121.

3. The Wrestling Match of the Two Buddhas: A rich man sets his gold Buddha to a wrestling match with a wooden Buddha owned by a servant. The rich man's house and property are the prize. The wooden Buddha wins the contest because the servant had worshiped it three times a day, giving it great strength, while the rich man never worshiped his statue.

4. The Magic Mortar: See entry 123.

5. The Tubmaker Who Flew to the Sky: A hoop snaps while a tubmaker is making a barrel, striking the man so hard that he flies up to a cloud on which the Thunder God is standing. The god engages the man's help in making some rain, but in the excitement, the man slips from the cloud and lands on the top of a huge tree. Eventually he is forced to jump into a "safety net" held by some villagers.

6. Three Tests for the Prince: A prince comes to ask for the hand of Susano's daughter in marriage, but the god tries three times to kill the prince. Through the help of the god's daughter and a field mouse, the prince survives, and he and the princess eventually flee from Susano's palace.

7. The Deer of Five Colors: A man's life is saved by a deer with a five-colored coat, but the only reward that the animal asks is that the man never reveal the deer's existence. When the lord of the province offers a great reward for the capture of a deer with a five-colored coat, the man treacherously leads the lord's forces to the deer. When the deer tells the lord about having saved the man's life, the deer is set free and the man is punished.

8. The Golden Axe: An honest man accidentally drops his old steel ax into a pond. The goddess of the pond appears holding a gold ax and asks the man if it is his. He says no, and she gives him both his own ax and the golden ax. A greedy neighbor tries to duplicate the honest man's fortune, but when the goddess appears, he claims that the gold ax is his. The goddess disappears, and the evil man not only does not receive the gold ax, he loses his own steel ax.

9. The Mountain Witch and the Peddler: A peddler meets a mountain-witch on his way to the village and in his eagerness to escape he mistakenly hides in her house. He manages to trap the witch in a kettle and burns her to death.

10. The Man Who Bought a Dream: See entry 97, tale 45.

11. The Fox and the Bear: Twice the fox and bear agree to grow food together, and twice the fox manages to trick the bear into doing most of the work while the fox takes all the crops. Then the fox tricks the bear into getting stung by a hive of bees. In revenge the bear tricks the fox into tying its tail to that of a horse and being dragged around a field.

12. The Tiny God: A tiny god comes to the Japanese god Okuninushi and teaches him various skills. After the tiny god leaves Japan, Okuninushi waits on the beach for his return until a messenger comes from the tiny god telling him to stop waiting and go help his people.

13. The Rice Cake that Rolled Away: A man follows a rice cake that rolls away until it comes to a statue of Jizō. The statue tells the man to climb onto its head. A group of demons will come to gamble, and after they have been there for a while, the man should crow like a cock. The man does as the statue says, and the demons think that dawn is breaking. They run off, leaving all their gold, which the man brings home. The man's greedy neighbor tries to duplicate the good man's fortune, but he is discovered by the demons and beaten.

14. The Grateful Stork: See entry 115.

104. Uchida, Yoshiko. *The Sea of Gold and Other Tales from Japan*. New York: Charles Scribner's, 1965.

This is a collection of 12 beautifully written tales. The stories are excellent for a storyteller to read aloud or for an older child to read alone. Each story has one full-page black-and-white illustration by Marianne Yamaguchi. See also Uchida's other two anthologies (entries 102 and 103).

1. The Sea of Gold: Hikoichi is such a fool that he cannot even learn to be a fisherman. Instead he becomes a cook on a fishing boat. All the people call him stupid, but he is really kind and gentle. Since he cannot keep the leftover food from the meals on board ship, Hikoichi throws it overboard every night, inviting the fish to come and eat and thanking them for their bountiful harvest. After many years, Hikoichi wakes up one night to find all the water gone from the ocean. He fills a bucket with the beautiful sand from the ocean floor. The "sand" proves to be pure gold, which the King of the Sea has given to Hikoichi in reward for his patience and kindness.

2. The Grateful Monkey's Secret: A poor wine seller helps a monkey whose hand had been caught by a crab. After the man bandages the monkey's paw, the monkey leads him to a magic pool in the mountains whose "water" is actually fine wine. The man then begins to take wine from this pool every day and is able to make a decent living, since this new source of wine is free. The pool gives him just enough wine to sell two large jars a day, teaching him that he must not be too greedy.

3. The Tengu's Magic Nose Fan: The good-for-nothing gambler Kotaro meets a tengu in the forest. The tengu exchanges his magic fan for Kotaro's dice. The fan will make any person's nose longer if fanned one way, and shorter if fanned the other way. Kotaro secretly makes the nose of a wealthy man's daughter a foot long. The father promises his daughter's hand in marriage to anyone who can cure her. Kotaro uses his fan to restore her nose to its normal size. After living in great luxury for a while, Kotaro goes out to his garden one day and begins fanning himself unconsciously with the magic fan. His nose grows so long that it reaches to heaven, where the people are building a bridge. They use Kotaro's nose as one of the pilings. Kotaro frantically fans himself to make his nose shorter, and he is pulled up into the sky. Halfway to heaven, he drops the fan and is left hanging between heaven and earth forever.

4. The Magic Purse of the Swamp Maiden: A poor farmer sets out on a pilgrimage to Ise. On the way he is lured into the Black Swamp, where he meets a mysterious young woman who asks him to deliver a letter to her parents in the Red Swamp. After much hesitation, the farmer agrees. The woman gives him a magic purse filled with gold. If a single gold coin is left in the purse overnight, by the morning the purse will be filled with gold. The farmer fulfills his promise and delivers the letter, whereupon the girl's parents give him even more gold. Because of his bravery and his honesty, he is now a rich man.

5. The Two Foolish Cats: Two cats are the best of friends. One day the larger cat finds a small rice cake, and the smaller cat finds a large rice cake. They begin to fight over who should eat which cake. Finally they go to a wise monkey and ask him to settle the argument. The monkey weighs the two cakes on a scale and begins to bite pieces from each to make them weigh the same, until the monkey eats up both cakes completely. The monkey then tells the cats that they have nothing further to argue about since both cakes are gone.

6. The Wise Old Woman: The young lord of a province orders that all the old people of the area be abandoned in the mountains, but a young farmer hides his old mother in a subterranean room in his house. Later the lord asks that three impossible tasks be performed: to make 1,000 ropes of ashes, to thread a single silk thread through a curved hole bent seven times, and to make a self-sounding drum. The old mother tells her son how to perform these tasks. When the lord asks the farmer how he obtained such wisdom, the farmer reveals that the knowledge is actually that of his aged mother. The lord decrees that old people will no longer be abandoned.

7. The Ogre Who Built a Bridge: A carpenter is unable to build a bridge across a raging river. Suddenly a huge ogre appears who says that he will build the bridge in exchange for the carpenter's eyeballs. The carpenter will be able to keep his eyes if he can guess the ogre's name in one day. The carpenter hears some children singing a nursery rhyme

about the bridge that was built by Oni-roku in exchange for a carpenter's eyes; thus the carpenter learns that the ogre's name is Oni-roku.

8. New Year's Hats for the Statues: An old man goes out to sell some reed hats so that he can buy food for the New Year's celebration, but he is unable to sell anything. He stumbles home through a raging snowstorm and comes upon six statues of Jizō standing exposed to the storm. The man takes his sedge hats and places them on the statues' heads, but he is short one hat. He unhesitatingly removes his own hat and places it upon the last statue. During the night, the six statues come to the old man's house and leave six sacks filled with food.

9. Gombei and the Wild Ducks: Greedy Gombei always traps just one duck a day, but once he tries to trap 100 ducks at once. The ducks are stronger than Gombei, and when they fly away, Gombei is carried into the sky holding the ends of 100 snares. Miraculously Gombei is transformed into a wild duck. But he is quickly captured in a snare and realizes how cruel it is to catch wild birds. Then Gombei becomes a man again. He gives up hunting and becomes a farmer.

10. The Wonderful Talking Bowl: A man sends his three sons out into the world for three years, telling them that he will leave his house and wealth to the one who learns the best skill. The oldest son becomes an expert archer, the second son becomes an expert weaver of hats, but the third son spends his three years helping a poor old woman. The woman gives the youngest son a magic talking bowl, which instructs the young man to tell his father that he has become an expert thief. When the man's uncle hears this, he challenges the youngest son to steal the moneybox from his house. With the help of the talking bowl, the youngest son succeeds in taking his rich uncle's fortune.

11. The Terrible Black Snake's Revenge: A man named Badger meets a huge snake that has been plaguing a village. The snake thinks that the man actually is a magic badger, and he confides that the thing he is most frightened of is hot melted tar. Badger says that he is afraid of gold. Badger tells the villagers how they can rid themselves of the snake. They attack the snake with the tar, but the snake escapes. Later the snake returns to take his revenge on Badger for betraying his confidence, and he pours a pile of gold into Badger's house.

12. Koichi and the Mountain God: Young woodcutter Koichi brings his lunch to the mountains every day, but it is always eaten by a strange old man. Koichi does not complain, and the man finally reveals that he is the God of the Mountain. He tells Koichi to make a pilgrimage to Tenjiku and to do whatever the people he meets along the way tell him. Koichi meets three people: a wealthy man who wishes to know how to cure his sick daughter, a man who wishes to know why two of his cherry trees never bloom, and a ghost who wishes to know how she can attain peace. When Koichi reaches the temple, he finds the God of the Mountain waiting for him. He tells Koichi the three solutions, the results of which make Koichi a rich man.

105. Ury, Marian. *Tales of Times Now Past: Sixty-two Stories from a Medieval Japanese Collection*. Berkeley: University of California Press, 1979.

These translations are of tales from the *Konjaku monogatari*. The stories include samples from each of the extant books of the *Konjaku* and are representative of the wide variety of story found in the collection. Ury's book begins with a very good introduction, and each story has notes explaining such things as names, unusual terms, and obscure phrases. There is also a selected bibliography that lists Japanese texts and relevant Western-language works.

1. How Sākyamuni Tathāgata Came to Dwell in the World of Men
2. How Sākyamuni Preached the Dharma to Five Bhikshus
3. How the Buddha Entered a City of the Brahmans to Beg Food
4. How the Buddha Converted Nanda and Caused Him to Renounce Secular Life
5. About the Death of the Buddha's Father, King Śuddhodana
6. How a God Heard the Dharma and Obtained the Clear Vision of the Dharma Eye
7. About King Prasenajit's Daughter Ugly Adamantina
8. What the Buddha Said to the Sangha When He Was about to Enter Nirvana
9. How Bodhidharma of India Went to This Place and That Observing the Devotions of the Monks
10. How Nāgārjuna, while a Layman, Made a Charm for Invisibility
11. How Two Brothers, Men of India, Carried Gold through the Mountains
12. How a Man for Love of His Child Went to King Yama's Palace
13. How a King Went to the Mountains to Hunt Deer and Was Robbed of His Daughter by a Lion
14. How the Three Beasts Practiced the Way of the Bodhisattva and the Rabbit Roasted Himself
15. How a Novice of the K'ung-kuan Ssu in China Viewed the Lotus-Matrix World and Returned to Life
16. How Sun Hsuan-te Copied the Wreath Sutra
17. How a Nun of Ho-tung in China Chanted the Lotus Sutra and How the Text She Read from Was Altered
18. How Someone in Lu-chou Killed a Neighbor and Was Not Punished
19. How Mo Yeh of China Made a Sword and Presented It to the King and How His Son, Broad-of-Brow, Was Killed
20. How Hou Ku Tricked His Father and Prevented an Unfilial Act
21. How Shih-huang of Ch'in Governed from His Palace at Hsien-yang
22. How Wu Chao-hsiao of China Saw a Poem on the Water and Loved Its Author

23. How Chuang Tzu Went to Someone's House and How His Host Killed a Goose to Serve with the Wine
24. How Chuang Tzu Observed the Behavior of Dumb Creatures and Fled
25. How E no Ubasoku Recited Spells and Employed Demonic Deities
26. How the Venerable Dōshō Went to China, Was Transmitted the Hossō Teachings, and Returned Home
27. How a Government Clerk of Higo Province Escaped a Rakshasa
28. How the Sutra Chanter Shunchō Exhibited the Lotus Sutra's Efficacy
29. About Two Men in Izumo Province, Reciters of the Wreath and Lotus Sutras
30. How a Monk of the Dōjōji in the Province of Kii Copied the Lotus Sutra and Brought Salvation to Serpents
31. About a Man Who Copied the Lotus Sutra to Save the Soul of a Fox
32. How a Priest of Chinzei Who Ate Carrion Was Reborn in Paradise
33. How Kaya no Yoshifuji, of Bitchū Province, Became the Husband of a Fox and Was Saved by Kannon
34. How Travelers from Chinzei, through Kannon's Aid, Escaped Being Killed by Bandits
35. How an Invisible Man Regained Corporeal Form through Kannon's Aid
36. About a Monk Who Prayed to Meet a Manifestation of the Bodhisattva Jizō
37. How Ki no Mochikata Worshiped Jizō and Benefited from His Favor
38. How a Monk through Bishamonten's Aid Begot Gold and Obtained a Means of Support
39. How a Falconer in the Western Part of the Capital Renounced Secular Life Because of a Dream
40. About the Monk Whose Name Was Entered on a Petition to the God of Mount T'ai to Take the Place of His Master
41. How Shinkai, a Monk of Mount Hiei, Suffered Retribution in This Present Life for Jealousy
42. How Great Minister Tokihira Got Major Counsellor Kunitsune's Wife
43. How Taira no Munetsune, Lieutenant of the Left Division of the Outer Palace Guards, Escorted High Priest Myōson
44. How Prince Kaya Made a Doll and Set It Up in the Rice Fields
45. How Minamoto no Hiromasa Ason Went to the Blind Man's House at Ōsaka
46. How the Lute Genjō Was Snatched by an Oni

47. How Fujiwara no Chikataka's Son Was Taken Hostage by a Robber and Freed through Yorinobu's Persuasion
48. How Men of Kaga Province Who Went to an Island Where a Snake Was Warring with a Centipede Aided the Snake and Settled in the Island
49. How a Woman Who Was Bearing a Child Went to South Yamashina, Encountered an Oni, and Escaped
50. How a Hunter's Mother Became an Oni and Tried to Devour Her Children
51. About the Two Wet-Nurses in the House of Middle Captain Masamichi Who Looked Exactly Alike
52. How the Fox of Kōyagawa Turned into a Woman and Rode on Horses' Croups
53. How Tamemori, the Governor of Echizen, Subdued the Junior Officers of the Six Companies of the Guards
54. How Kaishu, the Intendant of Gion, Was Given a Fee for Chanting the Sutras
55. How Fujiwara no Nobutada, Governor of Shinano, Took a Tumble at Misaka
56. How a Thief Climbed to the Upper Story of Rashō Gate and Saw a Corpse
57. How a Man Who Was Accompanying His Wife to Tanba Province Got Trussed Up at Ōeyama
58. How a Beggar Who Lived in the Area South of Kiyomizu Used a Woman to Lure Men into His House and Kill Them
59. How a Poor Man Left His Wife, and How She Became the Wife of the Governor of Settsu
60. How the Minor Controller of the Right Moroie no Ason Encountered a Woman and Died
61. About the Old Woman Who Sold Fish at the Headquarters of the Crown Prince's Guard
62. About the Great Oak in Kurumoto District in Ōmi Province

106. Wheeler, Post. *Tales from the Japanese Storytellers.* Edited by H. G. Henderson. New York: Japan Society, 1964.

Wheeler's original work was entitled *Hō dan zō* 放談雑 and comprised ten complete volumes. Wheeler collected the stories from the *hanashika* 話家, public storytellers. Most of the tales are from the Tokugawa era. Unfortunately, Wheeler's monumental work has never been published; Henderson's introduction to this edition explains the curious circumstances surrounding this unusual work. This edition presents 24 stories selected and edited by Henderson.

Shotoku Taishi and Princess Parsley: A girl is so busy gathering wild parsley to make soup for her sick and aged mother that she does not bow to the procession of Prince Shotoku when it passes. The prince is so moved by the girl's filial piety that he takes her as one of his wives.

The Daimyo and the Bullocks: A daimyo is in the habit of dressing as a peasant and going among his people to learn their true opinion of him. One day he sees a man plowing with two bullocks and asks him which of the two is better. The man takes him a far distance from the bullocks and then answers his question, saying that a person must not criticize anyone within his hearing. Thus the daimyo realizes that the man has recognized him.

The Sagacious Monkey and the Boar: See entry 89, tale 12.

The Subchaplin and Kiyomori's Concubine: Kiyomori's favorite concubine attempts to mortify a young priest who refuses to yield to her charms, but the priest addresses such a skillful sermon on the transience of beauty to Kiyomori and his company that it is the concubine who loses favor.

Kyusuke the Honest: A man is driven from his home by his stepmother. He takes service in the house of the headman of a distant village. For eight years he works industriously and saves 100 ryō to give to his father. On his journey back to his father's home, he is robbed of his money and fine sword by a bandit who gives him an old rusted sword in exchange. The sword proves to be an antique masterpiece worth 900 ryō. The man returns to the robber's home to give him part of the money, whereupon he learns that the robber is actually his long-lost elder brother. The man then goes to his father and buys the old man a large rice field. He finally returns to the home of his former employer who asks the honest man to become his son-in-law and heir.

The Crows and the Archers: Three crow fledglings are asked what they fear most. The first says an arrow, and the second says a skilled archer. But the third fledgling says the unskilled archer is the most dangerous. With a skilled archer one can jump to one side when one hears the bowstring, but with an unskilled archer one has no idea where the arrow will go.

The Painter and the Shirabyoshi: A traveler seeks shelter in the hut of a beautiful woman. During the night the man is awakened and sees the woman dancing skillfully before a statue of Kannon on a memorial altar. The woman tells him that she was a renowned shirabyoshi dancer who left the world because she did not wish to embarrass her high-born lover, but her lover went to search for her and died on his journey. She now dances nightly before his memorial tablet for the repose of his soul. Years later, after the man has become a famous painter, an old woman comes to his mansion. She proves to be the shirabyoshi dancer, and the man paints a portrait of her as she looked as a young woman performing her dance.

Winning without Hands: A bullying samurai is about to kill a workman for an inadvertent offense committed on a crowded barge, but the samurai Bokuden counsels mercy. The bully challenges Bokuden to a duel and jumps off the barge onto an isolated inlet. Bokuden, who has said that he was a master of the winning-without-hands school of swordsmanship, quickly pushes the barge off the inlet, stranding the bully.

The Fox in the Brothel: A woodcutter saves a fox from a snare. The fox comes to him in the guise of a beautiful maiden and convinces the man to sell her to a brothel. The fox-woman then pretends to commit suicide. The man then goes to buy back her contract and is paid a large sum of money for the death of his "daughter." The fox next comes and offers to become the man's wife, but he refuses since it is wrong for a human knowingly to marry a fox. Because of the man's virtue, the fox spirit is released from her entrapment in the animal world.

The Bonze's Three Prescriptions: A man has such unqualified faith in the wisdom of a certain bonze that the bonze cannot stand to disappoint him. Twice the man becomes sick and asks the bonze his prescription, and twice the bonze tells him to make a brew of wisteria vines and drink it. Both times the man is cured. Then the man's horse disappears, and the man asks the bonze how to get it back. The wearied bonze again says he should make a brew of wisteria leaves, but this time give it to the horse to drink. The ever-faithful man goes into the mountains to search for wisteria vines and finds his horse.

Taiko-sama's Eight Afterthoughts: When a humble warrior chastises Taiko Hideyoshi for frivolity, the Taiko at first orders that the warrior be cruelly executed. But as he thinks further on the matter, the Taiko revises his decision eight times until he finally decides that the man should be rewarded for his loyalty and his great courage in speaking out.

Lord Shunzen and the Talking Horse: After Lord Shunzen has worked some repairs on a certain shrine, his horse begins to talk. A diviner shows that it is due to the curse of a robber who had been hiding in a tunnel beneath the shrine and who had inadvertently been walled in by the shrine repairs.

The Straw-Hat Temple: A noblewoman who has fallen to poverty prays daily to a statue of Kannon whose temple had been burned down so that the statue is exposed to the elements. One day it begins to rain, and the woman removes her straw hat and places it on the statue. A nobleman is passing by and sees this act of piety. Moved by the woman's goodness, he takes her as his wife. He later rebuilds the temple.

Jinnai and the Bonze Dentatsu: The robber Jinnai tricks the bonze Dentatsu into safely escorting the robber across a provincial border and into providing a cloak of respectability while the robber ambushes a large shipment of gold headed for the provincial government. Jinnai for his turn watches out for the bonze's safety on the road and finally gives him a large contribution for his temple.

Ooka and the Lawless Stripling: Although fishing in the sacred ponds at Ise is strictly forbidden, the Lord of Kii's son constantly violates this law. Ooka has the boy and his companions arrested, and during the course of their trial he says that he knows this boy cannot be the lord's son, since the lord is an upright man and his son would have the pride that comes from knowing he will soon inherit one of the highest positions in the land. The boy is humbled enough by this lecture to give up his evil habits.

Ooka and the Pilfered Tachibana Fruit: When two oranges are missing from an order that Ooka had sent his most trusted servant to fetch, the man is put to torture before all the judges in Ooka's district. The man finally confesses to the crime. Ooka then reveals that he himself had stolen the fruit and had engaged his servant in this way to show that many innocent men were wrongfully forced to confess guilt when put to torture. After that, torture was no longer used in Ooka's districts.

Ooka and the Pickpockets: Ooka is commissioned to rid the city of its pickpockets. He issues a decree saying that henceforth pickpockets must be licensed and that each pickpocket must carry his license on his person at all times. Any pickpocket who is arrested for not having a license will be put to death. All the pickpockets sign the government roster for their license, whereupon they learn that the "license" is a three-foot red-painted wooded sign that says "Legally Sanctioned Pickpocket." All the pickpockets then leave the city, since they are now known to the authorities and could not possibly ply their trade successfully while wearing the sign.

Ooka and the Arithmeticians: The shogun asks Ooka to recommend one of three men as controller. Ooka asks each of the men a trivially simple calculation. The first two men answer immediately, but the third man, although he was well able to figure the answer in his head, nevertheless checks his calculation on an abacus. This man is made controller.

Ooka and the Carpenter-Convert: A group of adherents of the Hokke sect of Buddhism try to convert a carpenter who believes in the Jodo sect. They promise him increased wealth, wisdom, comfort, and they also give him ten ryō. The man stays with the Hokke sect for six months, then he returns to the Jodo sect. The Hokke sect sues the carpenter for return of their ten ryō. The man says that they had promised him increased wealth, wisdom, and comfort, none of which he received. Ooka decrees that since the man had chanted the invocation of the Hokke sect about 20,000 times in the past six months, the Hokke followers can have their ten ryō back if they will chant the invocation of the Jodo sect 20,000 times. They refuse, and the carpenter happily keeps his ten ryō.

Ooka and the Thumb-Tied Moneylender: A moneylender swindles a woman of 500 ryō. After ten years of trying to regain her fortune, the woman goes mad and sets the man's house on fire. She is captured and condemned to death for arson. Ooka, realizing that the moneylender had indeed stolen the woman's money, has the man's thumbs tied together as a charm to refresh his memory. The man is unable to do anything for himself, and he finally admits that he had the woman's money. Ooka computes all the interest that the moneylender owes the woman for holding the money for ten years. He then decrees that the moneylender will pay her a certain amount per year until the woman is 99 years old, at which time her death sentence can be imposed.

The Three Bridges: While crossing a bridge a man sees someone drowning in the river. He saves the man and learns that it is his drunkard nephew. The man upbraids the nephew, but the nephew retorts that he has come to this danger through the uncle's own advice: the man drank half as much wine that night, just as the uncle had requested. Usually after a night of drinking, the man would see three bridges spanning the river and would cross the middle one safely. But this evening he saw only two and chose the wrong one, falling into the river and nearly drowning.

Ii Naoto and His Wife Osada: The young samurai Ii Naoto lives such a life of dissipation that he loses both his martial skills and his family's fortune. His wife challenges him to a fencing match and beats him so badly that he is humiliated into giving up his evil ways and begins to study fencing under an expert master. Realizing that his wife had done this out of love for him, he returns home, and the two live the rest of their days together in happiness.

The Tale of Chobei: Chobei offers to hire out his brainpower to the rich merchant Kibun. Chobei figures out a way to build a great reservoir where wood can safely be stored against fire. When a fire does indeed break out in the city, Chobei takes a fortune of Kibun's money and uses it to set up shelters for homeless and injured people and to provide rice for all those who need it. After the emergency, Kibun makes back far more money than was spent in this charitable operation, but his fame as a benefactor and the gratitude of the people thus helped remain unabated.

The "How Now!" Teacup: A connoisseur of teacups stops at a teahouse and is appalled by a cup of such poor quality that it seeps tea even though it has no crack. A man who recognizes the connoisseur mistakes his careful examination of the cup as a recognition of the cup's great value. Through a series of events, the cup passes from owner to owner, and due to the presumed admiration of the great master becomes more and more valued until it is finally acquired by the wealthiest daimyo in Japan.

107. Whitehorn, Alan Leslie. *Wonder Tales of Old Japan*. London: T. C. & E. C. Jack, 1911.

1. Momotarō: See entry 125.
2. The Wonderful Tea Kettle: See entry 112.
3. Why the Jellyfish Has No Shell: See entry 137.
4. A Wonderful Bell
5. The Idol and the Whale: See entry 73, tale 19.
6. The Great Queen

7. The Mirror of Matsuyama: See entry 124(a).
8. The Story of the Monkey and the Crab: See entry 113.
9. The Cunning Monkey and the Boar: See entry 89, tale 12.
10. The White Rabbit and the Crocodiles: See entry 136.
11. The Story of Urashima, the Fisher Boy: See entry 134.
12. The Tongue-cut Sparrow: See entry 133.
13. Kachi Kachi Yama, or the Crackling Mountain: See entry 114.
14. The Old Man Who Made Withered Trees to Blossom: See entry 129.
15. The Old Man with the Wen: See entry 128.
16. The Story of Lazy Taro: See entry 90, tale 10.
17. The Story of Kintaro, the Strong Boy: See entry 120.
18. Hidesato of the Rice Bale: See entry 127.
19. The Travels of Two Frogs: See entry 73, tale 2.
20. Tamanoi, or the Jewel Spring: See entry 122.
21. The Story of Princess Hotaru

108. Williston, Teresa Peirce. *Japanese Fairy Tales*. New York: Rand McNally, 1904.

This collection contains Williston's rewritten versions of eight tales. There are color illustrations on most of the pages of text and eight full-page color illustrations. Each page of text is surrounded by a picture border in shades of pale green-gray. Illustrations are by Sanchi Ogawa.

The Wonderful Kettle: See entry 112.
The Woodcutter's Saké: A woodcutter spares the life of a badger. In gratitude the badger shows the man a magic waterfall that gives pure saké to the woodcutter, but only regular water to anyone else.
The Mirror of Matsuyama: See entry 124(a).
The Eight Headed Serpent: See entry 117.
The Stolen Charm: A boy is given a magic charm by the fairy of the sea foam. When the charm is stolen by a demon, the boy falls seriously ill. The boy's pet fox cub and puppy set out to recover the charm, and with the help of a rat they meet along the way succeed in their quest.
Urashima: See entry 134.
The Tongue-cut Sparrow: See entry 133.
Shippei Taro: See entry 77, tale 7.

109. Yanagita, Kunio. *Japanese Folk Tales*. Translated by Fanny Hagin Mayer. Tokyo: Tokyo News Service, 1954. *Japanese Folk Tales: A Revised Selection*. Translated by Fanny Hagin Mayer. Tokyo: Tokyo News Service, 1966; reprint edition Taipei: Oriental Cultural Service, 1972.

The first work is a translation of Yanagita's *Nippon no mukashibanashi*, and the second work is a translation of his *Nippon no mukashibana-*

shi kaiteihan. (For information on the Japanese editions, see A}
A.) Both translations are delights to read and are invaluable
books of Japanese folktales. Because the contents of the two works are so
different, they are annotated separately.

A. Japanese Folk Tales

Mayer's original translation appeared in *Folklore Studies* (9, no. 2
[1952]) and was revised for the Tokyo News Service printing.

1. Why the Monkey's Tail Is Short: The bear tricks the monkey
into using his tail as a fishing line through a hole in the ice of a frozen
lake. When the monkey tries to pull his tail out of the water, it is frozen
solid and snaps off.

2. Why the Jellyfish Has No Bones: See entry 137.

3. The Sparrow and the Woodpecker: When the sparrow and the
woodpecker hear that their mother is dying, the sparrow flies home
without giving a thought to her appearance, while the woodpecker does
not leave until she has finished dressing herself very finely. That is why
the sparrow is plain but can eat the grains of the field, while the woodpecker is beautiful, but must bang on trees and eat insects.

4. The Pigeon's Obedience to His Mother: The pigeon never
obeys his mother. When she is dying, she asks to be buried by the river,
thinking that he will thus bury her in the mountains, but he repents of
his past disobedience and buries her by the river. When it rains, he
runs around frantically, worried that the grave will wash away.

5. The Cuckoo Brothers: An evil older brother wrongfully kills
his younger brother. When he realizes his mistake, he is so filled with
remorse that he becomes a cuckoo. The cuckoo's sound is the older
brother calling to his younger brother's spirit.

6. The Cuckoo and the Shrike: The shrike owes the cuckoo
money. The cuckoo is always flying around demanding payment from
the shrike, while the shrike is always trying to pacify the cuckoo.

7. The Owl Dyer: When the dandyish crow asks the owl to dye
him a unique suit, the owl dyes him a suit that is completely black.

8. The Cicada and the Daishi Sama: A farmer turns a beggar away
from his house and then realizes that it was Kobo Daishi. The farmer
runs out and tries to call the saint back, until the farmer finally turns
into the shrilly calling cicada.

9. The Wren Counted among the Hawks: A wren is accepted into
a band of hawks after he kills a wild boar by flying into the animal's ear
and causing it to run into a tree. One of the hawks then tries to kill two
boars at once, but when he grabs them with his talons, the boars run off
in opposite directions and tear the hawk apart.

10. The Badger and the Mudsnail: The badger and the mudsnail
run a race. The snail attaches to the badger's tail. When the badger
reaches the finish line, he turns around to see where the snail is. The
snail falls off but is the winner.

11. The Badger, the Monkey, and the Otter: The three animals find some items on the road and divide them among them. The badger manages to give the monkey and otter useless things, while keeping some beans for himself. Later the badger pretends to have gotten sick from eating the beans.

12. The Monkey, the Cat, and the Rat: A man is shot when he tries to prevent a hunter from killing a monkey. The monkey gives the man a magic coin that makes him rich. When it is stolen by an evil neighbor, the man tells his cat that she must find it or be killed. The cat catches a rat and tells him that he must find it or be killed. The rat is able to slip into all the houses unnoticed, so that he does indeed find the coin.

13. The Rice-Cake Race of the Monkey and the Bullfrog: The monkey and the bullfrog steal a mortar full of rice cake. The monkey proposes that they roll the mortar down the hill and that the first one to reach the rice cake will have it all. The monkey reaches the mortar first, but the rice cake had fallen out along the way, and the frog had reached that first.

14. The Monkey Bridegroom: A man rashly promises his daughter to a monkey. The girl asks for a huge earthen jar full of needles as her dowry. While the monkey is walking along carrying the jar, he crosses a bridge over a river. The girl pushes the monkey off the bridge.

15. The Quiver of the Mountain Spirit: A blind minstrel who loses his way in the mountains plays for the mountain-deity in exchange for spending the night on the mountain. A hunter comes and gives the man food and later leads him down to the village. The "hunter" turns out to be a wolf.

16. The Eagle's Eggs: A man rashly promises his daughter to a snake in exchange for the life of a frog. When the girl becomes pregnant, a soothsayer says that the girl will die unless she has some eagle's eggs. The snake-bridegroom goes for the eggs, but is killed by the mother eagle. The girl recovers, and it is discovered that the soothsayer was really the frog the man had saved.

17. Kosai Osho and the Sea Turtles: A priest who has gone to buy gold for his temple saves the life of some turtles. Later the priest's ship is attacked by pirates, and he is thrown overboard. He is saved by a huge turtle. Still later, when he has returned to his temple, some men come to sell him gold. He recognizes them as the pirates who had robbed him, and they recognize him as the priest they thought they had murdered.

18. Monkey Masamune: Two courtiers save a monkey from an octopus. The monkey then steals the important letter that the courtiers were carrying to force them to wait. The monkey returns with the letter and with a fine antique sword.

19. From a Meadow Lane in Spring: A man finds the skeleton of a young girl in a meadow. Her ghost appears and tells him that she had

died of a sudden illness, but her parents had been unable to find her body. She takes the man to her parents' home, where the old man tells them of his discovery.

20. The Little Hand Mill that Ground Out Gold: A man is given a magic mill by a swamp maiden. The mill will turn a grain of rice into a grain of gold. The man must dig a pond in his yard and offer a little of the water from it twice a day to the mill. The man's greedy brother learns of the mill. He tries to turn a whole bowl of rice into a bowl of gold, but the mill slips from his hands and rolls into the pond in the yard.

21. Little Runny-nose Boy: A woodcutter offers some wood to the River Goddess. She gives him a little boy who can grant the man's every wish provided that the man feed him shrimp three times a day. After the man has become wealthy, he tires of going to buy shrimp every day, so he sends the boy away. All the man's wealth then disappears.

22. Matsuko's Pilgrimage to Ise: A mysterious couple from a certain village stop at an inn on a trip to Ise, but they do not have enough money to complete their pilgrimage. The innkeeper gives them the money, saying that the next group of pilgrims from the village can return it. The people who next come from the village do not recognize the description of the previous travelers. Later it is learned that they were the spirits of two pine trees in the village.

23. The Water Spider: A man is fishing in a certain pond when a spider comes out of the pond and attaches a string to the man's toe. The man moves the string to a log, which is very soon dragged into the water.

24. The Chief of the Snapping Turtles: A man catches a huge snapping turtle that he hears speaking. He sells the turtle to a fish market, but the turtle manages to escape.

25. The "Yaro-ka (Here Goes)" Flood: When a great flood is about to break through a certain dike, the flood waters cry out, "Here goes!"

26. Goshinro (You've-All-Been-to-Great-Trouble) Pond: When some villagers have almost drained a certain pond, a mysterious man rises up from the water and says, "You've all been to great trouble." At once the pond fills up again.

27. The Best Lacquer of Mera: A man finds some lacquer of the best quality on the bed of a river. When the man's brother also learns of this lacquer, the man has a woodcarver make a lifelike dragon so that he can set it into the river and scare away his own brother. When he does this and he is about to dive in for the lacquer himself, the dragon comes to life and keeps him out of the river.

28. Crab Pool and Princess Yasunaga: When a man accidentally drops an ax into a pool, the Water Spirit appears and says that he has cut off the arm of a crab that had been menacing her. He drops the ax into the pond again, and it kills the crab. After that the Water Spirit grants the man's every wish and also brings rain when the villagers pray to her for it.

29. The Bell from the Dragon Palace: A samurai who has built a temple saves the Dragon King by shooting a huge serpent that is threatening the undersea kingdom. In gratitude the Dragon King gives the samurai a magnificent bell for his temple.

30. What the Yamachichi Observed: A yamachichi feels that he has no trouble overcoming human beings since he can read their thoughts. Then he meets a man who accidentally drops a bamboo hoop and hits the yamachichi. The creature realizes that humans are dangerous since they can do things without thinking about them.

31. The Wife Who Didn't Eat: A man says that he wants a wife who does not eat anything, and sure enough a woman comes to him who claims she does not eat. Soon the man learns that she is really a demoness with a huge mouth on top of her head. She tries to carry him to the mountains, but he escapes and hides in a patch of mugwort and irises. When the demoness tries to catch him, she is pierced by the plants and killed. This is why iris and mugwort are used in the May fifth festival to ward off evil demons.

32. The Ox-driver and the Yamauba: A man meets a mountain witch, but in his haste to escape her, he inadvertently hides in her house. He is able to trick the witch into climbing into a wooden chest. The man then drills holes through the chest and pours boiling water on the witch.

33. O Sun, the Iron Chain: See entry 97, tale 21.

34. The Demon and Shinriki-bo: A demon always bothers a priest for food and wine. The priest tricks the demon into thinking that rocks are bean curd and bamboo roots are sprouts, so that the demon thinks that humans are much stronger than he is.

35. Kongo-in and the Fox: A priest frightens a sleeping fox. The next day the fox appears before the priest's friends as if he does not notice them and assumes the priest's shape. Later when the priest comes, his friends set upon him thinking that he is the transformed fox.

36. Suddenly Becoming a Priest: A man is tricked into thinking that he has committed a murder by some foxes in human guise who shave off his hair to make him a priest.

37. The Acolyte and the Fox: See entry 95, tale 5.

38. The Old One-eyed Man: An old man has only his right eye. One night he comes home with only his left eye. His wife realizes that he is really a fox, and she tricks the fox into getting cooked into soup.

39. The Fox at Hijiyama: An actor wearing a Noh mask meets a fox. The fox asks for the mask, not realizing that it will not turn his entire body into a human shape. The fox appears before a group of samurai wearing the mask and is instantly killed.

40. Shibaemon Badger: Two badgers decide to test their powers of illusion. One badger tricks the other by saying he will give the illusion of a great lord's procession. What the second badger sees is indeed a

lord's procession, and when he runs up to congratulate his rival, he is killed by the attendants.

41. How the Mountain Priest Overcame the Badger: After the prayers of a number of priests have failed to overcome a troublesome badger, a certain priest says he will try to rid a household of its pest. The man simply leaves in the house a parcel that proves to be a rice ball tainted with poison.

42. The Pile in the Harbor: A badger disguises itself as a pile in the harbor and floats away any boats that the sailors tie to it. A group of men pretend that they are looking for a pile on which to tie their boat. When one appears, they know it is the badger. They wind a rope around him and hit him.

43. Foxes Laugh: A fox comes to a man's house poorly disguised as a samurai. The man brings a pail of water so that the fox can see himself and realize that he still looks like a fox. The next day the man and the fox have a good laugh over what happened.

44. Sanya, the Rich Man Who Bought a Dream: A man dreams that he finds a large amount of gold in a valley near a mountain. The man's friend buys the dream and finds a gold mine in the valley.

45. The Horseflies of Takoshima: A boy dreams that three Buddha statues from a certain temple turn into horseflies. A man buys the dream, goes to the temple, and catches the three flies. When the man returns home, the flies turn back into beautiful statues.

46. Damburi-chōja: A farmer becomes a chōja through the help of a dragonfly, which shows him in a dream where there is a spring of wine.

47. A Straw that Brought Riches: See entry 130.

48. Kogorō, the Charcoal Maker: A rich girl receives an oracle to marry a certain poor charcoal maker. The wife gives her husband some gold with which to buy rice, but he carelessly throws it at some ducks. When the woman chastises him, he says that the area around his kilns is covered with gold.

49. Nijikki-ga-hara, the Field of Twenty Mounted Warriors: A chōja's ten sons go out to a certain field to practice archery. Watching them all, the man says that he would have liked to have had even twice as many sons. His wife then reveals that each boy had a twin brother who has been raised separately.

50. The Chōjas' Treasure Match: Two chōjas compare their wealth. One man displays his large amount of gold, but the other man displays his 20 sons.

51. The Stork Barrow at Aizu: A very rich man who has no children keeps a pet stork that he treats like his child. When the stork dies, the man has a barrow raised for it.

52. Koyama (Lake-Mountain) Lake: When the transplanting of his rice fields is delayed, a chōja beckons the sun three times to cause it to

reascend in the sky so that the work will be completed in one day. Because of his audacity, the man's rice fields eventually become a huge lake.

53. Plum Tree Estate: A rich man has a plum tree that has been passed down from his ancestors with the injunction that it never be sold. When the man falls on hard times and is about to move, he digs up the tree to bring it with him and discovers a large amount of gold buried at the base of the tree.

54. Mototori (Clearing-the-Old-Score) Mountain: People of a certain village are able to borrow beautiful lacquer dishes from a cave until a dishonest man borrows them and does not return them. Later a baby boy is born to the couple. When he is ten years old, he suddenly grabs two huge sacks of rice and runs off into the cave from which the dishes had been borrowed.

55. Uguisu-hime: See entry 100. In this version the Shining Princess is born from a nightingale's egg found in the bamboo patch. She is taken back up to heaven on a cloud, not by a delegation of moon men.

56. Uriko-hime: An old woman finds a melon floating in the river from which a beautiful little girl is born. When the old couple who raise her leave her alone one day, a demon comes, ties Uriko-hime to a tree, and assumes her shape. The old couple return, but they hear Uriko-hime calling from the tree, and the old man cuts off the demon's head. He throws the severed head into the millet patch. This is why millet stalks turn red.

57. Komebukuro and Awabukuro: Komebukuro, the stepdaughter, is abused by her new mother. Her real mother's soul comes to her in the shape of a white bird and gives her a beautiful kimono. When the stepmother takes Awabukuro to a festival, she leaves Komebukuro home with a great deal of work to do. Komebukuro's friends come and help her do the work. She goes to the festival wearing her fine kimono, where she is seen by the lord. He comes the next day to take her as his bride, but the stepmother tries to have him take Awabukuro instead. He compares the two girls and sees that Komebukuro is far more beautiful.

58. The Magic Straw Cloak of the Yamauba: A young girl becomes lost in the woods and goes to the house of a mountain-witch. She gives the girl a magic cloak that can let the girl assume any form and that will also give her anything she requests. The girl assumes the form of an old woman and takes service in the house of a kindly rich man. One day the man's son sees the girl in her true shape. After locating the girl's parents, the rich man arranges a marriage between the girl and his son.

59. The Origin of the God of the Kitchen Hearth: A man overhears the local deity saying that the man's son who was born that day has poor luck, while the girl born next door at the same time has good luck. The man arranges a marriage between the two children. After the children grow up and are married, their house prospers, but the husband finally drives the wife away. She takes another husband, and her new house

now flourishes, while her former husband falls into utter poverty. Later the former husband comes to the wife's new house by chance. When he recognizes his former wife, he is so embarrassed that he dies. The woman buries him behind the stove and makes offerings for his soul, saying that she is worshiping the god of the hearth.

60. Yasuke of Yamura: The farmer Yasuke frees a copper pheasant from a snare. Later a beautiful woman comes to his house and becomes his bride. One day a demon starts to haunt the area, and the woman reveals that the demon can be killed only with an arrow feathered with the tail feathers of the copper pheasant. She tells her husband that she is the pheasant whose life he had saved, gives him the required feathers, and flies away.

61. The Fox Wife: A man comes home and finds two copies of his wife in the house. Realizing that one is a fox, he drives away the wife who seems suspicious to him. Later he learns that he had sent away the wrong wife. As the fox wife is leaving, she casts a spell over the man's rice fields so that they will always have a fine harvest, but they will appear to have failed when the tax assessor comes to look at them.

62. The Blind Water Spirit: A man saves the life of an eel, and later a beautiful woman comes to his house and becomes his bride. He discovers that she is really a serpent, and she leaves his house. She gives him one of her eyes to use in nursing their child, but this rare treasure is confiscated by the local lord. The woman gives the man her other eye, but this too is stolen by the lord. The serpent then causes a huge earthquake in the province.

63. The Old Man Showered with Gold: See entry 96, tale 5.

64. The Hearth Fire on New Year's Eve: A man finds a beggar lying injured in the road. He brings the man home and cares for him as best he can. In the morning the man and his wife go to see how the man is, but they find a huge piece of gold in the man's bed.

65. The Jizō with Sedge Hats: A man who sells sedge hats is unable to sell anything to buy food for New Year's. While he is returning home, he is caught in a snowstorm and comes upon six Jizō statues standing unprotected on the road. He places the five hats that he had been trying to sell onto five of the statues, then he takes off his own hat and places it on the sixth statue. During the night the six statues come to the man's house and leave him sacks full of treasure to reward his piety.

66. Dumpling Paradise: See entry 103, tale 13.

67. The Tumor Doubled: See entry 128.

68. The Old Man of Ōshū Who Scattered Ashes: See entry 129.

69. Why the Sea Is Salty: See entry 123.

70. Hachikoku (Eight Koku) Mountain: A woman divides a field in half and gives half to her own son to plant with beans and half to her stepson. One night the woman digs up the stepson's beans so that the field will be barren. She overlooks one bean plant, which grows so tall

that it produces more beans than the half field that the woman's real son planted.

71. Dog's Head Thread: A girl makes her living growing silk, but all her worms except one die. The last silkworm is eaten by her dog. Then the dog starts to sneeze, and silk threads of the finest quality come running out of the dog's nose. The dog produces a large quantity of thread and then dies. The girl buries the dog in her yard, and the next season silkworms appear from the dog's grave and continue to give fine silk.

72. How a Fox Returned a Kindness: A fox eats all the beans in a man's field. Then the fox turns itself into a fine peony so that the man can sell it. Later the fox turns into a kettle, which the man also sells.

73. The Listening Hood: See entry 87, tale 8, except that in this version the rich man's daughter is the one who falls ill.

74. Sparrow Shrine: An evil man puts a needle into the food that he gives another man to eat. By watching a sparrow, the man learns that he can cure himself of the swallowed needle by eating leeks. He then builds a shrine to the sparrow that helped him.

75. The Deified Giltheads: A fish merchant saves a copper pheasant from a snare, replacing it with three giltheads. When the people of the village see this, they think that it is a manifestation from heaven, and they build a shrine for the giltheads.

76. The Hilt Ornament Carved Like a Lizard: A man sees a lizard in his garden and begins to carve ornaments in its shape. His fame spreads, but soon the man realizes that the lizard in his garden is an unearthly creature. He finally kills it, whereupon the man's good fortune ends.

77. The Fish-stone of Nagasaki: A Chinese man sees a stone in a Japanese man's garden and offers a large amount of money for it. Although the owner realizes that the stone is very valuable, he does not know why, but he refuses to sell it. The owner eventually splits the stone apart and finds two fish swimming in a small amount of water inside the stone. The Chinese man comes back again with an even larger offer for the stone. When the Japanese man reveals what has happened to the stone, the Chinese man tells him that the stone with the fish in it had had magical powers that could extend a man's life. Because of their greed, both men lose the benefits they could have obtained from the stone.

78. The Great Affair of the Melon: A shipment of melons is delivered to a palace, but an augurer says that one is poisoned. A conjurer determines which is the poisoned melon, a physician draws off the poison, and a warrior slices the melon, killing the snake that was inside.

79. An Augury Left by the Father: When a woman's father was dying, he told her that a man would come in ten years who would give her 1,000 ryō. Ten years later a diviner comes to the house, and when

he hears the story, the diviner walks through the house and discovers that the specified amount of money is hidden within a pillar.

80. The Beggar's Money: A man has a dream in which Daikoku tells him to borrow 300 ryō from a beggar so that he can make a fortune. The beggar does not have that much money, but the first man draws up a contract for it anyway. The man later finds the money in his own house, but he honors his contract with the beggar so that both men become wealthy.

81. Picking Up Too Much: A man slips on a street and drops his wallet. Later he returns to pick up his money and finds less than he originally had. The man returns home and discovers that his original money was in his wallet undisturbed all the time.

82. The Mountain Bandit's Younger Brother: A man is robbed by some bandits, but they take pity on him and give him a rusted old sword to take with him. The sword turns out to be a fine antique, and the man makes more on its sale than the bandits had stolen from him. He returns to the bandits to give them back the difference. The bandit leader then realizes that this man is his younger brother. Moved by the young man's honesty, the older brother quits his life of thievery and returns to his home to become a priest.

83. The Strong Man and the Woman in Travail: A man meets a woman in the mountains, and she asks him to hold her baby while she runs an errand. Although the child gets heavier and heavier, the man does not put it down. The woman then returns and rewards the man for his perseverance with great strength.

84. Strong Women: As a reward for helping a princess from the Dragon Palace, a man is given great strength on the condition that he never hand anything to a woman. If he does so, his strength will pass into the woman. One day the man accidentally hands something to his wife. After that his wife becomes very strong, and that strength is passed on to her daughters.

85. Oiko's Rice Balls: The strong woman Oiko makes rice balls that are packed so densely that a wrestler is unable to bite into them until he has practiced for seven days.

86. Kidaiyū of Hida: When the wrestler Kidaiyū is ordered to engage in a match with another renowned wrestler, he prays to a certain deity for help. The deity reveals to him the other wrestler's weakness.

87. Inazuma Daizō: A wrestler who has the strength of a tengu deliberately loses one of his matches, whereupon his strength immediately leaves him.

88. Fujinuki Kinai: A samurai comes to challenge the strongman Kinai. He meets Kinai in a field, but thinks that he is just a servant. Seeing the man's great strength, the samurai despairs of overcoming the master and he leaves.

89. The Wrestler from Awa and the Wrestler of Kumano: The

wrestler from Awa comes to challenge the wrestler of Kumano, but he soon realizes that he is no match for the other man.

90. Niō and Gaō, the Two Deva Gods: The two Deva Gods are going to have a match of strength, but they realize that they are equally matched and decide to cooperate with each other as guardian spirits from then on.

91. Tankuro and Takuro: Takuro, the younger brother, is crafty and is always swindling his dull-witted older brother Tankuro.

92. Clever Yasohichi: See entry 97, tale 56.

93. Two Bolts of White Cloth: A mother-in-law and daughter-in-law get into an argument as to what the name of a certain doll is. They agree to let the village priest decide the argument, but each woman secretly goes to the priest and bribes him with a bolt of white cloth. The priest then says that the doll has a name that is a pun on the phrase "two bolts of cloth."

94. A Silence Match: A man and wife have a silence match to see who will get the last of their mochi. A robber comes into the house, and the wife cries out. The man then says that the mochi is his.

95. A Leak-in-an-Old-House: See entry 121.

96. Seizo's Rabbit: Seizo sees a rabbit sleeping, but he thinks that it is dead. He makes a remark about the rabbit's being dead, but when the rabbit runs away, he tries to cover up his mistake with a second remark.

97. The Pigeons Might Overhear: A man whispers to his friend what he is planting in his garden so that the pigeons will not hear.

98. The Insect that Taps Along with a Stick: A man mistakes a blind minstrel carrying a lute for an insect walking along tapping a stick.

99. The Quilt on the Nape of His Neck: A father warns his children not to say that they sleep in straw, but to call it quilt. When they see a piece of straw on his neck, they say that he has some quilt on his neck.

100. Pretending to Know: A man who does not know what noodles are mistakes another man's name for the name of this new food. He later tries to show off his new knowledge.

101. Chilled Pride: A samurai boasts that he does not need a straw mat to cover himself as he sleeps, but in the night it becomes so cold that he makes up an excuse for using a mat after all.

102. The Hoarder: An old woman is such a grasper that she never lets anything pass her by if she can get it for free.

103. Stinginess: See entry 97, tale 58.

104. Temptation to Steal: A man comes from the sunlight into a dimly lit room. He steals a small hatchet, thinking that no one can see him, but as his eyes adjust to the light, he realizes that he has indeed been seen. He manages to make it seem that placing a hatchet in one's clothes will help one's eyes adjust to the light.

105. The Son-in-Law's Chat: A dull-witted son-in-law tries to impress his new father-in-law with his "clever" conversation.

106. The Roof of the Underground Country: Some people dig for many days trying to finish a well until they come to a layer of straw. A loud voice calls out that the straw is part of his roof.

107. The Gambler's Trip through the Sky: See entry 104, tale 3.

108. A Trip through the Sky: A man catches a whole flock of geese at once and is carried into the sky. He lands on the top of a pagoda and is forced to jump into a "safety net" held by four priests. The force of his fall is so great that it starts a fire.

B. Japanese Folk Tales: A Revised Selection

Because 45 of the tales in Yanagita's original anthology were later classified as "legends," a revision was undertaken to replace these with 43 "genuine folktales." This translation by Mayer is of Yanagita's revised anthology. This book also includes a reference index that gives full bibliographic information for literary sources of the tales in Japanese; titles and authors are given only in romaji.

1. Why the Monkey's Tail Is Short: See entry 109A, tale 1.

2. Why the Jellyfish Has No Bones: See entry 137.

3. The Sparrow and the Woodpecker: See entry 109A, tale 3.

4. The Pigeon's Obedience to His Mother: See entry 109A, tale 4.

5. The Cuckoo Brothers: See entry 109A, tale 5.

6. The Cuckoo and the Shrike: See entry 109A, tale 6.

7. The Legging on One Leg: A mother bird is putting on her leggings when she hears that her son is choking on some wheat. She flies off with only one legging on, and that is why this type of bird has feathers only on one leg.

8. The Meadow Lark Money Lender: The meadow lark was a moneylender, and he now flies around demanding payment from those who owe him money.

9. The Earthworm Who Wears a Reel: The worm weaves a dress of such fine thread that she must wind it around her neck. That is why worms have a mark around their necks. The toad makes her dress from very coarse thread, which is why the toad has rough skin.

10. The Owl Dyer: See entry 109A, tale 7.

11. The Wren Counted among the Hawks: See entry 109A, tale 9.

12. The Badger and the Snail: See entry 109A, tale 10.

13. The Badger, the Monkey, and the Otter: See entry 109A, tale 11.

14. The Monkey, the Cat, and the Rat: See entry 109A, tale 12.

15. The Rice-Cake Race of the Monkey and the Bullfrog: See entry 109A, tale 13.

16. A-Leak-in-an-Old-House: See entry 121.

17. The Monkey Bridegroom: See entry 109A, tale 14.

18. The Eagle's Eggs: See entry 109A, tale 16.

19. From a Meadow Lane in Spring: See entry 109A, tale 19.

20. The Golden Axe and the Silver Axe: See entry 103, tale 8, except that in this version the god of the pond brings both a gold and a silver ax.

21. The Little Hand-Mill that Ground Out Gold: See entry 109A, tale 20.

22. Little Runny-nose Boy: See entry 109A, tale 21.

23. The Snake Son: An old couple find a snake in their storeroom and keep it as a pet. After many years, the snake becomes so big it no longer fits in the storehouse and it eats more rice than the couple can afford to feed it. The snake goes to a certain bridge and will not let anyone pass. The lord offers a huge reward to anyone who can get rid of the snake. The old couple convince the snake to swim out into the open sea. They then collect the reward.

24. The Water Spider: See entry 109A, tale 23.

25. What the Yamachichi Observed: See entry 109A, tale 30.

26. The Wife Who Didn't Eat: See entry 109A, tale 31.

27. The Ox-driver and the Yamauba: See entry 109A, tale 32.

28. The Flower that Reflected a Human Form: A woman is kidnapped by a bandit who possesses a magical flower that indicates how many men and women are in the house. The woman's husband comes to rescue her. When the bandit sees two male flowers, the woman says that she is pregnant. The bandit celebrates this news and becomes drunk, whereupon the woman's husband kills him. The couple then bring the flower to their king.

29. "O Sun, the Chain": See entry 97, tale 21.

30. The Mountain Pears: A mother of three daughters becomes ill and needs some mountain pears to cure her. She gives the daughters instructions on how to find them. The two older daughters do not heed the instructions and are killed on their quest, but the youngest daughter obeys her mother and is successful.

31. The Three Charms: See entry 97, tale 19.

32. The Old Winnowing Basket, the Old Furushiki, and the Old Drum: A traveler spends a night in a temple that is thought to be haunted. The ghosts prove to be the spirits of some inanimate objects that were not disposed of properly.

33. The Sudden Tonsure: See entry 109A, tale 36.

34. The Novice and the Fox: See entry 95, tale 5.

35. The Old One-eyed Man: See entry 109A, tale 38.

36. Tanokyū: See entry 65, tale 7; in this version the name "Tanokyū" is confused with the Japanese word "tanuki," meaning badger.

37. Comparing Disguises: A fox and a badger have a contest to see who can assume the best disguise. The fox dresses as a bride. On the

road to a temple, she comes upon a delicious-looking dumpling. When she picks it up, the dumpling announces that it is the badger.

38. The Cat and the Hunter: A hunter's cat becomes angry when the man's wife scolds it. The cat counts the hunter casting 13 bullets. That day the hunter encounters a strange animal in the woods. He shoots all 13 bullets without effect, then he shoots it with an iron charm bullet that he is carrying. The last shot kills the animal. It proves to be the man's cat who had protected itself from the first 13 bullets with the lid of the hunter's tea kettle.

39. The Pile in the Harbor: See entry 109A, tale 42.

40. Misokai Bridge: Chōkichi has a dream telling him to go to Misokai Bridge. He does so and meets a man who says that he has had a dream that there is a large amount of gold buried under a tree in the yard of a man named Chōkichi. Chōkichi hurries home and unearths the treasure.

41. The Boy Who Had a Dream: A boy has a dream that he refuses to tell to anyone. The boy acquires a magic fan that can make him fly and the needles of life and death from creatures trying to learn his dream, but he still does not reveal it. Finally the boy flies to a town where the lord's daughter has died, brings her back to life, and becomes very wealthy from the reward given him by the lord.

42. Netarō Sansuke: Lazy Netarō Sansuke tricks the local chōja into thinking that the god of Izumo has decreed that he should marry the chōja's daughter.

43. Damburi-chōja (Dragonfly Chōja): See entry 109A, tale 46.

44. Warashibe Chōja: A chōja says that he will give his daughter as a bride to a poor man if the poor man can make a fortune from a single piece of straw. Through a series of clever exchanges, the man does indeed succeed.

45. Kogorō the Charcoal Maker: See entry 109A, tale 48.

46. The Golden Camellia: See entry 97, tale 49, except that in this version the wife is exiled for yawning, and the boy claims to have a branch of camellia that gives gold flowers.

47. Uguisu-hime (Nightingale Princess): See entry 109A, tale 55.

48. Uriko-hime: See entry 109A, tale 56.

49. Takenoko Dōji: A man finds a tiny celestial being named Takenoko Dōji trapped in some bamboo. After the man releases him, Takenoko rewards him by making him a great warrior.

50. Komebukuro and Awabukuro: See entry 109A, tale 57.

51. The Treasure Cloak of the Yamauba: See entry 109A, tale 58.

52. The Old Woman's Skin: A man rashly promises one of his daughters to the guardian spirit of the rice fields. His youngest daughter agrees to become the bride. Using the treasure that gets water, 1,000 needles, and the treasure that gets fire, she succeeds in destroying the spirit. A frog from the pond gives to her the skin that makes her look like an old woman. Wearing the magic skin, the girl goes and takes

service in a certain house. The son of the house sees the girl in her true shape and falls ill from longing. Every person in the house tries to bring the young man food until only the old lady is left. When the father of the man decides that even she should try, the girl removes the magic skin and appears in her true form.

53. The Wife Like a Picture: A man has a wife who is so beautiful that he cannot take his eyes off of her long enough to work in his fields. The woman gives him a picture of herself to hang in the fields, but it is blown away to the lord's mansion by the wind. The lord says that the man must hire two wrestlers to fight two of the lord's wrestlers. If the man loses, the lord will take his wife. The wife brings two old men as the wrestlers, but they easily win. Later the man learns that the wrestlers had been two male deities, while his wife had been a female deity.

54. The Origin of the God of the Kitchen Hearth: See entry 109A, tale 59.

55. The Driftlog God: A man uses a piece of driftwood as a pillow, not knowing that it is a deity. He learns from the deity's conversation that his daughter will face great peril from water on her eighteenth birthday. When the fateful day arrives, the man remembers the prophesy and is able to save the girl's life.

56. Yasuke of Yamura: See entry 109A, tale 60.

57. The Fox Wife: See entry 109A, tale 61.

58. The Frog Wife: A man saves the life of a frog, and several days later a beautiful woman comes to his house and becomes his wife. When the wife says that she must return home for a memorial service, the man follows her and sees her jump into the pond. He realizes she is a frog and drops a rock into the pond. The woman comes home the next day and says that the service had been fine until a huge rock had fallen into the midst of everything.

59. The Snake's Treasure: A man sees a beautiful woman going to pray at Miidera, and he arranges for her to become his wife. When she is about to give birth to a child, she asks him not to look at her while she is giving birth. The man disobeys her and sees that she is a snake. She leaves the house, but she gives the man one of her eyes to use in nursing the child. The lord learns of this rare treasure and confiscates it. The woman then gives the man her other eye, asking that he arrange for the bell to be rung at Miidera twice a day.

60. Money to the Old Man: See entry 96, tale 5.

61. The Fire for New Year's Eve: See entry 109A, tale 64.

62. The Toad that Talked: A man saves the life of a toad. The toad can talk and sing, and it goes with the man to perform for some villagers to make the man some money. A greedy neighbor borrows the toad, but it will not talk for him and the man kills it. The good man takes half of the toad and buries it. A tree grows that showers the good man's house with money. The evil man tries burying the remaining half of the toad, but the tree that grows showers his house with dung.

63. The Jizō with Sedge Hats: See entry 109A, tale 65.

64. The Ghosts of Coins: A man prays to his tutelary deity for good fortune. The deity says that the man should strike the leading samurai of a procession that will be passing by his house that night. When the procession comes, the samurai looks so regal that the man cannot strike him. A second procession passes that is less regal, but still too much for the man. The third procession is truly shabby, and the man strikes the leading samurai. He instantly turns into a pile of meager copper coins. The first samurai had been gold, and the second had been silver.

65. The Forbidden Room: A man is taken to the house of a spirit. She tells him that he can look into any of the rooms representing the 12 months except for the second month. The man obeys her and is rewarded with a magic ladle that turns plain water into any kind of food the user requests. The man's evil neighbor tries to duplicate the good man's fortune, but he violates the taboo and receives nothing.

66. Rat Paradise: A woman drops a dumpling down a hole and follows after it. She sees some mice pounding rice in a mortar and meows like a cat to scare them off. She then takes the mice's magic rice mortar and all their gold. An evil neighbor tries to duplicate the first woman's fortune, but when she meows, the mice realize she is a human being and pound her to death.

67. The Hidden Village: A man sees his cow being dragged by a number of ants, and in trying to stop them, he is dragged with the cow into a cave. There he meets a strange man who says that he can have money anytime just by coming to the mouth of the cave and asking for it, provided that he never tells anyone about the cave's existence. After some years, the man tells people where his money comes from. He then finds the cave completely sealed up, and his money eventually is all spent.

68. Dumpling Paradise: See entry 103, tale 13.

69. The Wind God and the Children: A mysterious man flies a group of children to a place where there are many good things to eat. He later leaves them, telling them to go home by themselves. The frightened children find a woman who is the mother of the wind gods. The man had been one of her sons, and she has another of the winds fly the children back to their village.

70. The Two Tumors: See entry 128.

71. The Old Man Who Scattered Ashes: See entry 129.

72. The Old Man Who Swallowed a Bird: See entry 97, tale 34.

73. The Sound of Chewing Acorns: An old man who has picked up some acorns on the path stops to spend the night in a dilapidated shrine. During the night some demons come and gather together gold and silver. The old man bites into the acorns, causing the demons to think that the shrine is collapsing. They run away, and the man takes the fortune. His greedy neighbor tries to duplicate his good fortune, but the demons discover him and give him a beating.

74. The Jizō Made of White Rice Cake: See entry 96, tale 4.

75. The Wolf's Eyebrows: A man meets a wolf who gives him a hair from his eyebrow. By looking through it, the man can tell if a person is really a human being or an animal in human guise.

76. How a Fox Returned a Kindness: See entry 109A, tale 72.

77. Chōja from a Wooden Image: See entry 103, tale 3.

78. The Listening Hood: See entry 87, tale 8, except that in this version the rich man's daughter is the one who falls ill.

79. The Deified Giltheads: See entry 109A, tale 75.

80. The Mountain God and the Boy: See entry 104, tale 12.

81. The Success in Life of the Three Brothers: Three brothers are driven from their home because of their laziness. They each go a different way, settling on the day and place when they should meet again. The first brother becomes a carpenter, the second an archer, and the third a thief. After the three return home, the lord's daughter is kidnapped by a demon. Using the skills that they have learned, the brothers are able to free her and slay the demon.

82. The Star Carrying a Lance: With the help of a mountain ascetic, a poor boy wins two contests against the seven sons of a chōja. The chōja's sons attack the poor boy with a lance, but their teacher intervenes. All nine people are then turned into stars. This is the origin of the Pleiades.

83. Why the Sea Is Salty: See entry 123.

84. The Rice-Cake Tree: A crafty younger brother tricks his dull-witted older brother into buying a tree covered with rice cakes, saying that the cakes actually grow on the tree. When the cakes are all taken down and no more are produced, the younger brother explains that the largest cake had been the "parent" and had to be left behind if the tree were ever to produce cakes again.

85. Clever Yasohichi: See entry 97, tale 56.

86. The Two Bolts of White Cloth: See entry 109A, tale 93.

87. Niō and Gaō, the Two Deva Gods: See entry 109A, tale 90.

88. A Silence Match: See entry 109A, tale 94.

89. Rat Sutra: An old couple ask a hunter to teach them a sutra, but he is unable to remember the words. Seeing a rat cautiously slipping into the room, the hunter makes up a sutra based on what he sees. Later a thief slips into the house, and hearing the old couple chanting their "sutra" thinks that they have seen him.

90. The Frog Who Imitated Men: A frog tries to imitate men by walking up on two legs. He sets out on a journey, but when he stands up and looks around, he sees that the place where he is going looks just like his home. The frog's eyes are on the top of his head, so when he stands up to look, he is really looking back at where he has come from.

91. The Black Line on the Broad Bean: The bean, the piece of straw, and the charcoal go on a journey. The charcoal tries to cross a stream using the straw as a bridge, but they both fall into the water. The

bean laughs so hard that it bursts. A girl comes along, and she sews up the bean, but she only has black thread with her. That is why the bean has a black line on it.

92. The Centipede's Errand: The flea and the louse send the centipede to buy some wine. After waiting a very long time, they go to see what has happened. They find the centipede still on the porch fastening his many pairs of sandals.

93. Seizo's Rabbit: See entry 109A, tale 96.

94. The Pigeons Might Overhear: See entry 109A, tale 97.

95. The Insect that Taps Along with a Stick: See entry 109A, tale 98.

96. The Quilt on the Nape of the Neck: See entry 109A, tale 99.

97. The Kinomata Letter and the Black Letter: A woman's daughter goes as a bride to a distant village. When a man is going to that village on business, the mother gives him a letter for her daughter. After it is delivered, the girl gives the man a letter in reply. In fact, neither the mother nor the daughter could write, but they covered the paper with signs that the other person was able to understand.

98. Pretending to Know: See entry 109A, tale 100.

99. Chilled Pride: See entry 109A, tale 101.

100. The Hoarder: See entry 109A, tale 102.

101. Stinginess: See entry 97, tale 58.

102. Temptation to Steal: See entry 109A, tale 104.

103. The Son-in-Law's Chat: See entry 109A, tale 105.

104. The Roof of the Underground World: See entry 109A, tale 106.

105. The Gambler's Trip to the Sky: See entry 104, tale 3.

106. A Trip through the Sky: See entry 109A, tale 108.

110. Yanagita, Kunio. *The Legends of Tōno*. Translated by Ronald A. Morse. Tokyo: Japan Foundation, 1975.

Yanagita's *Tōno monogatari* 遠野物語 is truly a cornerstone of Japanese folklore studies. The collection is composed of 119 entries and contains a wide variety of folk materials, including tales of local gods, tales of supernatural creatures, discussions of local geography, descriptions of folk religious practices, and a transcription of a folk song. All the entries are short; some are only two or three sentences, the longest about two pages. The introduction by Morse is excellent. There is also a foreword by Richard M. Dorson and a translation of Yanagita's preface to the original edition. This edition contains three full-page maps and is illustrated throughout with photographs and drawings. Yanagita's work is an outstanding example of a local folklore study, and Morse's translation is an outstanding example of a researcher making an important work available for use by colleagues.

111. Yasuda, Yuri. *Old Tales of Japan*. Rutland, Vt.: Charles E. Tuttle, 1956.

This collection contains 12 tales and almost 100 illustrations. Although the book is meant for children, there are many Japanese words and names included that could cause difficulty for English-speaking children.

The Story of Shitakirisuzume, the Tongue-cut Sparrow: See entry 133.

The Story of Kintaro, the Strong Boy: See entry 120.

The Story of Nezumi no Yomeiri, the Marriage of a Mouse: See entry 126.

The Story of Sarukani Kassen, the Monkey-and-Crab Fight: See entry 113; this version of the tale is given in the form of a play performed by six children.

The Story of Urashima Tarō, the Fisherman and the Tortoise: See entry 134.

The Story of Kaguyahime, the Luminous Princess: See entry 100.

The Story of Momotarō, the Peach Boy: See entry 125.

The Story of Kachikachiyama, the Kachi Kachi Mountain: See entry 114.

The Story of Hanasaka Jijii, the Old Man Who Made Trees Blossom: See entry 129.

The Story of Kobutori Jisan, the Old Men with Wens: See entry 128.

The Story of Bunbuku Chagama, the Lucky Cauldron: See entry 112.

The Story of Issunboshi, the One-Inch Boy: See entry 118.

Chapter 3

Classic Folktales of Japan

112. The Badger Tea Kettle. Bumbuku Chagama 文福茶釜

A man releases a badger from a hunter's snare. In gratitude the badger turns itself into a tea kettle so that the man can sell it. The kettle is sold to the abbot of a certain temple. When the abbot gives the kettle to some acolytes to polish, the kettle starts to scream that they are rubbing too hard. The abbot puts the kettle on the fire to make some tea. Suddenly the kettle sprouts the head, tail, and legs of a badger. It cries out that it is too hot, jumps off the fire, and runs around the room. After the creature resumes its plain tea kettle form, the abbot returns it to the man who sold it to him. (In some versions the abbot sells the kettle to a tinker.) When the man who now owns the kettle learns that it is a badger, he treats it kindly. The badger then proposes a plan by which the man can become wealthy. The man goes to the center of town and advertises that he has an acrobatic tea kettle. Many people pay to see the badger-kettle dance and perform tricks. After the man has made his fortune, he returns the kettle to the temple with money so that it can be maintained on an altar and given daily food offerings. As long as the badger spirit remains in the kettle, the badger eats the offerings. One day, however, the offerings are left on the altar, and the priests of the temple realize that the badger spirit has left. (Several temples in Japan own tea kettles that are claimed to be this famous badger tea kettle.)

113. The Battle of the Monkey and the Crab. Saru Kani Kassen 猿蟹合戦

A monkey finds a persimmon seed; a crab finds a rice cake. The monkey convinces the crab to exchange items, then eats the rice cake. The crab plants the seed, and soon a tree grows and produces fruit. The monkey offers to help the crab harvest the fruit. He climbs into the tree, but he eats all the ripe fruit himself and bombards the crab with the hard, green fruits. The crab is badly injured and vows revenge. (In some versions the crab is killed, and vengeance is exacted by the crab's son.) The chestnut, needle, dung, and mortar help the crab. When the monkey enters his house, the hot chestnut explodes in his face. The crab pinches him and the needle stings him, causing him to run out of the house and slip on the dung. The mortar then jumps on him and crushes him.

114. Crackling Mountain. Kachi Kachi Yama かちかち山

An old man traps an evil badger and brings it home for his wife to make into soup. While the man is gone, the badger tricks the old woman into releasing it, kills her, assumes her shape, and makes her into the soup. The badger then tells the old man what really happened and runs away. The rabbit finds the old man crying, and when it learns of the old woman's death, it vows to avenge her. The rabbit asks the badger to help carry some firewood. When the badger has the load of wood on its back, the rabbit sets it afire. The badger hears the wood burning and asks the rabbit what the sound is. The rabbit replies that the mountain they are crossing is called "crackling mountain" because it makes a sound like a burning fire. The badger is deceived and becomes badly burned. The rabbit then comes to the badger's house to apologize for the "accident." The rabbit says that it has some soothing medicine that will help heal the badger, but the rabbit covers the wounds with an irritating substance, like hot mustard. Next the rabbit offers to take the badger out boating. The rabbit has built two boats, one of wood and one of mud. The rabbit gives the badger the mud boat. While they are out on the lake, the badger's boat begins to disintegrate. The rabbit then reveals that it is avenging the old woman, strikes the badger with an oar, and makes the badger drown.

Most of the versions end at this point. In some tales, the rabbit recovers the badger's body and makes it into soup. The rabbit either eats all the soup, which angers some farmers whose kitchen it had used, or it gives the badger's bones to the farmers to chew on, which causes them to break their teeth. The farmers then decide to kill the rabbit. They catch it and send their children for a knife, but each time the child returns with the wrong object. The farmers then leave the children to guard the rabbit, but it tricks them into letting it go and escapes. The farmers return just in time for one of the farmers to hurl a knife at the rabbit and cut off its tail. This is why rabbits have short tails.

115. The Crane Wife. Tsuru Nyōbō 鶴女房

A man releases a crane from a hunter's snare. Later a beautiful woman comes to his house and becomes his wife. (In some versions the crane is saved by an old man who is married but childless. The girl comes and becomes his daughter.) The woman is an expert weaver who produces cloth of such beauty that the house soon becomes prosperous.

However, no one is allowed to look into the room where she is weaving. The man finally cannot restrain his curiosity. He looks and sees a crane sitting at the loom, removing feathers and inserting them into the warp. Because the husband has learned her true nature, the wife is no longer able to remain with him.

116. The Creation of the World

Originally the universe was chaos. Heaven and earth were mingled together as a great egg. Then the lighter elements spontaneously began to separate from the heavier elements. The lighter part formed the heavens, while the heavier part formed the earth. Five heavenly deities then came into existence, followed by myriad other heavenly deities and ending with Izanagi and Izanami (see entry 119). For further details, including the long and difficult names of the various deities, see *Kojiki*.

117. The Eight Headed Serpent. Yamato no orochi 大和の大蛇

When Izanagi banishes Susanō to the underworld, Susanō goes up to heaven to bid farewell to his sister. While there, he commits numerous crimes, including breaking down the rows of the rice fields and contaminating Amaterasu's dining hall with excrement. Finally he skins a horse and throws the skin into a hall where the celestial weaving maidens are working. One maiden is so startled that she accidentally strikes herself with a weaving shuttle and dies. At this, Amaterasu becomes terrified, and she hides herself in a great rock cave, plunging the plain of heaven and the earth into darkness. The heavenly deities forge the sacred mirror and set it up before the entrance of the cave. The goddess Uzume then performs a rousing dance, while she and the other deities sing of their celebration of a goddess of unequalled beauty. Amaterasu peeks out of the cave to see what is happening and sees her own reflection in the mirror. Entranced by the beauty of the "unknown goddess," she slips out of the cave, while one of the deities strings a sacred cord across the cave's entrance so that Amaterasu can no longer enter it. The heavenly deities then punish Susanō and banish him to the earth. When he descends into Izumo, he sees a pair of chopsticks floating in a river and realizes that there must be someone living upstream. He finds an old couple and their young daughter weeping. The family has been plagued by an eight-headed serpent, which has killed all of the older daughters. He is coming soon for this youngest daughter. Susanō agrees to slay the dragon in exchange for the girl's hand in marriage. Susanō has the couple pour eight large jars of wine, which he poisons. He sets them near the place where the dragon will come for the girl. In one version he has the girl sit in such a way that she is reflected in each of the jars. In another version, he turns the girl into a comb, places her into his hair, then sits where he can be seen in the jars. The serpent comes and drinks the wine in its attempt to kill the girl (or Susanō). Susanō then easily kills it. He starts to dismember the body, but when he tries to cut the dragon's tail, he strikes something metallic inside. He discovers a fine sword, which he later offers as a peace token to Amaterasu. (This sword is one of the three imperial treasures. It is the sword used by Yamato-dake and obtained the name "Grass-Cutter" [see entry 138]).

118. Issunboshi 一寸法師

An old childless couple pray for a child, even if he is no bigger than one inch. A one-inch child is born who never grows any larger. When he reaches maturity, Issunboshi sets off to find his fortune, carrying a rice bowl, a chopstick, and a needle. He uses the bowl as a hat until he comes to a river, when he uses it as his boat. He uses the chopstick as an oar and the needle as a sword. He comes to the house of a minister, where he is taken into service as a companion for the minister's daughter. One day while the princess and Issunboshi are on an outing, she is attacked by a band of ogres. Issunboshi fights the ogres until one of them swallows him. He then stabs the insides of the ogre until the ogre coughs him back up. The ogres run away, dropping their magic hammer, which can grant anything one wishes by being struck. The princess uses it to strike Issunboshi, chanting that the hammer should make him taller. He is made into a fine, tall young man. The princess and Issunboshi are married.

119. Izanagi and Izanami

At the request of the heavenly deities, Izanagi and Izanami descend to the earth. While they are standing upon the floating bridge of heaven, Izanagi takes the Jeweled Spear of Heaven and plunges it into the firmament below. The brine that drips from this spear after it has been pulled back up forms the first of the Japanese islands. The deities descend to the island and construct a palace with a heavenly pillar. Izanami walks around the pillar to the right, and Izanagi walks around it to the left. When they meet, Izanami exclaims that she met a fair young man, then Izanagi exclaims that he met a fair maiden. They become husband and wife, but the child born of this union is the Leech Child. They set him adrift in a boat, then ask the heavenly deities why such a deformed offspring was born. The deities reply that it is because the woman spoke first when they met after circling the heavenly pillar. Izanagi and Izanami then repeat the ritual, but when they meet Izanagi speaks first. The children that are born after this are successful. First they give birth to numerous islands, then to various deities. But when

Izanami gives birth to the Fire God, she is so badly burned that she dies. Izanagi pursues her to the land of Yomi. Izanami tells him that she will ask the gods of Yomi if she can return to the earth with him, but while she is doing so he must not look at her. He breaks the taboo and sees Izanami's rotting corpse with eight deities of Yomi on it. He flees in terror, and she pursues him in anger along with the eight deities. By throwing various magical objects behind him, Izanagi slows their pursuit. When he reaches the border between Yomi and the earth, he places a huge boulder across the opening so that the two worlds are severed from one another. He then goes to a river to perform ritual ablutions to cleanse himself of the pollution of death. Numerous deities are born as a result of this ablution, including Amaterasu and Susanō. Izanagi appoints Amaterasu to rule the heaven and reside in Takamagahara. He appoints Susanō to rule the oceans of the earth. But Susanō neglects his duties, saying that he wishes to join his mother Izanami. In his anger Izanagi banishes Susanō to the underworld. (The story of Susanō continues in the tale "The Eight Headed Serpent," entry 117.)

Kaguyahime: See entry 100.

120. Kintarō 金太郎

After a courtier falls from favor and dies, his widow goes to live in the forest. She gives birth to a son who grows into an extremely strong boy. He makes friends of the animals in the forest and is their leader. One day Kintarō and his animal companions come to a huge ravine. Kintarō uproots a tree and makes it into a bridge. This act of strength is witnessed by a courtier who is journeying through the forest. When he reports what he has seen, the lord has the man locate the boy and his mother. They are brought back to the city with great honor. The boy is made the lord's retainer and grows up to be a fine warrior.

121. The Leak. Furuya no mori 古屋の漏

During a rainstorm an old man remarks that what he fears most in the world, even more than a wolf or a thief, is a leak. He is speaking about his old thatched roof. At that moment a thief is on the roof of the house and a wolf is walking through the yard. They both wonder what sort of terrible creature this "leak" must be for the old man to fear it so. The thief slips off the roof and falls onto the wolf. Each thinks that the other is the leak, and they are both terrified. The wolf runs off to the forest with the man on its back. The man manages to catch onto a tree branch and swing himself off the wolf. The wolf tells the tiger and the monkey about his terrible experience. The monkey happened to see the wolf running, and he knows that the "leak" is just a human being. He offers to capture the "leak" single-handedly. When the thief sees the three animals approaching the tree, he climbs into a hole. The monkey sticks his tail into the hole, trying to lure out the man. The thief grabs the monkey's tail and pulls so hard that it is ripped off. The animals run away and the thief makes good his escape.

122. The Luck of the Sea and the Luck of the Mountains. Umisachi Yamasa-chi 海幸山幸

The grandson of Amaterasu, Ninigi, is sent down to rule the earth. He meets a beautiful earth deity, Princess Flowers Blooming, and makes her his wife. Her father also offers him the older sister, Princess Long-as-Rocks, but Ninigi is put off by her plainness. If Ninigi had accepted the older daughter, his descendants would have been as long-lived as the rocks, but because he refused her and took only the beautiful younger sister, his descendants become mortal. This is how the descendants of the Sun Goddess lost their immortality. Ninigi and his wife have two sons. The older is Prince Fire-shine and the younger is Prince Fire-fade. Fire-shine possesses a magic fishhook with which he catches abundant fish from the seas. Fire-fade has a magic bow with which he shoots many animals in the mountains. At the younger brother's insistence, the two brothers exchange their treasures for a day. Fire-shine can kill nothing with the bow. Fire-fade can catch no fish, and moreover he loses his brother's fishhook. Fire-shine insists on its return, even refusing to accept 500 fishhooks that Fire-fade made from his sword as a peace offering. Fire-fade is lamenting by the seashore wondering what to do when he is approached by a mysterious old man. The man makes a boat in which Fire-fade travels to the palace of the Sea God. The Sea God assembles all the fish of the sea, and the fishhook is found caught in the throat of one fish. The Sea God returns it to Fire-fade, telling him a curse to lay upon it when he returns it to his brother. He then gives to Fire-fade the jewels of the flow and ebb of the tide. When Fire-fade returns to the earth, Fire-shine attacks him, but Fire-fade holds forth the tide-flowing jewel and submerges his brother in a flood. Fire-shine surrenders, and Fire-fade holds forth the tide-ebbing jewel, causing the flood to recede. After that Fire-shine's descendants are the retainers of Fire-fade's descendants.

In most versions of this tale, Fire-fade marries the daughter of the Sea God. When she is about to give birth to their child, she comes to the land, but she instructs Fire-fade not to look at her while she is giving birth. He breaks the taboo and sees that she has turned into a huge crocodile. She leaves her child with Fire-fade and returns to the sea. Her younger sister comes to nurse the child until it is grown. When the elder daughter returns to the sea, she closes off the border between the land and the sea.

The Magic Listening Cap: See entry 87, tale 8.

123. The Magic Mortar. Shio-hiki usu 塩ひき臼

A poor man goes to borrow some rice from his wealthy older brother, but the brother refuses. Returning home in despair, the man meets an old man who gives him a rice cake. He tells the man to take it to the "little people" in the forest and exchange it for their mill. The man does so and learns that it is a magic mill that will produce whatever is requested when it is turned in one direction; it stops when it is turned in the other direction. With the magic mill, the man becomes very wealthy. The man's greedy brother learns of the mill and steals it. He escapes by boat. While he is sailing along, he has the mill make some salt, but he does not know how to turn the mill off. The mill produces so much salt that the boat sinks. The mill is still at the bottom of the sea producing salt, and that is why the sea is salty.

The Magic Straw Cape of Invisibility: See entry 83, tale 7.

124. The Mirror of Matsuyama. Matsuyama no kagami 松山の鏡

(a) A man goes on a trip and brings back a mirror for his wife. The wife later falls seriously ill. As she is about to die, she gives the mirror to her young daughter, telling her that when she wishes to see her mother after the mother's death, she should look into this object. The girl does not know what a mirror is and thinks that the reflection is the soul of her mother, appearing as she did when she was young and healthy. The girl gazes into the mirror often, talking with her "mother." In some versions the father becomes suspicious as to what the girl is doing; in other versions the father remarries, and the stepmother accuses the girl of practicing witchcraft against her. The father goes to see why the girl spends so much time by herself in her room and finds her staring into the mirror. The girl tells her father of the mother's dying words, and the father realizes that the girl thinks the reflection is her mother's spirit. (In versions where the stepmother is involved, the stepmother realizes what a good and filial daughter the girl is and asks forgiveness for her suspicions.)

(b) A young man whose father has recently died sees a mirror for the first time. He thinks that the reflection is his father's soul that has somehow been trapped in this object. He quickly buys the mirror and takes it home. His wife begins to wonder why he spends so much time looking at something in secret. She finally finds the mirror. When she sees her reflection, she thinks that her husband has bought a beautiful courtesan to be his concubine and is keeping her in the mirror. A terrible argument ensues between the man and his wife. A nun is called to decide the argument. She looks in the mirror and sees her reflection. She says that the "woman" who has caused the argument has repented of her causing strife in the marriage and has become a nun. She takes the mirror to the nunnery.

125. Momotarō 桃太郎

An old woman finds a huge peach floating down a river. When she brings it home to serve for dinner, the peach splits open and at its center is a baby boy. He grows to be very strong and goes off to subdue the ogres of ogre island. He brings with him some dumplings, by means of which he secures the help of a dog, a monkey, and a pheasant. With the help of these three animals, Momotarō is able to overcome all the ogres on the island and capture their huge treasure.

126. The Mouse's Marriage. Nezumi no yomeiri 鼠の嫁入り

The mouse wishes to arrange a marriage for his daughter with the most powerful being in the world. The sun says that the cloud is more powerful; the cloud says that the wind is more powerful; the wind says that a wall is more powerful. The mouse then realizes that the mouse is the most powerful, since it can chew through a wall. He accordingly arranges the marriage of his daughter to another mouse.

127. My Lord Bag-of-Rice

The warrior Hidesato comes upon a dragon lying on a bridge that he is crossing and calmly steps over it. The dragon then says that it has been looking for a warrior just this fearless for a long time. The dragon is threatened by a huge centipede, and it requests Hidesato's help in fighting its enemy. When the centipede appears, Hidesato shoots it with an arrow and kills it. In gratitude the dragon gives him a self-filling rice bale. Because of this, Hidesato came to be called "Lord Bag-of-Rice."

128. The Old Man Who Lost His Wen. Kobutori jiisan 瘤取り爺さん

An old man with a lump on his cheek spends the night in a hollow tree trunk. During the night a band of demons appear and have a party by the tree. Although the man is frightened, he becomes so fascinated by the ogres' dancing that he jumps out of the tree and begins to dance too. (In some versions the man is discovered by the demons and told to dance by them.) The man dances so well that the demons insist he return the next night. They remove the lump from his face and keep it as a "pledge." The man returns to his village and tells what has happened. His neighbor, who has a lump on the opposite cheek, goes to the tree the next night in the hope that he will have his lump removed. The neighbor dances so poorly that the demons send him away, fastening the lump they had taken back onto the man's cheek. Thus the neighbor ends up with lumps on both cheeks.

129. The Old Man Who Made Withered Trees Blossom. Hanasaka jijii 花咲か爺

An old man's pet dog shows him where to dig so that he finds a huge treasure. A greedy neighbor borrows the dog, but the dog only points to places where filth is buried. The neighbor finally kills the dog. The old man buries the dog's body in his yard. In the morning a tree has grown from the grave. The old man cuts it down and fashions it into a mortar. When the man puts in a grain of rice, the mortar turns it into a grain of gold. The neighbor borrows the mortar, but he only gets filth. He burns the mortar. The old man takes the ashes of the mortar and climbs a withered cherry tree on a road where a lord's procession is passing. He announces that he can make the blossoms bloom. The lord tells him to demonstrate, and the man scatters the ashes, causing the tree to blossom. The lord gives the man a reward. The neighbor takes some ashes and climbs a tree, but when he scatters them, the ashes blow into the eyes of the lord and his attendants. The evil neighbor is punished.

130. A Piece of Straw. Ippon no wara 一本の藁

A poverty-stricken young man prays to Kannon for good fortune. The goddess appears to him and tells him that he will grow rich from the first thing that comes into his hand when he leaves the temple. On his way out, he stumbles and catches hold of a piece of straw. As he walks along, he catches a dragonfly and attaches it to the straw. A boy and his mother pass by. The woman gives the man three oranges for the dragonfly on the straw. A noblewoman's procession passes by, but one of the women faints from the heat. The man gives her the three oranges to revive her, and the noblewoman gives him a bolt of fine cloth. He walks farther and meets some men from a lord's procession standing by the body of a dead horse. The man gives them the cloth for the horse, whereupon the horse revives. The man rides the horse to a house where the farmer is ready to leave for a trip. He gives the man a large price for his horse and also asks him to watch the farm while he is gone. If the farmer does not return within a certain amount of time, the man will be the new owner of the farm. The farmer does not return. Thus the man became a wealthy landowner through the help of Kannon and a single piece of straw.

131. The Princess Who Wore a Bowl on Her Head. Hachikatsugi 鉢かつき

A beautiful young girl is called to her mother who is dying. The mother explains that the girl's beauty will actually be a problem for her now that she is about to become an orphan. The mother places a wooden bowl on the girl's head that hides her face, telling her not to remove it until she marries. The girl wanders around until she is taken in as a servant at a rich man's house. While she is there the rich man's son sees under the bowl and falls in love with her. (In some versions, the girl removes the bowl at night when no one is near, and the son sees her.) The son insists that the girl be allowed to become his wife. When the girl tries to remove the bowl, she cannot. No one can remove the bowl from her head, but it is finally decided to go ahead with the wedding. As soon as the three wine exchanges are completed, the bowl bursts and pours forth a great treasure of gold and jewels.

132. The Robe of Feathers. Hagoromo 羽衣; Tennin nyōbō 天人女房

A fisherman finds a number of feathered robes belonging to some Celestial Maidens and steals one. The maiden is unable to return to heaven without it. (a) The maiden agrees to perform a dance for the man. He gives her the robe, she dances for him, and then she ascends to the heavens. (b) The man takes the robe and gives it to the feudal lord. The woman manages to become a lady at the lord's mansion. When the day arrives for the yearly "airing out" of all the clothing in the castle, the servants foolishly put out the robe of feathers. The woman retrieves it and ascends to heaven. (c) The man takes the robe home and hides it. He forces the woman to become his wife. Several years go by, during which time a number of children are born, but the woman is never able to find her robe. One day she hears her oldest son singing a lullaby to the baby in which he reveals that the robe is hidden behind some millet sacks in the storehouse. The woman finds the robe and ascends to the heavens. In some versions the woman takes her children with her. In some versions the husband attempts to follow his wife up to heaven. (This is an extremely complex tale cycle. For more information on the structure of variants, see entry 28.)

133. The Tongue-cut Sparrow. Shitakiri suzume 舌切リ雀

A man keeps a sparrow as a pet. One day his bad-natured wife prepares some starch to use in doing her laundry, but the bird eats the starch. The angry old woman cuts the sparrow's tongue with a pair of scissors and drives the bird away. The man goes to search for the sparrow and comes to her house in the woods. He is lavishly entertained there. As he is about to leave, the sparrows bring him two boxes, one large and one small, and ask him to choose one as a gift. He chooses the smaller box. When he arrives home, he opens it and finds it full of gold and treasure. The old woman goes to the sparrow's house. When she is about to leave, she chooses the large box. On the road home, the box becomes heavier and heavier, so the woman finally stops and opens it. It is filled with snakes, centipedes, and demons who jump out of the box and kill the woman. (In some versions the woman is rescued by her husband and repents of her past wickedness.)

134. Urashima Tarō 浦島太郎

A fisherman, Urashima Tarō, saves the life of a turtle. The turtle then brings Urashima to the palace of the Dragon King beneath the sea. He remains there for three years, after which time he decides to return to his home. The daughter of the Dragon King gives him a box with strict instructions that he not open it. When Urashima arrives at his village, he learns that 300 years have actually elapsed. He returns to the beach, and in his despair, he opens the box. A white smoke comes out that is the supernatural lapse of time. Urashima instantly ages the 300 years and dies.

135. The Weaving Maiden and the Herdboy. Tanabata 七夕

The Celestial Maiden who is responsible for weaving the fine cloth used to make the robes of the celestial deities falls in love with the herdsboy who is responsible for looking after the celestial cattle. They spend so much time together that the heavenly ruler decides they must be parted. He causes a great river, the Milky Way, to spring up between them. However, the Weaving Maiden stands on one bank lamenting while the herdsboy stands on the opposite bank lamenting. The heavenly ruler then decrees that the two can meet once a year if they attend to their duties on the other days of the year. The night of their meeting is July 7. On that night the flock of celestial magpies forms a bridge across the Milky Way, which the Weaving Maiden can cross. July 7 is celebrated as the Tanabata festival in Japan. The lovers are the stars Altair and Vega. (The male heavenly ruler is a Chinese mythological figure. According to the indigenous religion of Japan, the ruler of heaven was the Sun Goddess Amaterasu.)

136. The White Hare of Inaba. Inaba no Shirousagi 因幡の白兎

A white hare that lives on the island of Oki wishes to cross to the Japanese mainland. He devises a plan whereby he can cross by deceiving some crocodiles. When the rabbit is talking to a crocodile, he proposes a challenge to see which animal has more relatives. The crocodile assembles all the other crocodiles, and the rabbit has them line up so he can count them. They stretch from the shore of Oki to the shore of Inaba. The rabbit jumps from crocodile to crocodile counting off, but when he reaches the last crocodile he foolishly reveals that he has deceived them. The last crocodile catches the rabbit and rips off all its fur. The rabbit is lying by the shore when a number of gods arrive. They are the evil older brothers of the god Ōkuninushi. They tell the rabbit that his pain will be eased and his fur will grow back if he bathes in the salt water of the sea. The rabbit does so and is left in even greater pain. Ōkuninushi then arrives carrying his brother's baggage. He tells the rabbit to bathe in a pond of clear water and rub himself with a certain grass that grows on the pond's shore. The rabbit does so, and he is cured. The brothers are on their way to court the Princess Yagami. The rabbit predicts that Ōkuninushi will be the successful suitor and will become the ruler of the land.

137. Why the Jellyfish Has No Bones. Kurage hone nashi 水母骨なし; Saru no ikigimo 猿の生ぎも

The wife or daughter of the Dragon King under the sea becomes ill. It is learned that she can be cured only with the liver of a live monkey. A turtle is sent to lure a monkey to the Dragon Palace. When the monkey is there, he is treated well and entertained. However, the jellyfish foolishly reveals the real reason why the monkey has been sent for. The monkey pretends that he has left his liver hanging on a tree back on the land. The turtle returns the monkey to his home so that he can fetch his liver. Once they reach the land, the monkey climbs into a tree where the turtle cannot reach him. He also warns all the other monkeys about the Dragon King's plan. The turtle is forced to return to the Dragon Palace without a monkey. When the Dragon King learns that the jellyfish is responsible for the loss of the monkey, he orders his courtiers to beat the jellyfish until his bones turn to pulp. That is why jellyfish have no bones.

138. Yamato-dake

The son of the Emperor Keiko is sent to destroy a band of robbers. By disguising himself as a beautiful maiden, he is able to gain access to the robber leader and kill him. The prince then acquires the name "Yamato-dake." Later he is sent to suppress a rebellion. He is given the great sword that had been found by the god Susanō in the tail of the eight-headed dragon and that had been kept at the sacred shrine at Ise. When Yamato-dake reaches the place of the rebellion, he is lured out into the middle of a reed plain, which the rebels then set afire all around him. Yamato-dake takes the great sword and begins to cut down all the grass around him. (In some versions, the goddess Amaterasu appears and uses the sword to cut the grass.) Wherever the grass is cut, the flames turn back on the rebels and destroy them. The sword is named "Kusanagi," the grass-cutting sword. On one of Yamato-dake's crossings of the Bay of Yedo, the Sea God causes a great storm to arise in retaliation for a previous slight by Yamato-dake. The prince's wife, Azuma, throws herself into the sea as a sacrifice. In his final adventure, Yamato-dake kills a huge serpent, but the prince is poisoned by the snake's breath and dies before he can return to the capital.

Appendix A: Japanese-Language Sources

Folklorists who have studied Japanese may prefer to examine works in the native language.

The K.B.S. (Kokusai Bunka Shinkōkai 国際文化振興会) *Bibliography of Standard Reference Books for Japanese Studies* is one of the most useful general references available. Volume 8, *Manners and Customs, and Folklore*, was published in 1961.

Nihon mukashibanashi shūsei 日本昔話集成 by Seki Keigo 関敬吾 (Tokyo: Kadokawa Shoten, 1950–58) is a monumental collection in six volumes and three parts. Part one deals with animal tales; part two, with proper folktales; and part three, with jokes. This work includes samples of over 600 tale types and over 15,000 variants.

Seki's *Nihon no mukashibanashi* 日本の昔話 (Tokyo: Iwanami Shoten, 1956–57) is a collection in three volumes of 240 tales selected from the larger *Shūsei*. This is the anthology used by Robert J. Adams for his *Folktales of Japan* (entry 97).

Nihon mukashibanashi shū 日本昔話集 by Yanagita Kunio 柳田国男 is a collection of 108 tales, originally published by Ars in Tokyo in 1930. It was published under the revised title *Nippon no mukashibanashi* by Shunyōdo Shōnen Shōjo Bunko in 1934, by Mikuni Shobo in 1942, by Jiipusha in 1951, and by Kadokawa in 1953. This is the anthology used by Fanny Hagin Mayer for her *Japanese Folk Tales* (entry 109A). Because 45 of the tales in Yanagita's collection were later classified as "legends," a revision was undertaken that replaced these with 43 "genuine folktales." The revised collection, *Nihon no mukashibanashi kaiteihan* 日本の昔話改訂版 was published by Kadokawa in 1960. This is the anthology used by Mayer for her *Japanese Folk Tales: A Revised Selection* (entry 109B).

The *Konjaku monogatari* 今昔物語 is a source of many tales. For Japanese editions of this work, see the bibliography in Marian Ury's *Tales of Times Now Past* (entry 105).

Fanny Hagin Mayer's article "Available Japanese Folk Tales" (*Monumenta Nipponica* 24, no. 3 [1969]: 235–47) lists five sources for folktales in Japanese:

1. Collections of stories from all over Japan
2. Collections of local stories gathered by official or private concerns
3. Collections gathered by local associations and/or schools
4. Collections gathered by individuals
5. Collections recorded in journals

Mayer discusses each of the five types, lists prewar and postwar materials, and gives full titles, with kanji for authors and titles in footnotes. This is an extremely valuable reference work. (This article is included in Mayer's *Introducing the Japanese Folk Tale*, entry 38.)

Four of the works listed in this bibliography give references in romaji for folktale collections in Japanese:

1. Ikeda's "A Type and Motif Index of Japanese Folk Literature" (entry 25)
2. Seki's "Types of Japanese Folktales" (entry 46)
3. Dorson's *Folk Legends of Japan* (entry 69)
4. Yanagita's *Japanese Folk Tales: A Revised Selection* (entry 109B)

For studies in Japanese on Japanese folklore, especially folk religion, see the end notes for Wakamori Tarō's articles "Folklore" (entry 51) and "The Study of Folklore" (entry 52).

Appendix B: Glossary of Japanese Terms

Ama no ukihashi 天の浮橋
The floating bridge of heaven; it extends from the heavenly reed plain to the land of Japan.

Amaterasu-ō-mikami 天照大神
Shinto deity; the Sun Goddess, daughter of Izanagi, ruler of the heavens and the celestial deities.

chōja 長者
A very wealthy landowner, a "millionaire."

daimyō 大名
Feudal lord.

Emma 閻魔
Ruler of the Buddhist underworld; the souls of people who have died are judged by Emma, who then assigns them to one of the various Buddhist hells to exact punishment for sins.

furushiki (furoshiki) 風呂敷
A cloth used for wrapping parcels.

geta 下駄
Wooden clogs.

-hime 姫
Suffix indicating a highborn young woman, a "princess."

Izanagi 伊邪那岐
Celestial deity. He descended from the heavenly reed plain to the earth and became the primeval "father" of all earthly creation; father of Amaterasu and Susanō.

Izanami 伊邪那美
Sister and wife of Izanagi, primeval "mother" of all earthly creation.

-ji (-tera) 寺
Suffix indicating a Buddhist temple.

Jimmu Tenno 神武天皇
Descendant of the Sun Goddess Amaterasu and legendary first emperor of Japan; founding ancestor of the Japanese imperial family.

jinja 神社
A Shinto shrine.

Jizō 地蔵
Buddhist deity, the Bodhisattva Ksitigarbha, patron guardian of children.

kakemono 掛け物
A hanging scroll.

Kannon 観音
Buddhist deity, the Bodhisattva Avalokitesvara, Goddess of Mercy.

kappa 河童
Water spirits. A kappa has a monkeylike, childish body with webbed hands and feet, a shell like a turtle's, and a saucer-shaped indentation on the top of its head. The saucer contains a heavy liquid that is thought to give the kappa its tremendous physical strength.

kitsune 狐
A fox.

Kōbō Daishi 弘法大師
Posthumous name of the Buddhist saint Kūkai 空海 (744–835), founder of the Shingon sect of Buddhism.

kujira 鯨
A whale.

kurage 海月; 水母
A jellyfish.

mochi 餅
Rice cakes.

mon 文
An ancient monetary denomination of very low value.

mujina 貉 *(also called tanuki)*
A badger.

nekomata 猫股
A cat demon.

nezumi 鼠
A mouse, a rat.

Ninigi 爾爾芸
Shinto deity, grandson of the Sun Goddess Amaterasu, father of the Princes Fire-shine and Fire-fade.

nushi 主
Guardian spirits of trees and ponds.

Ō-kuni-nushi-no-kami 大国主神
Shinto deity, descendant of Susanō, youngest of many brothers. He cures the rabbit in the tale "The White Hare of Inaba."

oni 鬼
A demon. Demons often appear as horned giants with one, two, or three eyes.

rōnin 浪人
A masterless samurai.

ryō 両
An ancient monetary denomination of very high value.

ryū (tatsu) 竜
Dragon.

Ryūgū 竜宮
The submarine palace of Ryūō.

Ryūō 竜王
Shinto deity, the Dragon King, God of the Sea.

shōjō 猩猩
Magical humanoid creatures of the sea with red hair and skin. Shōjō are very fond of saké.

Susanō-ō-mikoto 須佐之男命
Shinto deity, son of Izanagi and younger brother of the Sun Goddess Amaterasu. He slays the dragon in the tale "The Eight Headed Serpent."

Takamagahara 高天原
The reed plain of heaven on which stands the palace of the celestial deities.

tama (tamashii) 魂
Soul; spirit.

tanuki 狸 *(also called mujina)*
A badger.

tatsu (ryū) 竜
Dragon.

tengu 天拘
Long-nosed, winged goblins. Tengu originally were depicted as having a birdlike appearance, but in later representations they became more human in their form. Tengu sometimes had brightly colored blue skin.

-tera (-ji) 寺
Suffix indicating a Buddhist temple.

Uzume 鈿女
One of the Shinto celestial deities. Uzume performs the dance that lures the Sun Goddess Amaterasu out of her cave (see "The Eight Headed Serpent").

yamabushi 山伏
A mountain priest. Yamabushi were ascetics who often possessed magic powers.

yamachichi 山父
A one-eyed, one-legged monster of the mountains that can read the minds of human beings.

yamauba 山姥
A mountain witch.

yanagi 柳
A willow tree.

Yomi 黄泉
The Shinto underworld, the realm of the dead.

zashiki bokko 座敷ぼっこ *zashiki warashi* 座敷わらし
Boylike spirits that live in the tatami room.

Subject Index

Article Index

Folktale Index

Titles are listed alphabetically according to first word following parentheses. The following words and phrases are ignored in alphabetizing: about (a, the), an account of, concerning, history of, how (a, the), legend(s) of, the romance of, sad story of, story (about, of how, of) the stories of, the strange story of, the tale(s) of the, the wonderful adventures of, when.

onstrated the miraculous power of the Ninnō Sutra, 120

(How a) priest out visiting sneaked some troutlings, 117

(How a) priest prayed for the mitigation of his sins, changed grave sins into lesser ones, and attained enlightenment, 26

(How a) priest put the magic incantation of the Bodhisattva Zuigu into his forehead, 115

(How a) priest put Seimei to the test, 118

(About) priest Shunchō, 25

(How a) priest took his master's place and had himself entered in a letter to the court of King Emma at rites to Taizan Hukun, see (About the) monk whose name was entered on a petition . . .

The priest who ate the corpse, 74

(About the) priestly gentleman who was Takashina Shumpei's brother and the magical art of laying sticks, 120

(How the) priestly nobleman from Mikawa retired from the world, 116

The priest's towel, 73

Prince Hosokawa's most valuable title-deeds, 92

(How) Prince Kaya made a doll and set it up in the rice fields, 154

Prince Ruddy Plenty, 130

The princes, Fire-shine and Fire-fade, see The luck of the sea and the luck of the mountains

The princess and the fisherman, 148

Princess fire-fly, see The fire-fly's lovers

(The story of) Princess Hase, 125, 126

(The story of) Princess Hotaru, 160

Princess Peony (The peony flower), 68, 97, 109

(About) Princess Toyosaki, 118

The princess who became a human sacrifice, 84

The princess who wore a bowl on her head (The black bowl; Hachikazuki; The wooden bowl), 11, 31, 44–45, 71, 72, 107, 109, 111, 124, 127, 188

The procession of ghosts, 92

(About the) promise of a thousand tales of gold, 120

Punishment worse than death, 88

The quail and the badger, 134

The quarrel between the mountains, 141; see also Contest in height between two mountains

The quilt on the nape of the neck, 170, 177; see also Bedding in one's ear

The quiver of the mountain spirit, 162

The rabbit and the bear, 134

The rabbit and the crocodiles, see The white hare of Inaba

(Stories of) Raiko (The goblin spider of Oyeyama), 67, 100, 127

Raitarō, the son of the Thunder God (The child of the thunder; The good thunder), 69, 99, 101, 109, 130

Rapunzel (The maiden in the tower), 2, 36–37

(About the) rat and snake of Shinano Province, 25

Rat paradise, 175; see also The roly-poly dumpling

Rat sutra, 176

The red nose of the image, 74

The reed mower and the lady (The ashikari tale; How a poor man left his wife and how she became the wife of the governor of Settsu), 33–34, 122, 155

(The story of how the) refectory of the Yakusizi burned but the main hall did not burn, 63

Reflections, see The mirror of Matsuyama (b)

(About the) regent from the First Ward and some verses, 116

Reincarnation, 93

Relics of Benkei, 81

(About the) retainer of the Tada neophyte, 116

(How the) retired Emperor Shirakawa was attacked by an evil spirit, 116

(How the) retired Emperor Shirakawa's guards held a mock provincial governor's procession, 118

Reunion with death, 124

The revengeful spirit of Masakado, 78